THE
LAWS
OF THE
SPIRIT
WORLD

" There is no religion in the Spirit World. We worship one God only."

KHORSHED BHAVNAGRI

D1557270

JAICO PUBLISHING HOUSE

Ahmedabad Bangalore Bhopal Bhubaneswar Chennai
Delhi Hyderabad Kolkata Lucknow Mumbai

Published by Jaico Publishing House
A-2 Jash Chambers, 7-A Sir Phirozshah Mehta Road
Fort, Mumbai - 400 001
jaicopub@jaicobooks.com
www.jaicobooks.com

THE LAWS OF THE SPIRIT WORLD
ISBN 978-81-7992-985-8

First Jaico Impression: 2009
Thirteenth Jaico Impression: 2015

Printed by
Kadambari Printers Pvt. Ltd.
114, Patparganj Industrial Area
Delhi – 92

Mrs. Khorshed Bhavnagri
27 September, 1925 – 13 August, 2007

To
God
The One
To Whom We Owe
Everything
&
My Dearest Sons
Vispi And Ratoo

VISPI'S PRAYER

My dearest God Almighty,
Please our Lord,
Help us to avoid all evil
and save us from such evil creatures.
Please take us in Your hands and guide us.
We are Yours, our God,
and will be Yours always.
Keep us with You, our Lord, for eternity.
So always and forever we will be blessed,
guided and helped by You and only You.
Thank You, God Almighty.

CONTENTS

FOREWORD

All my life I have been asking questions. I always perceived things differently from most people, which was a result of my thirst for knowledge. Ever since I was young, I would gaze at the stars and somehow know that we were not alone in the universe, that I had friends in the Spirit World — my guardian angels who always love and look after me.

My family taught me to be respectful of all religions. An inborn curiosity led me on a journey. In time I became a firm believer in Sai Baba of Shirdi*, and I told Him about my deep yearning for a spiritual master on Earth. It was then that I came across a lady, whose name was Khorshed Bhavnagri. The first day I met her and spoke to her departed sons, Vispi and Ratoo, I felt a great kinship when they called me "Small Brother."

The knowledge that I gained about the afterlife through Khorshed Bhavnagri — or Khorshed Aunty, as I called her — was *recognition* more than discovery. It was something my soul already knew. To me, the afterlife is simply an

---

* Sai Baba of Shirdi was an Indian guru who died in 1918. Sai [Sa'ih] is the Persian term for "holy one" or "saint" whereas Baba is a word meaning "father" used in Indian languages, thus referring to him as "holy father" or "saintly father".

extension of this life. We are all spokes of a wheel, coming to a centre, which is ONE GOD. We are all connected.

In the 25 years of learning with her, Khorshed Aunty was much more than my spiritual master. She was my best friend, someone I could trust, someone who was open-minded, non-judgemental, aware, had a great sense of humour, and possessed a luminosity and healing energy.

She helped me appreciate the value of experiences. She made me understand that the positive experiences were my blessings, ones that I should be grateful for, and that the negative ones were not to be feared, for they were my real teachers. A simple "God Bless" and "All will be well" from her were enough to put all my fears to rest.

I was completely open with her and discussed everything — God, my relationships, my work, the difference between religion and spirituality, karma, past lives, the purpose of rebirth, prophets, angels, psychic phenomena, extra-terrestrials, why human beings are self-destructive, death, old age, loneliness, fear, the healing nature of crystals, the importance of now, the power of intention, thought and prayer, whether God is kind or punishing, how I could understand the meaning of it all and evolve — and realise my place and function in the grand design and scheme of things.

Khorshed Aunty answered all my questions, but always told me that in the end, the most important thing was to be a good human being on Earth and always follow the Godly Good Path. She made me realise that I was solely responsible for my actions and that I could not blame God or anyone else for whatever came my way. She also taught me the importance of selfless service, controlling the mind, spreading God's knowledge and guiding and comforting people who had lost their loved ones. When I needed guidance most, Khorshed Aunty and her husband, Rumi Uncle whom I was also extremely close to, offered me a loving environment, full of wisdom and laughter, in which my spirit was nurtured, trained and eventually freed.

Even though they are not alive anymore, I feel I have two more angels in the spirit world looking after me. I do not mourn their absence because I know that they are with me all the time. Moreover, they have left with me the most valuable of all guides — spiritual knowledge. Please read this book with an open mind and understand how simple and powerful the truth really is. Vispi always emphasised that this knowledge could be understood even by a child, and that the truth is always simple.

Fortunately, I am not the only one whose life has been changed by Khorshed Aunty and Rumi Uncle. Over the last 25 years, thousands of people came to them and received spiritual knowledge, guidance, comfort and healing.

I hope this book does the same for you.

God Bless

Shiamak Davar

Rumi and Khorshed Bhavnagri
at their Byculla residence

PREFACE

Khorshed and Rumi Bhavnagri lived in Byculla in Bombay, India with their two sons, Vispi who was born on August 9th, 1950, and Ratoo, on December 13th, 1951. As the boys grew up they were extremely interested in all aspects of motoring. Eventually, Vispi and Ratoo set up a garage for motor services and repairs. They also participated in several motor rallies.

In the fateful year of 1980, Vispi and Ratoo were to enter a 1,632 mile cross-country motor rally. The rally was to start on February 23rd, and Vispi and Ratoo decided to take the car out for a trial run from Bombay to Khopoli, before the event. Khorshed narrated what happened just before their sons set out on their journey. "Ratoo hugged me tight, said goodbye and went out. He hardly went down a few steps (we lived on the 2nd floor), then he came running back to the door, to me. Again he hugged me tight and kissed me. I could not understand why, because this was unusual for Ratoo. He went down one floor, then once more he came running back to me and held me tight and hugged me. By then Vispi came to wish me goodbye as well. I told them to drive carefully. They said, 'Don't wait for us, mama, we will go till Khopoli and return, or we may stay overnight and come back tomorrow morning.'"

Just as they got into their car, the boys met their father. Rumi told them to drive carefully. Ratoo replied, 'Why are you worried, daddy? In any case, we can't go over 30 [miles per hour] since we have just overhauled the engine. We will be alright.' So, at 8.30 that night, Vispi and Ratoo set out in high spirits along with two mechanics and a friend.

When they did not return by 8 o'clock the next morning, Khorshed and Rumi began to worry. At 8.30 am a mechanic from the boys' garage came over saying that there had been an accident somewhere near Khopoli, and that both Vispi and Ratoo were in hospital.

Rumi rounded up a few friends and sped towards the accident site at Khopoli. There they found Vispi and Ratoo's car smashed into a tree. Nobody was around, but they learned that the boys had been rushed to the hospital a few minutes away. When Rumi got to the hospital, he was told that both Vispi and Ratoo had been killed on the spot, but the other occupants of the car had escaped with minor injuries.

Rumi asked the mechanics what had caused the accident. All they said was, "We were asleep one minute and the next minute there was a crash." Everything felt unreal to Rumi. He was fortunate to have his friends and neighbours with him to help with the formalities in the hospital. With a heavy heart he returned home and wondered how to break this tragic news to his wife.

As Rumi painfully climbed the stairs to his apartment, Khorshed kept asking him from the landing, "Why have you taken so long? Where are Vispi and Ratoo? Why can't you move faster?" When Khorshed heard the news, she broke down. She felt she had nothing to live for.

Khorshed's faith in God was shaken. "I had been very religious," she said. "Now, for the first time, I began to question whether there was a God. If there was a God then why should He do this terrible thing to me, snatch my sons away when I have never harmed a hair on anyone's head? I was ready to give up God, religion and life."

Then something wonderful happened. On the 29th day after the funeral, a neighbour named Mrs. Dastoor told Khorshed and Rumi an amazing story. Mrs. Dastoor's sister-in-law had gone to a concert and, during the intermission, overheard a lady speak of two boys who had recently died in an accident and wanted to send a message to their parents. So Mrs. Dastoor's sister-in-law had taken down the lady's telephone number.

The next day, Khorshed and Rumi got in touch with this lady and she invited them to her house. She had lost her brother and was in contact with him through seances organised by a powerful medium named Mrs. Kapadia. On one such occasion, the seance was interrupted by a cry from two young boys. The boys said they had died in an accident and that their parents were shattered. They wanted their parents to know they were happy in the spirit world and not to worry as they could see their parents.

On March 22nd, 1980, Khorshed and Rumi attended a group seance at Mrs. Kapadia's residence on Napean Sea Road. Mrs. Kapadia, the medium, sat in the centre and the

others were seated around her. She moved from one person
to another to assist them in their communication with
their dear ones who had died. When Mrs. Kapadia came to
the Bhavnagris, the first words uttered by her were, "Hello
Mummy, fatso." That was what Vispi had always called his
mother. The fact that a stranger knew such an intimate
detail was what gave Khorshed and Rumi proof that it was
their sons, and this restored their faith in God.

Vispi and Ratoo then told their parents that they wanted
to talk to them alone. So Mrs. Kapadia gave them the
name of another medium, an elderly lady called Mrs. Rishi.
A few days later the Bhavnagris spoke to their sons
through Mrs. Rishi. They said, "Mom and Dad, this is
Vispi and Ratoo. Yes, we died and reached the spirit world
within minutes of our death. It is God's will and God
knows what is best for each one of us. God is good. You
must not cry for us or miss us, we are much happier here.
We can see you all the time, and are looking after you. We
cannot communicate with you until you are completely
relaxed and happy. You have to develop powers of
concentration." They also told her that she had to stay on
Earth to do her spiritual mission, which was to help
people and spread spiritual awareness.

Over the next few months, Khorshed and Rumi, with the
help of their sons, developed powers of complete
concentration and relaxation which made direct
communication between the parents and their sons
possible through a process known as 'Automatic Writing'.
She would hold a pen lightly onto a book, concentrate
intensely, and gradually the spirits of her deceased sons
would use her hand to move the pen slowly and unevenly

over the page. At first there were mere scratches, but with days of practice, words formed and she could ask questions aloud, to which the answers would come, written onto the book.

Shortly after the boys' death, a very unfortunate family problem arose and Khorshed and Rumi had to resort to litigation. Contrary to the advice of some lawyers who said they should not fight the case, Khorshed and Rumi chose the lawyer on the advice that their deceased sons conveyed to them telepathically. To their surprise, against all odds, the litigation came to a successful conclusion. This was one more sign that the Bhavnagris were indeed being guided and protected.

After some time, Vispi and Ratoo conveyed to their parents a desire to dictate, by the same process of automatic writing and then telepathically, a book containing the laws of the spirit world, for which they had obtained special permission from higher souls. They thought it would be of considerable benefit to human beings on Earth to know the true laws of God and the spirit world, which, if followed, would help them advance spiritually. It was the desire of Vispi and Ratoo that the book be dictated, published and distributed widely. However, Vispi and Ratoo were very clear that their teachings and beliefs were not to be forced on anyone.

As friends, and even strangers, heard of Khorshed's communication with her sons, they came pouring in at the Bhavnagri residence. Khorshed and Rumi slowly realised that by reducing the pain of others through selfless service, their own pain was being considerably reduced.

This was how they found solace after the death of their sons. They provided guidance and comfort to both young and old. By sharing their story, they prevented people who had suffered a similar loss from being consumed by sadness. They counselled people regarding problems ranging from addictions to physical abuse, but eventually they nourished those souls who had a true thirst for spiritual knowledge and a desire to improve spiritually. People posed questions, both spiritual and personal. Many of those questions have been reproduced in Part II of this book.

As there is no religion in the spirit world, questions and answers that relate purely to any particular religion have been excluded.

Rumi and Khorshed Bhavnagri passed away in 1996 and 2007 respectively, and are happily reunited with their sons in the spirit world.

NOTE

Khorshed Aunty would communicate with Vispi at least twice a day, sometimes three to four times a day, only between sunrise and sunset, with no fixed agenda or plan. She received messages on various topics, the sequence, conversational tone and language of which have been preserved exactly as they were received. The messages reproduced here are the ones she received in English even though her mother tongue was Gujarati.

Ratoo Bhavnagri
13 December, 1951 – 22 February, 1980

Vispi Bhavnagri
9 August, 1950 – 22 February, 1980

PART I

Spirit Communications
from the
Journals
of
Khorshed Bhavnagri

14-04-1981

THE REAL LAWS OF GOD

My dearest Mom and Dad, this is Vispi and Ratoo speaking from the spirit world to make people on Earth understand, through you, how to follow the right path, God Almighty's own path. So, my dearest Mom, write this book for us and let your world know about the spirit world, about the laws and rules of God Almighty, which are misunderstood by people on Earth, and about the Realms[1] in the spirit world.

It is quite wrong to believe everything that your priest tells you, and what great philosophers preach, about the real justice of our God Almighty. They don't know all — they or you will come to know all only when you leave from your Earth plane and go to the spirit plane. Well, it will not take just a few pages or a few chapters, not even a few books to explain to you what *real* justice is. It will take you ages to learn what our God truly wants from us. So our efforts to explain this to you may not prove quite satisfactory. But we, from the spirit world, want our dear

---

1. There are seven Realms or planes of existence in the spirit world, with one being the lowest and seven the highest.

ones and all Earth people to know what the truth is, to know that you are making many, many mistakes just because of some silly notions, or because of what some man who is *supposed* to be holy and philosophical tells you. Sometimes what they say is quite the opposite of our God Almighty's *real* rules and regulations.

At this time on Earth, when evil and bad souls are on top and good souls are suffering, we feel this book will explain to you why — yes, why — bad souls seem to succeed and good souls suffer. Good souls want to blame our dearest God Almighty for being unjust towards them. So read on, my dears, and you will find many answers.

15-04-1981

IMPROVEMENT THROUGH SELF-ANALYSIS

Bad souls can be helped by God Almighty, if the bad soul so desires. Bad souls must have the inner instinct and may pray to God Almighty to change them. God Almighty will definitely help them. It is entirely in each soul's hands to be good or bad. Those souls who are bad but want to change can be changed to good souls in no time. On Earth, we have often heard you say, "Confess and God will forgive you". This is true, but you must confess your sins to *yourself* and not to a priest. A priest has no power to forgive you. Who is that priest to forgive you? He may be more sinful than you are, so don't confess to a priest, confess to yourself. Tell yourself that you are bad, ask God Almighty to help you, and you can be sure that He will. You must be *absolutely sincere*. I repeat, absolutely. If you ask God Almighty half-heartedly, it will not help. But if you are completely sincere and positive that you *need* to change, let us assure you that He will help you change for the better in no time.

Now suppose a person thinks he is good but in reality, he is not. What about such souls? Many people think what they are doing is as per God's laws. They never have an ounce of realization of how sinful they are. They will say, "I believe in God. I read holy books. I pray everyday. I go to the temple or church every day or every week. I give plenty in charity. I give food, clothing, and jobs to the poor and needy. What more does anyone want? I will surely go to heaven." Sorry to say, these poor souls think that heaven's door is wide open for them, but they will never even reach the lowest ladder of heaven. It is really difficult for a soul on Earth to understand this, but it is true, they will not even see the lowest step of heaven. So listen carefully with an open mind. Why are they going to a place of worship every day? Some go to show people around them that they are so pious that they think of God often. Ask yourself, "Can God Almighty ever be fooled?" **You can fool your fellow men, but you will never be able to fool God Almighty.** You call yourself a God-fearing person? If you really were a God-fearing person, would you ever try to fool God?

Some go to a place of worship every day or every week to ask God for more money, more happiness, and more success. What is this? You are going there for your own selfish motive — not for God, but for yourself. Can a selfish motive carry you to heaven?

Suppose you are giving a great deal to charity. First ask yourself why. What is your *motive* behind giving to charity? **Your motive is most important.** If your motive is entirely selfless – for example, if your motive is only to help someone, and it comes automatically – then, of course, God is pleased and He knows why you gave, which was not to impress Him. But suppose your motive is to get into heaven, to impress God Almighty by saying, "If I give this to a poor person, God will send me to heaven." You can be sure that God knows your motive and you won't be sent to heaven. **You can fool each other, you can try to fool yourself, but you can never fool God Almighty.** So your motive behind that charity is very, very important. Be sincere in whatever you do. Even a tiny spark will bring you to heaven if you are sincere. But even the largest of charities will take you to hell if you are selfish and try to fool God Almighty. So this is entirely in your own hands, isn't it?

16-04-1981

JUSTICE

We are very thankful to God that He needs no proof for our actions right or wrong and His justice is absolute. In your world most of the justice, even by the highest judges, may not always be correct, but God's justice is always right as He knows you inside out. If you try to hide something from your fellow man it may stay hidden, but you cannot hide even a tiny bit from God Almighty, and His justice is always perfect. If you believe this you will never go wrong. You can be sure that this is absolutely true and whatever you do or say is always recorded. So lead a moral, sincere and com-passionate life.

Try to improve yourself. You may think that no man on Earth is perfect, so how could you be? My dear readers, even we here, on a higher plane or Realm in the spirit world are not perfect, so how can you be?

We are trying so hard to become perfect by gaining the good and discarding the bad. Every soul's goal should be self-improvement so that you can reach God Almighty – the Perfect Being – and it takes eons to reach Him. So in your life, try very hard to do good, speak good and never harm your fellow man. Never be unkind and try very hard not to be a hypocrite. You can achieve this if you want to – but the genuine desire should be there.

Now, since you are on Earth, you have more scope to try to improve yourself. Once you come to the spirit world, you progress very slowly. So if you really want to improve yourself, do it *now*. Yes, *now* is most important.

SPIRIT COMMUNICATIONS

We are all trying to improve; you on the Earth plane, and we on the spirit plane. But there is a vast difference between us. You cannot know all truths and we know most of them. You will not know how bad or good your fellow men are, but we know exactly how good or bad a soul is. You cannot read each other's minds. We can read minds up to a point. You cannot see or hear us, but we can see you, hear you and even know your mind and thoughts, so we can know you better than you can yourself.

If you think this is all humbug, let me give you an example. Our dearest Mom, who is writing for us, never realised what some people around her were really like. She had a bad opinion about a man, whom we saw to be a good soul. And those who she thought were good souls we saw them as the biggest hypocrites – jealous and harmful people. So we advised her. At first she did not believe us, but when she and our Dad asked questions all around, they found, to their surprise, that what we said was true. They found out what they might not have if we hadn't told them about how bad and sinful some souls near them really were.

So, my dear readers, if you can communicate with your dear ones who are in the spirit world, and take their guidance, you will definitely know which person is good and which one is not. In this way, you can know whom to trust and whom not to.

You all have fixed ideas about so many things, which cause you to go wrong. This is why we are guiding you all through this communication. Evil souls are very difficult to improve, but there are countless chances to improve even evil souls once you gain their confidence. Numerous wonderful things have happened through spirit communications. You can even take souls on Earth out of their misery by conveying a message from their loved ones who have departed from your world. Not everyone can receive messages from the spirit world, but we are sure that those who can communicate are willing to help others. I am sorry to say that people on Earth can be very foolish sometimes. Even a cupful of happiness near their mouths is like poison to them. They are foolish not to believe in spirit communications, or in the soul and life after death. We feel very sorry for such souls, as they are stunned when they come to the spirit world.

18-04-1981

THE STORY OF THE OLD MAN AND THE BROOK

Now, we would like to tell you a very good story about something that happened with us a little while ago in the spirit world. There was an old man sitting near our favourite brook. It is very rare to see an old man here, for as a soul becomes wiser it becomes younger here, so we were very surprised to see him.

We asked him, "Are you a newcomer, sir?"

He said, "Yes, young men, how did you know that?"

We said, "It was instinct!"

He said, "You seem to be wise young men, so I am sure you will show me the way home."

We asked, "Well, where is your home?" And he gave us the address of his home on Earth.

We laughed and told him, "Sir, you are not on Earth, you are in the spirit world." We told him that he was a newcomer to the spirit world.

He looked at us as if we had come out of an asylum, and then said, very meekly, "I thought you were wise, as I have somehow arrived at this vacation spot. Yes, I am a newcomer to this place."

"Vacation?" we said. "Sir, you have come *home* from your vacation."

He replied, "My God, these are real mad men, I must run away." And he fled. We felt very sorry for him, so we called one of our higher souls to join us, and approached him again.

His face went white, and he said, "My God, now there are *three* lunatics. What can I do?" And he began shouting out a name. Later, we learned that it was the name of his son on Earth. No matter how much we tried to explain the situation to him, he refused to believe that the spirit world could be so beautiful, that you could live in a place of such beauty after your death on Earth.

We had to call some more high souls, who could tactfully explain the situation. We all got together, explained everything to him, and showed him around. After some time, he believed us and realised that we were telling him the truth. Then he became very friendly and said, "All the while I was afraid to die on Earth, thinking that after death we would have to sleep in eternal peace on a very barren cloud where only angels can fly."

We laughed and told him we had never seen an angel flying here! So he said, "Oh, that means we are not in heaven, so how beautiful must heaven be!"

We laughed again and explained to him, "This is a higher Realm and it *is* heaven, but the highest Realm is of course the most beautiful — beyond our imagination." He became a little less old then, as wisdom seeped into his Subconscious Mind[2] which began to open. He got a bit

---

2. According to Vispi the Subconscious Mind is your true spiritual mind. It is also known as the Higher Mind or the Conscience. It is not to be confused with any other definitions of the Subconscious Mind.

wiser, but he still had a lot to learn. He was very surprised that the land of "eternal peace" could be so beautiful and that instead of resting, we were all so lively and full of zest.

From this story, you can tell how people on Earth are so ignorant of the spirit world and are traumatized when they find out what it is really like. So, dear people on Earth, prepare yourselves for the spirit world through spirit communications, and be sure to lead your life according to the Godly Good Path, so that you can reach the higher Realms.

19-04-1981

UNDERSTANDING GOD'S LAWS

Our fellow spirit beings here would like us to let the people of Earth know what the real laws of God are, as people from Earth are ignorant of such laws. We would like to give this knowledge to them and, by all means, we have full faith that they will believe us and use this knowledge for the good of humanity. There are many false notions that lead you entirely astray from the laws of God Almighty.

Many of God's laws have been misunderstood. Just try this game — we played this game at parties when we were young. Sit in a circle, and have a person start a sentence by whispering it to the person beside him, then pass on the sentence by whispering it from one person to the next. By the time it reaches the one who started it, it will be absolutely different. In the same way, the laws of God Almighty started from a point where they were absolutely correct, but when they were passed down through the ages some truths were altered. Not wholly, but partly.

20-04-1981

HOW WE DIED AND THE REALMS OF THE SPIRIT WORLD

Now we would like to tell you more about the spirit world so that you can understand how we live here and what a wonderful spirit world you could be in if you follow God Almighty's laws and lead a good life. We would also like to tell you what lower Realms are like, what evil souls should expect and what good souls can expect.

Let's start from our death so that we can explain to you what happened, how we went to the spirit world, and where the spirit world is.

We were travelling by car, slow and steady, as we had to free the engine, which we had worked on a few hours earlier. We were driving home on the highway and as I, Vispi, slowly drove the car, I realised that all the others were asleep. I slowed down some more as the potholes were so bad that a bumpy ride might have woken everyone up.

We drove towards our Earth home, but at the time I never realised, of course, that my brother Ratoo and I were actually moving towards our real heavenly spirit world home.

All of a sudden a terrible form — black, huge and horrible — came in my way. I swerved the car a little to my left and tried to apply the brakes, but the brakes failed and I saw a tree ahead of me. The car smashed into that tree.

Then I saw myself outside of my physical body. I saw my physical body lying on the grass and I realised I was no longer in my physical body, but in my light spiritual body. I also realised that I felt no pain or discomfort. That's when I knew I was dead to the Earth world. I looked all around me and saw no one. A shout escaped from my lips, "O God, no one has come to welcome me to the spirit world." After a few seconds, I noticed a soul standing beside me and I was overjoyed as he looked like my brother, Ratoo. I hugged and kissed him and said, "Ratoo, at least we are together." The soul smiled and said, "Vispi, I am not Ratoo. Ratoo is over there, still breathing in his physical body." I looked down at Ratoo, but the other soul looked so similar that I pleaded, "Whoever you may be, please, please for God's sake, save Ratoo – don't let him die on Earth as my Mom and Dad will be alone. Who will look after them?" He very kindly told me, "Vispi, my dearest, it's not in our hands, it's in God's hands. And Vispi, I am your grandfather." So this was my Mom's father, whom we used to call Pappa or Popsie. I had not recognized him as he was much younger looking than when he had died in 1974. At the time of his passing, he was 93 years old and now, in 1980, when we left Earth, he looked about 30 years old, and somewhat like my brother Ratoo. I hugged him and requested him again to do something to save Ratoo.

Pappa explained again, "Vispi, my dearest, it is not at all in our hands. Just let us pray to God as I am also feeling miserable about this. What will my dearest daughter do without you two?" As we joined our hands in prayer and said, "O God..." Ratoo came out of his physical body, too. We stood there, sad and miserable, thinking of my Mom and Dad.

Ratoo saw me and then noticed his smashed-up car, but he did not see his physical body lying on the grass. He shouted at the top of his voice — he had a loud hoarse voice — I heard his same earthly voice, but much louder: "What have you done to my car?"

Then, he saw Pappa and recognized him. "Pappa, you are here. Where am I? Pappa, you are dead. What are you doing here?" Then, he spoke to me again, "Tell me, what have you done to my car?"

We explained to him that we were dead to the Earth world. Like me, Ratoo also said, "O God, what will happen to Mummy and Daddy?"

We sat staring at our physical bodies, wondering if there was a way for us to go back into our bodies for the sake of our dearest Mom, Dad and Gina (Vispi's 2 ½ year old daughter), but we were summoned up. Some of our friends and relatives also came, and we all prepared to go up together. There was a High Good Soul[3] with us, who said, "Vispi, Ratoo, close your eyes," and we felt as if we were going up at great speed. When we arrived at our destination we were asked to open our eyes and we saw the most wonderful place — our beautiful spirit world home.

Because we were very sad and in a state of shock we were

---

3. A High Good Soul refers to a spirit being from Realm 6 Stage 7 and above.

taken to a huge hall by a few High Good Souls. That hall is called **The Hall of Rest**. We were asked to lie down on a soft and feather-like, or shall we say cloud-like couch where we fell asleep.

After a while, I awoke and saw Ratoo lying beside me on a couch. Some rays were being given to him. A High Good Soul came to me and told me to follow him. I said, "I will stay here as Ratoo is still not properly rested." The High Good Soul said, "No, you must come with me. You cannot stay here any longer. Ratoo will meet you outside when he is properly rested." I was led outside and there I saw Pappa, my friends and my relatives all waiting for us to come out of the Hall of Rest. After some time, we saw Ratoo come out too. Then we decided that since we could not go back to our Mom and Dad, we would have to help them take this horrible blow courageously.

21-04-1981

THE 7 REALMS OR PLANES

If you come here after a short or long illness your departed friends and relatives may be around to welcome you, but if your death is sudden they may take a while to come down to welcome you. But you can be sure they will come, except if you are in the lower Realms. In that case, don't expect any good soul to welcome you. Evil souls, however, will be ready to take you to the low Realms.

There are 7 Realms, or planes, in the spirit world. In each Realm there are 10 stages, from 0 to 9. So Realm 1 – 0 would mean Realm 1 Stage 0.

Realm 1 is the lowest and darkest and also the nearest to Earth. It is the most horrible place. There are bare rocks with crawling creatures – human souls with disfigured bodies and horrible minds, full of bad feelings. Their bodies are much heavier than ours and they live in a barren world, crawling about on rocks in pitch darkness. They never see even a tiny spark of light at any time.

Realm 2 is also horrible, but not as dark as Realm 1, nor are the bodies so heavy or disfigured. They also live in rocky caves, hating each other and using filthy, terrible language, seeing no light or good things.

Realm 3 is still better, but yet there is no light. The bodies are lighter than in Realms 1 and 2. The atmosphere is extremely heavy and foggy, and their bodies look human, but are older-looking, and imperfect. The souls on Realm 3 have bad feelings for each other and they blame each other for everything. They catch souls who have arrived on Realm 3 for the first time and make these souls their slaves, forcing them to help them in their evil ways.

Realm 4 is an in-between Realm. It is more or less like Earth, where there is both night and day. It is the Realm in which a human soul starts its life journey. You are given a chance to go up or down from Realm 4 Stage 5, and it is entirely in your hands.

Realm 5 is the beginning of heaven, which is like a beautiful place on Earth. There is a little brightness in the sky at *all* times. Souls on this Realm are helpful to each other. Their bodies are much lighter and there are no deformities.

Realm 6 is very beautiful, full of wonderful bright green grass, trees and flowers of colours you cannot see on Earth. It is always bright throughout, like a sunny day. The souls have nearly perfect, very light bodies and they all live in harmony and love, helping each other and doing work that they love. If you are on Realm 6 and above your subconscious mind (what you call conscience), which is your true, spiritual mind, will work in such a way that it will stop you from committing those sins on Earth that would take you lower than Realm 4.

Realm 7 is the highest. The people on Earth could never even imagine how beautiful it is. The beauty of Realm 7 has to be seen to be believed. It is beyond any power of description – yes, it is beyond imagination. Souls on this Realm have the brightest, most perfect, young-looking spirit bodies. They are as light as clouds. They live in utmost harmony and love. It is more than heaven.

After Realm 7, what? We don't know, just as people on Earth don't know much about the spirit world. After Realm 7 Stage 9 we do not reincarnate any more on Earth. But our spiritual journey continues.

Those on Realm 7 are almost perfect, purified souls. But if they reincarnate on Earth, and somehow sin even a little, they have to go down to Realm 5 or 6. So it is always in every soul's own hands whether to take God's good path or go down the evil, dark path.

22-04-1981

OUR REAL HOME

We all know that it is good to leave from Earth and go to the spirit world. The spirit world is our real home. We go to Earth for a short time and return home. We go to Earth to gain experience. Earth is our School where we have to learn, gain experience and try to purify our souls to reach a higher level.

Earth people have no memory of their real home – the spirit world. If you had that memory, you would never think of staying on Earth for even a minute. So God has given you no memory of your real home, your real loved ones and how beautiful the spirit world is. God has kept it this way so you will not be keen to return without first completing your training and schooling.

God is so sure that you would hate to live on Earth if you remembered the spirit world so He has entirely blocked that memory from your physical mind; but your spiritual mind, also known as your subconscious mind, has full memory of the spirit world. However, the subconscious mind does not reveal this memory to your physical, logical mind.

If the subconscious mind is dormant in a person on Earth, the person will not know God's real laws. We want you to be aware of this fact so you can awaken your subconscious mind, as people on Earth are going from bad to worse. We want you to know the truth and be brave enough to follow the right path.

23-04-1981

BEASTS OF BURDEN

Very good souls suffer greatly, and evil souls seem to go scot-free on Earth. We often hear people cry out, "Is this God's justice?"

Very good souls must go through all kinds of training and gain experience. For this, they must suffer to rise to a higher level. The more success evil souls reap on Earth, the deeper in hell they will go. There is no other way out because one day everyone has to die and come to the spirit world. So the more success bad people experience on Earth the more pitiful is their experience when they come to the spirit world. If evil or bad souls succeed in harming others, pity them because they will definitely go down to the lowest Realm and suffer the utmost – so don't envy them and say, "See the evil person is happy and successful." Instead ask God to do what is best for that person. The person must die in your world and the day will come when his soul has to face the lowest Realm and endure extreme suffering for ages and ages to come.

You must not say that there is no such thing as God's justice. When evil souls go beyond a certain limit they suffer the most. The lowest Realm means pitch dark, humid, cold, bare rocks and creepy things crawling all over you. There is no hope to see even a tiny bit of light or anything good. These evil creatures have distorted limbs and are therefore forced to crawl. They have horrible-looking faces and their clothes are old tattered rags. They are half-human and half-beast.

There is another way of going through your punishment.[4]
If you truly repent and your call to God is genuine, you
get to be born and suffer as a beast of burden, which will
be a little better than the lowest of the low Realms. **As a
beast of burden, you have full memory of the sins of
your previous lives on Earth.** You go on suffering,
remembering every sin you had committed and you repent
for it. You can be sure that such souls do become beasts of
burden and not pets that are treated kindly. (This does not
mean that human beings should treat any living being
unkindly.)

Good souls never want to sin, as they would hate to be in
an evil soul's place. It is so very terrible that we have no
words to describe it – if you can, try to improve evil souls
so that they don't go to the lowest of the low Realms. If
they are successful in their evil ways be sure it will be
worse for them in a few years. So it is your duty to try
hard to improve them by showing them what they are.
Never encourage them in their ways by being nice to them,
but show them how wrong they are.

24-04-1981

IS IT GODLY TO HELP EVERYONE?

It is a great privilege to know the real laws of God
Almighty. You must have heard people say, "It is
Godly to help everyone." Yes, of course, it is Godly to

---

4   This refers to your karma – what you sow you reap. It is not God who
    punishes. Karma is the consequences of a soul's actions, good or bad.
    Negative Karma is not only your punishment. The higher purpose is that
    of learning. Positive Karma also exists – the blessings you receive for
    selfless good deeds done.

help, but *not* everyone. It is good to help your fellow men, but you cannot help *all* your fellow men, as some are positively evil. It is up to you to find out which people you should help and which people you should not — because if you help an evil soul, you are encouraging evil. So have you done right? Is this what God wants you to do? Think, and you will understand that you are harming yourself as well as that evil soul. You will say, "I won't help an evil person in murdering or harming anyone." We do understand you wouldn't do that, but if you help that evil person by even giving food, money or clothing to him, is it wrong? Yes, it is absolutely wrong. It is wrong because by giving him this he sustains his energy and continues to do more evil. So it is against God's laws to give even a little help to such souls, as they will go on harming others if you help them.

Be firm with an evil person. If you are not firm you are encouraging him. By doing so you are also of the same category, of the same sinfulness. Suppose you pass a starving man lying on the road and you feel it is your duty to give him some money or food. You cannot ask him whether he is an evil person and if he is evil he would definitely not tell you the truth. So you don't know at all whether he is evil or good and your heart tells you to give him something, because he is starving. If your heart says so, you have to give him something, because you are absolutely ignorant of that man's character. But if you *knowingly* give charity to an evil man or help him it means you yourself are also evil, otherwise you would not give an evil person any kind of help.

You would say, "But he was starving, so should I watch him die of hunger?" No, it is not humane, so give him food, but never help him in other ways, *except* when that evil person has repented for his deeds. This means he has really repented and keenly and genuinely wants to improve. In that case, you must help him in whatever way you can. It is your duty to help bring him out of evil influences and progress to a higher level. That is a real good deed. But you should only give him full support if he *really* repents and genuinely wants to improve.

Help a good man in doing good — go out of your way to help the good. **But make sure your deed is selfless. Your action should be purely selfless.** That's what you should know about helping people, and we are sure you will never go wrong.

25-04-1981

EARTHLY CRIMES vs. SINS

Many times we have heard and also said, "God helps those who help themselves." This is absolutely true. It is a real law of God Almighty.

Suppose you are on a lower Realm, but have the genuine desire to go to a higher level and you truly try to improve, God will do His best to help you. God Almighty wants you to rise spiritually. He wants you to be really happy, so if you show a little inclination towards improvement, you will get a lot of help.

Many people on a lower level will say, "I have harmed no one. I was a God-fearing man and I have never committed crimes." **You may have never committed crimes, but you may have committed many sins.** God is not concerned with the laws people on Earth have made. What is considered a crime in your world may not be a sin, and what is a sin may not be a crime. For example, it is not a crime to be selfish; nor is it a crime to show the world that you are a good soul when inside you are black as darkness. No, it is not a crime, but it is a big sin.

So you see, many of your crimes — the breaking of man-made laws — are not sins. Sinning means breaking God-made laws. Many sins are not counted in your world as wrong, so the people on Earth are mistaken about God Almighty's real laws. There are many sins that are taken lightly and some that are not even thought of as sins. So isn't it better for the people on Earth to know which sins will put you on the lower levels of the spirit world, which is your real home?

26-04-1981

YOU HAVE TO PAY FOR YOUR SINS

Now, pay careful attention as this is very important. You must not make any mistake in understanding this. It is said that if evil people leave their evil ways and walk on the right path God will take over. Yes, God does take over and help them to rise higher, but this does not mean He forgives them and welcomes them to heaven as soon as the evil people say they want to be on the good side. Definitely not, **you have to pay for your sins, no matter what.** But if you have the genuine desire to change, God will definitely help you. That will only happen when you truly repent for your sins and God is sure that you will *not* go back to your old ways. Only then will He help you rise up sooner. Rising up sooner does not mean God will take you straight to the higher Realms, it means He will guide you and teach you to pay off your karma in a good manner. He will guide you in this way so you can reach the higher levels much sooner than you could otherwise.

You should by no means believe that if you are evil at one moment and then think of God and worship Him the next, you will reach heaven. It is silly to confess to a priest and think that God has forgiven you. As I said before, the priest may be more of a sinner than you. Who is he to forgive you? Only God Almighty can forgive you for your sins, but not before *you* truly repent.

Your inner motive — a genuine desire to change for the better — is the only thing that matters. Your inner desire must be to reach God Almighty by leading a true, honest and kind life.

A person may be quite ordinary and no one may bother to look at him twice, or no one may even care to answer his humble questions. He may be nobody in your world, but in the spirit world he may be even higher than any famous man on Earth. So you see, for you on Earth it is difficult to judge a real good soul from an evil soul. There is a vast difference between these souls, but you would still never be able to differentiate between them because **you are absolutely blind to the vibrations and the aura of a soul.** Yes, it is most difficult for you to understand who is a good soul and who is evil.

Many times people on Earth have thought a person to be very holy and pious, but that person may be an extremely evil soul. Our advice to you is that if you can communicate *safely* with the spirit world, take guidance so that you will not be fooled and dragged to a lower level by the constant company and influence of evil souls.

27-04-1981

THE DEVIL DOES NOT EXIST

It is said that there is a Devil who will tempt you. Well, let us tell you that **there is no Devil in our universe, but there are as many devils as there are evil people** — here, on the lower levels of the spirit world, as well on your Earth plane. These devils have made your world a hellish place to live in. On Earth you all live together — good souls, bad souls, and even evil souls — but here in the spirit world good souls do not live with bad or evil souls.

All good souls together.
All bad souls together.
All evil souls together.

In the spirit world, you need not fear that an evil soul will harm you, or a bad soul will fool you. Here all good souls live together in harmony, love and help each other, and never harm anybody.

Bad souls live together and fool each other. They have jealousy, dishonesty and bad feelings for each other. They harm each other, even torture each other mentally. But bad souls who want to improve just have to call for help. If this call is genuine, help will immediately come from higher Realms. Many kind souls from higher Realms will go to their aid and try to bring them out of their misery.

Evil souls on the lowest Realms find it very difficult to rise spiritually, as the evil souls around them will try to make them more evil and not let them improve. As evil souls allow no goodness to come out of their souls, it is most difficult — but not impossible — for them to improve. Even the worst kind of evil soul will improve in a very limited time, but some evil souls remain on the lowest Realms for centuries, as they have no desire whatsoever to improve. Such souls try to prevent others, who have the desire to advance, from improving because they don't want to be alone. So you see it is very difficult to rise from lower Realms, but as we said it is not impossible if you genuinely repent.

So dear readers, these are the real devils, the ones who try hard to make others evil like themselves. If others desire to rise to higher Realms, they try their level best to discourage them and even harm them as much as possible so that they don't rise.

Now let's talk about God Almighty. There is no need to tell you about God, as everyone knows about Him — our heavenly Father, **King of our universe and several other universes.**

God is full of love, kindness, justice and wisdom. He is a just Lord of Heaven, who will never misjudge a soul. His sole intention is to improve you, help you throw away all your evil feelings, purify your soul and make you happy. He has several helpers to guide souls on even the lowest of Realms. So you can be sure that His kindness and love will never fail and that He is the one who can bring even the most evil of souls to the higher Realms.

28-04-1981

YOU TRULY REAP WHAT YOU SOW

Many people on Earth simply refuse to believe in life after death. Those who do believe, believe in eternal peace, thinking that eternal peace means you sleep forever — what a silly conclusion, what a misguided thought!

In the spirit world, we are more alive than you are on Earth, as we are free of bodily aches and pains. We are *almost always happy* and most of all we are spirits with no burden of the physical body. We can work at what we like the most. We don't quarrel with each other, we don't hurt each other and we never steal or do any harm to anybody and therefore we don't need to protect our homes. We are absolutely free and our freedom is given to us by God Almighty. If we like to study, we study; if we like to work, we work; if we want to rest, we do; if we would like to visit a friend, we go; if we feel like praying, we pray. We can do whatever we feel like doing. So does that not mean we are freer than you all are? Are we not more alive and do we not know more than you know, even about yourself? We just want you to keep in mind that whatever we tell you will be better than what you know, do, or think, and at the same time we would like to tell you that we are not perfect. We are also learning. We will be perfect and completely purified only when we reach God. Now, as you fully understand us, we from the spirit world want to send you these messages so that we can guide you. From the Earth world you can reach a higher level much sooner than when you are in the spirit world.

There are certain laws of our God Almighty that are

observed very strictly by all souls. Most important of all is this, **"Whatever you sow, you reap"**.

God Almighty is very kind-hearted and full of love, so humans began to take advantage of His love and kindness. But God has given you a subconscious mind, or conscience. This subconscious mind operates on the principle of, "Whatever you sow, you reap". You get good for good and evil for evil. There is no injustice. If you have been good you will get happiness in the spirit world. **If you have harmed someone you have to pay for it and your own subconscious mind will make you suffer.** It is your own subconscious mind that gives you real justice, no one else. Your own subconscious mind, without your knowledge, gives you justice, as your physical mind does not even know why you are suffering. You automatically get your reward or punishment, as the case may be. From this, you will see that God Almighty is extremely kind and full of love and that He never punishes anyone. Whatever you sow, you reap.

29-04-1981

REBIRTH

It is not possible for us, in the spirit world, to know all future events. We do know some, but we are not supposed to tell you about them unless we get instructions or permission from high souls to tell people on Earth. As soon as people on Earth contact the spirit world they ask hundreds of questions regarding their future. Only a few refrain from asking such questions. We don't blame you for this, but we request you never to bother us about the future.

Aimai Navrojee Batliwalla reincarnated as Khorshed Rumi Bhavnagri
(Khorshed Bhavnagri's great grandmother)   nee Screwalla
Date of Death: 1800s   Date of Birth: 27 September, 1925

Rumi P. Mehta   reincarnated as   Burzin Vispi Mehta
(Burzin's father's brother)
Date of Death: 5 January, 1969   Date of Birth: 5 August, 1980

Jal Dumasia   reincarnated as   Vistasp Nozer Kanga
(Vistasp's maternal grandfather)
Date of Death: 15 January, 1994   Date of Birth: 1995

As we will explain, no one knows the exact future, as no one can know how others will act. For example, we might tell you that you will live for 90 years, but the next day you might be killed in an accident or be assassinated. It is all about a human being's free will and the choices one makes. On Earth, one cannot predict beforehand what is going to happen.

Sometimes we do know what will happen — if it is a definite thing that should happen — but we may not be permitted to tell you. We are permitted or even instructed to tell you some things for the good of others and yourself. For the most part, the future is rarely correctly predicted on Earth and if we do know and are not permitted to tell you then it is absolutely senseless to ask us about it. So please refrain from that.

We, in the spirit world, can know a lot about what will happen to us as we want to improve and reach higher levels. We ask God Almighty to send us back to Earth and we ourselves decide as to where we will take rebirth. We always choose our mother. Our father comes to us automatically because, many times, we may not know who our mother will marry. However, sometimes, we can also pick our fathers.

We mostly choose a mother who will look after us, love us and care for us until we can look after ourselves. We usually pick a mother who is very dear to us, but sometimes, to gain experience, to pay off karma and to advance higher, we pick a bad or evil soul as our mother.[5]

---

5. Read "Soordas' Story" on page 83 to learn about evil mothers and spiritual advancement.

No one can force us to go to one mother when we want to go to another. If we need rough handling and punishment for our sins, we naturally choose a bad soul as our mother so that we will suffer and be good after going through a rough childhood. In that case, we take a huge risk, as that mother may even ruin our life if her influence is too strong and we are not able to control our minds. We must, however, take such risks for our improvement — to purify our soul.

You will ask, "Isn't there another way to improve and to rise to a higher level?" Yes, there is another way, but it would take ages and ages to reach our goal. **On higher Realms you can choose never to be reborn on Earth and try to advance in the spirit world itself, but this process is extremely slow.**

Most souls take the risk and are born even to bad mothers in order to improve. Others choose rebirth just to help their loved ones. They are the ones who choose their mothers from among their loved ones and try hard to follow the good path, as they never want to fall spiritually.

From this you can understand how free we are. In the spirit world we can do what we like. If it is wrong, our subconscious mind will never permit it. **There is *no* risk of going lower if you are on a higher level in the spirit world.**

If you choose the risky way to improve you might ruin your life by not following the laws of God Almighty, as you will have absolutely no idea what is right and wrong because your subconscious mind does not work full time on Earth. Only those on a high level who take rebirth can be guided by their subconscious mind on Earth.

We, Vispi and Ratoo, both chose our mother, whom we loved the most.

30-04-1981

FIGHT EVIL

We all do some work here, each and every one of us. Whatever we like best, we do with joy. Some of us send messages to people on Earth to bring them out of their misery and guide and help them to rise up higher than they currently are. Many souls do this — some are successful and some are not.

We are very keen to relieve the people on Earth from the aches and pains of daily physical fatigue, but that can only be done when you discard your physical body, so it is not in our hands. But it is in our hands to guide you all as to what the real laws of God Almighty are.

Some of God's laws you never knew, and some you misinterpreted. So we are here to put you on the right path. If you are nice to evil souls you are encouraging them. Don't be nice to them; don't help them in any way. If that evil soul wants to change, be sure of it first and then help that soul wholeheartedly. That is your duty. *But be sure of that person's intentions.* How can you be sure? If you are absolutely sure, you would not ask how you could be sure, which means you are in doubt. That means you may be right or you may be wrong. This is where we spirit beings come in for your guidance. We can guide you on whether to believe that person or not. But, for those who have no contact with the spirit world, we advise you to pray from the bottom of your heart and ask God Almighty to help you in that matter and God will somehow lead you to the right path.

So remember, never be nice or encourage evil people. **Fight evil. That is an important rule of God Almighty.**

01-05-1981

ONLY GENUINE DESIRE CAN LEAD TO CHANGE

God Almighty is full of love and kindness. He is absolute, a perfect judge. He wants every soul to come up to a higher level, so He has many helpers to guide sinful and bad souls as well. His helpers are as kind and loving as He is.

Now, suppose an evil soul wants to rise to a higher level but has no desire to improve, then what? He will languish on whichever level he is. He will never come up because he has no desire to improve his wrong ways.

Your own genuine desire works wonders. You may tell yourself, "I have a great desire, but I don't think I am moving to a higher level." Just think for yourself, and ask yourself, "Do I have a *real* desire to improve myself or am I just pretending that I want to improve?"

There is a vast difference between the two — to have a genuine desire, and a make-believe desire in which you fool yourself. By analysing yourself you will most probably understand which of the two you are actually feeling. If you are really keen on improving you will definitely stop fooling yourself and go about it genuinely.

Nowadays, good souls are few and bad souls are many. So it is the duty of every good soul to improve a bad soul. But no one can force another; it should come from within. A bad soul saying, "Yes, I want to improve," hundreds of times will not help. Advice and guidance from us will not help either. Only you can bring yourself off the wrong path and onto the right one.

No matter how much we, from the spirit world, try, no one, not even God Almighty will be able to bring you out of your wrong ways as He has given you a subconscious mind to guide you and He will never interfere with it. Your subconscious mind will definitely punish you if you are wrong and you will stay on the same lower level until you genuinely try hard to progress. There is only *one* way to rise to a higher level and that is to genuinely improve yourself. No other way will ever help you – no prayers, no pleas to God Almighty – if you do not have the genuine desire. So start immediately, before it is too late.

02-05-1981

VISITING ANOTHER REALM IN THE SPIRIT WORLD

There are 7 Realms in the spirit world. The lowest of them is Realm 1 and the highest is Realm 7, so according to your good deeds and sins your own subconscious mind takes you to the Realm you deserve to be on. No one can go higher than he deserves, no matter how much he tries.

It is impossible for a soul to visit a higher Realm, as that Realm is invisible to him — you can only see your own Realm and the ones below you. From Realm 5 onwards, however, a soul can visit a higher Realm if certain requirements are fulfilled:

1.   Someone from a higher Realm should invite him.

2.   Permission should be granted by the High Good Soul of that higher Realm.[6]

3.   He has to undergo certain training.

4.   He must wear a protective cloak so that the extra bright light won't blind him and the extra-light atmosphere won't suffocate him. As his soul is a little heavier than souls in the higher Realm, he needs a cloak that makes him lighter.

You cannot stay in that higher Realm for long and you cannot go often. You can go from Realm 5 to 6 and from Realm 6 to 7 very rarely and for a very short time.

We have made such visits. Some of us have had the great privilege and honour of visiting Realm 7. However, we can all go to the lower Realms to visit or to improve someone as often as we would like.

If we must visit the lower Realms, such as Realms 1, 2 or 3, we also need a protective cloak. **This protective cloak makes us invisible to all evil and bad souls, so that they and their bad vibrations don't harm us.**

Those on Realms 1, 2 and 3 can never leave their Realms,

---

6. The Ruler, King or Head of each Realm is called the High Good Soul of that Realm.

except when they have repented greatly and genuinely and have been shown the way out by kind souls from higher Realms. This only occurs when the good souls are sure that the soul from the lower Realm will never again commit those sins. The soul then has to repay those he has harmed by taking rebirth and paying off his karma. This can sometimes take hundreds of years, whereas at other times, can take only a few years. This is entirely in the hands of each individual soul.

Many have risen from the lowest Realms to the highest Realm in a few hundred years. There are also some good souls that have never seen Realms 1, 2 or 3 in their entire spiritual life.

Every soul starts its spiritual journey from Realm 4, Stage 5.

Many souls have risen very rapidly, others have taken thousands of years, and still others have been in the lowest Realms for eons. There is no fixed rule or time for souls; it depends on the individual and if the desire to improve is definite and genuine it takes a shorter time to rise spiritually.

03-05-1981

GOD'S JUSTICE

God Almighty is very kind, loving and full of justice. No one ever gets treated unjustly. Many people think that God has been unjust to them because they don't really know what is right and what is wrong — that is the real reason so many feel God has been unjust.

For example, we know one soul, whom we will call Suresh. He was very popular on Earth and was quite famous. He had made donations of thousands of rupees to various charities. He created jobs and donated clothing, homes, and food to many, so he was absolutely certain he would go to the highest Realm. When he died on Earth, a grand funeral was held in his memory and people kept speaking of what a good soul he was. A statue of Suresh was erected in the charitable institute he had helped establish.

When he came to the spirit world he found himself on a low Realm. He was furious and shouted, "Where is God's justice? I gave so much to charity – people actually worshipped me on Earth – and God put me in this hell! Why? Where is His justice? He is most unkind and unjust. He is cruel."

Many good souls went to him and told him to calm down and listen to the reasoning behind this situation. They told him to ask himself why he acted so charitably – what was his motive?

He said, "I did those things so that I could go to heaven, but look at where I am."

The good souls explained to him, "Your act was not selfless. You did all of this to secure a place in heaven for yourself, isn't that true?"

He said, "Yes, it is true, but don't our holy people, priests, and philosophers say that if you help poor people and give them shelter, food and jobs, you will go to heaven? God, the priests and all the philosophers have fooled me."

They explained to Suresh that God Almighty had not fooled him, but rather he had fooled himself, as whatever he had done was not out of generosity. His deeds were neither good nor selfless. He did them for his own selfish motive, which was to go to heaven by bribing God after having committed sins. He had only been charitable to wipe away his sins.

He was furious and said, "This is wrong. I was done a great injustice. I should be in heaven. I deserve to be in heaven as I did so many good things to wipe away my sins, to gain heavenly bliss. Instead, God fooled me and is keeping me here."

He was so shocked to be on such a low Realm that he was unable to think straight. He cursed the priests, holy men and God, but he did not realise that the sins he had committed could not be wiped away by the *selfish* motive of giving thousands in charity.

You have to pay for your sins no matter how much you give in charity. Nothing will wipe away your sins except real, heartfelt repentance and somehow repaying the person you harmed. So you see, many people have the wrong notion that because they have given thousands in donations they will go to heaven. If you do good deeds with that motive forget about seeing heaven, as you will never even reach heaven's doorstep. You can be sure of that.

04-05-1981

SPIRIT COMMUNICATIONS

W e are here and you are there, but we can still see you, talk to you and exchange our thoughts. Most people on Earth don't know that, however, so that is why only few can communicate with us. We are exhilarated when a soul from Earth is able to communicate with us.

On Earth many believe that if anyone communicates with the spirit world they must be real devils and that it is very bad and harmful to do so. This is absolutely untrue. **It is entirely false to think that it is bad to communicate with the spirit world.**

Some are *forced* to believe it is wrong to communicate with the spirit world. They are convinced it will hinder us spirits and stop our progress by bringing us (our souls) down to Earth. These are all wrong ideas. On the contrary, God Almighty and High Good Souls are very happy if we seek permission to communicate with people on Earth.

You see, some of us spirit beings have to 'impress'[7] upon our loved ones to stop doing what is wrong, as we want them to be with us on the same high Realm. We face many difficulties while projecting our thoughts to them.

Most of the time, after working so hard to impress upon people on Earth, we fail very badly to even give you a tiny idea because many people do not accept our good thoughts

7. Spirit beings provide guidance to Earth souls through telepathic thoughts known as projected thoughts. These thoughts or 'impressions' can be intercepted by Earth souls through their subconscious minds.

and advice, because their minds are limited.

By communicating directly with people on Earth we can very easily tell them what is good for them and prevent them from falling spiritually and going to lower Realms. However, we are not allowed to reveal what the spiritual test might be. We can only help them by giving them **hints** and guidance.

It is easier for us to communicate directly with people on Earth, rather than trying to project our thoughts, which normally fail to penetrate your thick skulls. The few who can safely and easily communicate with us must place all their random thoughts aside, which will help both of us.

Our progress is faster when aided by communications, as we don't waste our precious time trying to put down good thoughts, ideas and wisdom in people's constricted minds, as only a small percentage of your subconscious mind works on Earth.

From now on, you must try to contact your departed loved ones. **BUT YOU CANNOT START ON YOUR OWN. IT IS VERY DANGEROUS TO START COMMUNI-CATING THROUGH AUTO WRITING ON YOUR OWN.** You have to build up a link through a person who is authorised and experienced at automatic writing.

It is easy for us to communicate continuously with our loved ones. It's just like sitting at home and talking on a two-way radio. There is not much difference between our method of communication and your two-way radios.

We rarely come down to Earth to talk to you. We simply

sit in our home and communicate via our expanded subconscious mind. **Our thoughts are extraordinarily powerful.** Like a two-way radio, we transmit and receive.

Some people on Earth have a God-given power of a two-way radio in them as well, so they can receive our messages in the same way and we can very easily gather what you say or think. Some people on Earth are lucky to have this power, but some are not. Always remember that it is best for both you and us when we communicate via this two-way radio of our mind. Ask for help from one who has this gift and you will see what a difference it can make in your life.

05-05-1981

HOW THE REALMS WORK

Together Realms 1, 2 and 3 are known as hell and Realms 5, 6 and 7 as heaven. Realm 4 is an in between Realm. It is neither heaven nor hell. It is the one from which human souls start.

The ultimate aim is to reach Realm 7. You have to work very hard to do this. What makes the difference is the inner instinct to rise higher. Then you never do things that bring you down and you reach your goal very soon. There are a few lucky souls who have done this. It is entirely in your hands.

Each of the 7 Realms is governed by a High Good Soul. By *governed* we mean he is the head of that Realm.

In higher Realms, no one commits sins or harms anyone.

Justice is always served by our own subconscious mind so there is no need for a police force or high-ranking officers. However, we do need permission to do certain things and if we need some advice or guidance we go to the High Good Soul of our Realm.

Sometimes even the High Good Soul of our Realm must ask permission or guidance or must seek advice for us from **His Highest Good Soul** – the head of Realm 7, who is also the head of *all* the Realms, like an Emperor.

Realms 1, 2 and 3 are each governed by one High Good Soul; it is the same with Realms 4, 5, 6 and 7. The leader of Realm 7, His Highest Good Soul, however, is the ruler of all.

They are very humble and kind-hearted that they will never make you feel they are superior to you. They will even laugh with you, joke with you and behave as if you are on the same level as them. Their light is so luminous and their shimmering cloak is so wonderful that, immediately you know they are pure, true and high good souls.

We cannot go down to the lower Realms. If we have to, we need protection as the atmosphere is bad, our eyes need to get accustomed to the darkness and the bad vibrations and evil influences could affect us by making us depressed and uneasy. So we have to take certain precautions, especially to go to Realms 1, 2 and 3. Mostly, when we go down to Realms 1 or 2 we wear a cloak that makes us invisible to the negative souls in those Realms.

We need permission and protection to go to the higher Realms as well, as their light is too bright for us, atmosphere too fine and vibrations too strong for us. You can only go up a Realm higher than the Realm you are on. No one can go higher than one Realm for a visit (thank God we were on Realm 6; in 1985 we reached Realm 7). You can, however, go down to the lowest Realm to advise, guide and improve a soul that has called for help. We need extra protection and so we must be invisible to all except the one who has called us, otherwise those awful souls might harm or attack us. They are very nasty and they sometimes capture higher souls and keep them as prisoners and resort to mental torture as they cannot do anything physically, for we do not have physical bodies. If we become their prisoners many High Good Souls must come and free us, so it is best to be invisible to them. Otherwise, it is best not to visit such places.

There are many good souls who spend most of their time in Realms 1, 2 and 3 to guide, advise and improve others. It is very rare that Realm 1 souls call for help. Even though the High Good Souls want to help the souls of Realm 1, these souls are so lost and gone so far on the wrong path that they are incurable. If they are helped without their genuine realisation and repentance, they will commit all those sins again. They spend hundreds of years on Realm 1. But the souls on Realms 2 and 3 are often helped by good souls, who go there to bring them up.

If a soul realises his mistakes, repents sincerely and asks for help, many good souls will rush to his aid at once. In this way, many souls from Realms 2 and 3 have had chances to rise, but souls from Realm 1 have little chance of rising. For them it mostly takes hundreds of years to rise.

For the souls of Realms 5, 6 and 7 it is also in their own hands to rise or stay where they are. They can stay in the spirit world where progress is slow and steady. Although progress is extremely slow, it is guaranteed that they cannot go down. It is entirely their free will to do what they want to do. No force is applied to anyone. Everyone is free to do only what they want. But this must be within the soul's capacity, otherwise their own subconscious mind will automatically stop them.

06-05-1981

YOUR SOUL NATURE IS YOUR TRUE SELF

You will have to live longer, much longer, in the spirit world, your true home, than on Earth, which is your temporary home or like a school. Before you commit sins please think about your future as everyone has to leave Earth one day. Then your subconscious mind will take you to the right Realm and you have to rise from there. So never go against your subconscious mind or conscience.

When your soul leaves your physical body it rises. It is much lighter than your physical body and all your pains, aches and deformities disappear along with your physical body, if you are fit for Realms 5, 6 and 7. The better your soul, the lighter and more colourful your spirit body. It is much lighter than you could ever imagine. You can even travel hundreds of miles in a few minutes.

Bad souls' bodies are heavier and full of deformities. On the Earth plane an evil soul may be good to look at, but when he comes to the spirit world, his spirit body will turn into one full of deformities.

On the contrary, **a good soul's body on Earth may be full of deformities, but when he comes to the spirit world his spirit body will be perfect.**

You just have to look at a soul in the spirit world and you will know whether he is good, bad or evil. Vibrations tell us everything. On Earth, however, you cannot judge a person by looking at them. Here, in the spirit world, we have no difficulty in recognizing people's virtues.

THE SILVER CORD

We know that many times things are hard for you to believe. For instance, we spirit souls and you Earth souls do meet constantly and almost every day. You will ask how? When you are in deep sleep, people on Earth leave their body and travel up to certain heights to meet their departed loved ones. Only a magnetic cord known as the **Silver Cord** joins you to your body. This cord will bring you back to your body if you are woken up suddenly. This happens only if your sleep is deep and dreamless. You have no memory of this, but we can assure you that you meet your departed loved ones almost everyday.

Let us make one thing clear, as it is most important. You can only meet loved ones who love you as well. If your love is one-sided this will not occur. Your loved ones should love you back. Suppose a departed soul says he loves you when he is on Earth, but on arriving in the spirit world, finds he cannot love you, he will never come to meet you, as he no longer wants any connection with you. Only near and dear ones who love each other can meet — whether they be mother and son, husband and wife, father and daughter, father and son, or even just friends. But there must be mutual love between them.

Remember that you do meet loved ones. **So *never* grieve for your departed loved ones, as your grief affects them.** It makes them depressed and miserable.

07-05-1981

WHEN YOU ARE ASLEEP, YOU ARE HEALED AND GUIDED

The spirit world is far from you and the Earth. It spans around the Earth, but miles and miles above you. The lowest Realm is closest to the Earth, above it is the 2nd Realm and so on.

You may meet your dear ones for a few minutes or for a few hours — it depends on your sleep, which should be deep and dreamless. Mostly everyone has a dear one to visit — even if he or she is not known to you in this life. Once again, the love should be mutual and not one-sided.

It is this link that keeps you going, no matter what you suffer. You have no memory of that visit, but its effect makes you face your problems and gives you courage to overcome your misery.

Have you noticed that after a good sound sleep you feel calm and less miserable than before? Well, the reason is this — you meet your loved ones and they calm you down and provide guidance through your subconscious mind, but your physical mind does not know anything about this. You are calmed down, but it is up to your subconscious mind whether it can force guidance upon your physical mind or not.

Every person on Earth needs good, sound sleep, even for a little while, which makes you visit us and allows us to help calm you down and guide you. When your subconscious mind fails to enforce guidance and advice into your physical mind we have to try hard to impress your physical mind, and make you understand what you should or shouldn't do. Most of the time, however, your physical mind rejects our advice and guidance, thinking it is just a passing thought that may be wrong. Most of the time you fail to understand our guidance and you often do what you shouldn't do. This is the worst part of your life on Earth, which often takes you to lower Realms because you ignore our guidance. You think, "Who is going to know about it – as long as I can be successful and rich on Earth, it is happiness to me." But have you thought of what will happen after a few years of happiness? You are on Earth for only a few years, but you are in the spirit world the rest of the time. **For a few years of temporary happiness on Earth, do you want to be on the lower Realms in the spirit world for hundreds of years?** This should help you understand why you should lead a good life on Earth.

08-05-1981

LIFE ON DIFFERENT REALMS

We are very happy here in the spirit world. In Realms 5, 6 and 7 we never harm each other. We laugh, joke, tease each other and are always in high spirits; we are *never* miserable or sad, except when our loved ones on Earth are sad.

The souls in Realm 4 are sometimes happy, sometimes sad, and sometimes they feel some jealousy towards each other, but still, they cannot harm each other much.

We have a spirit body so no one can kill us or torture us physically, but mentally it is possible and souls in Realms 1, 2 and 3 are experts in this.

The souls of Realm 4 sometimes fool each other, lie and try to make those who are disliked very unhappy. They have a little good and a little bad in them.

We don't need a police force or military to protect us, but in Realms 1, 2 and 3 you have to protect yourself or you will be tortured for centuries — unless you truly repent and call for help.

Even on Realm 4 you have to protect yourself, as someone may hound you mentally. On the Realms 5, 6 and 7 no protection is required, as no one would even think of harassing anyone.

Our main laws on Realms 5, 6 and 7 are these: help each other, make each other happy, do any work that you like, and help your loved ones on Earth.

We live so harmoniously on these Realms that when souls come here from Earth they feel completely free, without fear, sadness, bodily aches and pains. Love is all around. Above all, we live in an extremely beautiful place. So isn't it worthwhile to obey God Almighty's laws so that you can come to higher Realms? So people of Earth, do try hard to follow God's laws; be determined never to go wrong and we are sure God will bless you all!

09-05-1981

THE LOWER REALMS ARE FULL

As we mentioned before, you choose your mother. But why should you be born repeatedly, living out so many lifetimes? You, on Earth, know that you are reborn again and again to gain experience, but the main reason is to improve spiritually and rise to higher Realms. You are reborn to reach a higher level. But what do you do? Instead of rising high as God wants you to, *most* of you go down. Evil people rule your world. This is the reason the Earth is going from bad to worse.

Evil souls never want good to have the upper hand so they try very hard to suppress good and to bring out the evil in everyone. This is your world *now.*

So when you leave your world and come to the spirit world, those who are bad and evil are taken to the lower Realms by their subconscious mind. The lower Realms are absolutely full. The upper or higher Realms are very scarcely populated. A century ago it was quite the opposite. Many good souls have fallen to lower levels as negative vibrations and influences are too widespread in your world.

People who think they are successful on Earth are very happy that, by hook or by crook, they are rich and famous. They don't mind going to any extreme for money, sex and status. Only when they return to the spirit world do they realise the truth about what category they belong to, and how wrong they were on Earth. No one advised them, no one guided them, and then it is too late for them.

Some extremely evil souls don't mind going to even the lowest Realm, as their hearts are as dark as the darkest Realm. But those who have become bad through the influence of evil suffer the most. We pity them and we want them to read this book before it is *too late*.

10-05-1981

WHY SOME PEOPLE DIE YOUNG

We take rebirth to go higher, and most people on Earth go down because of the widespread evil influence in your world. Many good souls over here have to think hundreds of times before taking rebirth in your world, as no one likes to go down, except the real evil souls — the devils.

Many good souls are reborn in your world to do good, to fight evil and to spread harmony and goodness, but unfortunately the evil influence is so strong that their subconscious minds request God Almighty to bring them back home immediately. They hate to go down to lower Realms and their subconscious minds do not allow them to do wrong — extreme wrong — so they don't understand where to turn in a world so influenced by evil. That is why good souls are unhappy and miserable. **So without their conscious knowledge, their subconscious minds appeal to God Almighty to call them back to their real, spiritual home.**

This is the reason people on Earth have the saying, "Those who die young are God's favourites," or "God calls the young ones whom He loves the most."

Good souls who cannot go wrong due to their subconscious minds and cannot force good in your evil world do not know what to do. They constantly ask God, "Is this your justice?" But the subconscious mind knows what is wrong – it knows that good souls cannot cope in this evil world of yours and that's why many good souls return home sooner than they should. Only a few good souls live to be 90 or so and unfortunately, they suffer a lot.

Evil souls don't like to leave your world so they stick to their physical body and to the Earth like leeches. It is true that their subconscious mind knows very well where they will land once they die in your world, as the subconscious mind knows everything.

It is very strange that the subconscious mind tries hard to control and stop them when they do wrong, but they don't want to listen to their subconscious minds, as they are entirely blinded by evil forces. Such people *never* want to leave Earth as they fear they will land in lower Realms – and of course, their subconscious minds know the conditions there very well.

Some good souls try to stick to Earth as they feel they must protect some dear soul, or they may be given a mission to spread goodness, so no matter how much they suffer they still stick to their physical bodies and to Earth. There are those few who suffer very much yet stick to God's ways. They try to fight evil, but they get nowhere as evil has spread too heavily on Earth.

This book will give good souls some insight before they shout out to God, "Is this your justice, O God?" Our book reaches out to good souls who can be saved from evil influences with the hope that it will stop them from going down. We are sure that very few bad or evil souls will read this book and they will most probably think what is written here is nonsense.

Many don't believe in **Reincarnation**, so to them let us say that every soul is reborn hundreds of times, or sometimes over a thousand times to purify itself, but unfortunately many souls go down instead. There is not a single soul that would have lived only 10 or even 100 lives, but over many hundreds of lives you all come down to Earth.

It is wise to live your life such that it will take you higher, not lower. So, dear readers, lead your life in such a way that you will make God Almighty happy. Don't think that if you pray for hours God Almighty will be very pleased. By going to churches and temples every day or by giving to charities in thousands you take for granted that God will be pleased and He will welcome you to heaven. No, it won't work if your motive is to bribe God Almighty. He can *never* be bribed, but if you are very sincere and have given your time or money to charities with genuine kindness, if you worship God Almighty for a little while with no other motive than true love of God, of course God Almighty will be extremely happy and keen to make your place in heaven. **So dear readers, we urge you to lead a simple, honest, kind and selfless life.** This is more important than hours of prayers without concentration and giving thousands in charities to fool people and gain a place in heaven, or just to show others what a pious and holy person you are.

11-05-1981

GOOD SOULS ARE MISLED BY NEGATIVE SOULS

Many good souls have gone on the wrong path, influenced by evil and your world's evil ways, so it is about time people on Earth understood and believed in what is wrong and what is right.

We, in the spirit world, know what you are going through in your world. We know that evil has influenced the world so much that you find it very difficult to go on the straight path. Still, there are many who know they will suffer if they stick to the Godly Good Path, but they still stay on the right path. This is a great credit to them.

There are also some good souls who want to walk on the Godly Good Path, but because they *fear* that bad and evil souls might take revenge or harass and hurt them they stray from the right path. These souls must know that what they might suffer — the revenge or hurt from an evil man on Earth — will be nothing compared to what they will face in the lower Realms. They must also know that it will take hundreds of years and many more lives on Earth to come back to the level they left when they were in the spirit world, before rebirth.

If they only realised what awaits them, we are sure they would not fear an evil man's revenge or harassment. It is most necessary for them to know this. No, dear good souls, *don't go lower,* be sure that your few years of suffering at the hands of such evil persons will be much, much better than hundreds of years in the lower Realms.

We urge evil or bad souls to read and *reread* what we have

written about the lower Realms. It is no joke to live in such a state, even for a few days — how then, could you live there for hundreds of years? If you still want to continue on the path of evil, you are welcome to — it is your own folly — but please don't take others down with you. That is even worse as it will take you to the lowest of the low Realms. It is very wrong to make others suffer because of your selfish motives. Evil and bad souls should try to improve now and repent genuinely, otherwise the doors to the lowest Realm will open wide for them.

A famous person in your world will not be looked upon as higher in the spirit world. Here, a beggar from your world could be higher than a king or a very famous man. **Fame on Earth has absolutely *no value* in the spirit world.**

We are positive that no one in their right mind would be foolish enough to enjoy fame on Earth for a few years, only to suffer hundreds of years in the hellish darkness of the horrible lower Realms. You must try and take other souls to a higher level instead of trying to bring them down to the lower Realms. If you bring them lower, it is you who will suffer the most. The soul you have brought down will suffer too, but much less than you. It is up to you to heed our advice and guidance or ignore it.

12-05-1981

CONTROL YOUR MIND

Your senses on Earth have, in many ways, deteriorated because of your physical body. The physical body hinders a lot in spirituality, as it is a wall between your soul and the spirit world. It is the biggest nuisance, and creates many problems for your soul; you cannot be free from jealousy, hatred, dishonesty, hypocrisy, heartbreaks, revenge, or the sickness, aches, and pains of your body. The physical body is the prison, and your soul is the prisoner. This prison is so secure that it is difficult for a person on Earth to be free from all the negative feelings, except if you are on a very high level because your subconscious mind is much more open than that of ordinary people. If you have a genuine desire to be on a higher level you can control your physical mind and prevent it from going astray. **If you have good will-power you can control bad feelings and you will not commit sins.**

It is not easy in the beginning but, once you start walking on the Godly Good Path, it will come automatically and you will never go wrong. First, dear readers, you must try to control your bad feelings as much as possible. Once you are successful in this, it will become very easy and you will hate to do wrong. Sometimes, you may be overcome by bad feelings, but you will at once understand and immediately check yourself. So you just have to try very hard in the beginning and keep your bad feelings under control.

As we are without a physical body in the spirit world, we can control our minds in the very best way. On higher Realms every soul is free from such bad feelings, and we have no sicknesses, aches, or pains. But if you go to the lower Realms, you will find hatred, jealousy, torture, feelings of revenge – a place teeming with bad feelings. The souls on these Realms harm each other in such a way that sometimes it is beyond our imagination. There are no limits to their evil and ill will. They take pleasure in harming others, especially those who are weaker. The weaker souls go through hell on lower Realms. So imagine living there for hundreds of years. Think very hard before you act.

13-05-1981

OUR FEELINGS IN THE SPIRIT WORLD

We have all the similar feelings as you do on Earth – love, affection and kindness – but we love those dear to us more thoroughly and deeply, whether they are in the spirit world or your world.

As we don't have to cope with emotions like guilt, hate and jealousy, our love is pure and true. We love our dear ones selflessly, without wanting anything in return, for no other reason than for the sake of love itself.

Sex is out of question for us, so you see, our love is *not* physical but entirely spiritual and we have no desire for sex or any other reward. So whomever we love, we love truly, deeply, genuinely and very strongly.

We can easily forgive people on Earth than you can as we have no selfish feelings within us – we cannot hate anyone – it is out of question on these higher Realms.

We feel no jealousy here, even if we meet someone far superior to us. Instead of being jealous, we admire those superior souls and try to become like them. We shed all our bad feelings when we leave our physical bodies, but *all* the good feelings come back home, to the spirit world, with us.

The souls in the lower Realms are stuck with all of the bad feelings they had on Earth, even when they shed their physical bodies. Sometimes they become *more* hateful, vengeful and jealous, blaming God because they are in the lowest, darkest Realms.

JIMMY'S STORY:
ON EARTH, PEOPLE ARE NOT WHAT
THEY SEEM

We would like to tell you a true story about our friend, Jimmy Uncle (we have changed his name out of respect). He was an excellent speaker and very charming during his time on Earth. He showed the world that he was a good soul, who did not harm anyone. He showed us all that he always helped many people by giving them jobs, clothing, food, and plenty of money. He prayed regularly for hours and his wife and children were just like him. He constantly praised his wife, who was beautiful, but unwise. His children got through school by mere 'parroting'. He had high hopes for them and often praised their intelligence.

Like father, like son, they say. His children followed in their father's footsteps, and the people on Earth praised them all. They were very rich and famous, and very popular, so no one would ever have thought they would go anywhere but straight to heaven. We knew them very well, and when Jimmy Uncle died we were still alive on Earth. We prayed for his soul and consoled his wife and children, telling them that he must have immediately gone to heaven.

What fools we were! On Earth one cannot judge a soul

correctly. A while after we returned to the spirit world, we remembered Jimmy Uncle, so we began searching for him on our Realm (in 1981, we were on Realm 6). We couldn't find him, so we thought that a good soul like him would be on Realm 7, the highest Realm. Since we had wanted to surprise him, we hadn't called out to him with our thoughts at first, but when we couldn't find him on Realm 6 we projected our thoughts to Realm 7 and called out to him, "Jimmy Uncle, we are here in the spirit world, come and meet us on Realm 6." We did not receive a response.

Ratoo said, "Vispi, he must have gone beyond 7 as he was a real good soul." I added, "Must be. We will ask our High Good Soul."

As we were newcomers to the spirit world, it had never occurred to us to look for him on the lower Realms. We went to the High Good Soul and inquired about Jimmy Uncle. His High Good Soul smiled and said, "He is neither here on Realm 6 nor on Realm 7. When you go down to the lower Realms, try to find him there."

We were stunned and said, "That is impossible, Sir, he was a very good soul, much better than us." He replied, smilingly, "Yes, yes, I have heard that, but still go and look for him on the lower Realms when I send you there to do some work."

We felt bad and wanted to tell His High Good Soul all about Jimmy Uncle and the good deeds he had done on Earth, but we kept quiet because His High Good Soul knows better than us.

After some time, His High Good Soul called us and said,

"I am giving you two this opportunity to find out about your friend, Jimmy Uncle. I am giving you some work to do, so go down to the lower Realms, do your work and then try to find him." We were happy to go to work on the lower Realms. After finishing our work on Realm 3, we called out to Jimmy Uncle, but there was no response. We were happy, so we came back to our own Realm and told His High Good Soul.

His High Good Soul laughed and said, "Vispi and Ratoo, I want you to find him so that you can learn something that will be tremendously good for you. So I give permission and protection to you both. Go to Realm 2, find him, talk to him, and ask him why he is there."

We were very surprised and scared, as we had never been sent lower than Realm 3 for work. His High Good Soul assured us that we would be protected and sent us down.

The protection was excellent and no one could see or harm us. We went searching for Jimmy Uncle in that dark, horrible place. It was a shock to find him there in his state – stunned and miserable. We became visible *only* to him and he was surprised to see us. He felt very ashamed that we had found out what a bad soul he was. We could not stop ourselves from asking, "What did you do that brought you here, Jimmy Uncle?" And he poured out his story. It was a terrible story, and it was so startling that a man like Jimmy Uncle – so popular, nice, and good on the outside – was so terrible and mean within.

14-05-1981

JIMMY'S STORY CONTINUED:
YOU CANNOT FOOL GOD ALMIGHTY

Jimmy Uncle's story was so terrible, it was unbelievable. We could not believe it because we had always idealized Jimmy Uncle. He was always donating to charities, helping the poor, and had been a loving and friendly man. In Jimmy Uncle's own words, here is his story:

"Vispi and Ratoo, my dear friends, you thought I was a beautiful soul; you believed what I showed the world, and I believed it too. I believed that all of my horrible sins had been pardoned by God, as I was doing all of those good things *just to reach heaven* after I died on Earth. I gave money to charities and did good deeds thinking I wouldn't be punished for my sins, but I got what was due to me. I fooled myself and the Earth world, but no one can fool God. God can never be fooled.

"To start with, I began my life as the son of a very gentle, loving lady, who didn't even have any bad thoughts. My father was a crook; he harassed my mother and forced her to act wrongly. He was a very selfish man, and was even cruel to us. He forced us all — my mother, brothers, sisters and myself — to act wrongly. I watched my mother cry in agony so many times, telling us, 'It is wrong; it is all wrong; we are sinning.'

"My father joked about it and called her crazy. After a while, we, his children, were so impressed by our crooked father that my brothers, sisters, and even I began to see our mother as such — crazy and stupid. He saw to it that we would not respect our good, kind mother, and our love for her vanished.

"My mother was absolutely miserable seeing her children following in their father's footsteps. One day, my mother said, 'Jimmy, I want you to stop doing what your father tells you to because I believe it is wrong. As you are my eldest child, I want your co-operation to save your brothers and sisters.'

"I laughed at her, and said, 'Why don't you just jump from the cliff, since you cannot tolerate us all?' We lived in a cottage, near a deep valley, and from the window, I showed her a steep descent into the valley, and added, 'Nothing is fit for you but this death. Our father is an intelligent man; you are not fit to be his wife. Drown yourself in the river!'

"She did just that.

"The next morning, we were called by the police and we found her body lying by the riverside near our home. I was shocked, but still thought of her as a stupid and crazy woman. I considered her weak because she did not have the strength to stop herself from committing a sin like suicide. Our father was now very happy because he would not have to suffer any more interference from my mother.

"He started training us to become the worst type of crooks; he was such a thief, but we never knew about it until our mother's death for we were so impressed by him. We thought that all the nice things he brought us had been given to him by people he had helped. He had brainwashed us so much that we believed him absolutely and never questioned him.

"He trained us to con people and make them part with their valuables. He showed us how to fool them with sweet words, an innocent look, and a pious manner. To the world, we were all dutiful, good, kind and honest, but on the inside we were just like the devil our father was.

"Having taught us all these horrible things — even how to kill without leaving behind clues — he retired, telling us since he was the head he had a right to all the booty.

"He showed us boys how to approach old, widowed, or lonely ladies, win their love, make love to them and then take whatever they had, leaving them to a life of despair and poverty. He said with pride that he had done this to many women and had never been caught by the police. In fact, no one had ever even pointed a finger at him. We thought he was so great, intelligent and brave to have done such things that we must follow his example."

15-05-1981

JIMMY'S STORY CONTINUED: GOD'S JUSTICE ALWAYS CATCHES UP

"For a few years, we all did whatever our father told us to. We worshipped our evil father. He took us deep down to the darkest hell. We were really happy, living in admiration of him. His brainwashing did not let us think straight and we never realised at that time what devils we were.

"After a few happy years, our father began to suffer from a fever. Doctors said they could not diagnose what was wrong with him, so one of them told us to have his blood analysed. They found sugar in it, so we were told to put him on a strict diet. He was very particular about his health, so he did what the doctors told him. After a few months he felt a little better, and so he went out alone one day, but met with an accident. Both his legs and one hand had to be amputated. There was no other alternative.

"God's justice had begun but, like fools, we blamed God for harassing our beloved father. After some time, doctors detected cancer in his lungs. Just as before we blamed God, but went on with our horrible work. My sisters looked after our ailing father. The pain was unbearable and he became very weak, yet he would thrash my sisters with a long whip because he couldn't bear the pain. Our father abused us all, blaming us for his suffering.

"He shouted that we had neglected him and that we were very selfish. Our priest heard about our father's illness, his unbearable pain and came to our house. As usual, my father welcomed him, asking, 'Why am I suffering so much when I have never hurt a soul, have done only good deeds?' The priest never knew how evil my father was, so he prayed and asked God Almighty to help cure my father. After that day, he would come to our house every evening at 5 o'clock, so we all prepared for his visit and became virtuous, good souls just before 5 o'clock.

"One day, the priest happened to come earlier, when he entered the cottage he heard my father using absolutely rotten language to my sisters, blaming them for his suffering. He even mentioned how a dying old woman cursed him so that he would suffer horribly and he in turn cursed her, and many others who had cursed him.

"The priest was shocked – he turned and left without even announcing himself. The priest was an intelligent, pious man – he deduced that my father was evil and that he might have corrupted us, as well."

16-05-1981
JIMMY'S STORY CONTINUED:
GOD IS ALWAYS WATCHING

"The priest was a really intelligent and straight-forward man. He spoke to a police officer and asked him to find out everything about our family. By and by, the police found out almost everything – they got all the information, but unfortunately they had no proof.

"They did not know what to do. Meanwhile, my father's condition was worsening. He now felt unbearable pain throughout his body and his diabetes had worsened. He also suffered skin eruptions, which broke all over his body. His temper grew worse, and the sight of him was unbearable. He began throwing whatever he could lay his hands on, abusing and cursing us.

"The priest knew all about this as he was watching us all closely without our knowledge. One day, he came by when all of us were home, as our father's condition was very grave. We were all in his room, so he came straight in and said quietly, 'Look here, you will all see a miracle,' and he added, looking at my father, 'Calm down and watch this miracle.'

"He picked up all the objects from around the room, objects that could be thrown by our father, and ordered us to take them to another room. We took everything to the other room, thinking that the priest would somehow miraculously cure our father.

"He made sure there was nothing around that could be used against us, and he then made us sit around our father. As we were all under the impression that our father was going to be cured by some miracle, we never thought that the priest would perform an extraordinary miracle by fooling us all – we, who had fooled several people for many years.

"We sat around our father on his bed and the priest stood at the door. He began his prayer, loud and distinct. Then, he requested God to help him help us all. After that, he paused and began telling my father's evil and cruel story. At first my father shouted, cursed him and used horrible language. We tried to stop him, but we couldn't. At this point, we saw a few policemen appear behind the priest, guns in their hands.

"'Don't blame God Almighty, you evil people. This is the right punishment for you, you cruel man. You are getting your dues,' said the priest. He continued, 'Only God knows how much more you will suffer in hell for your horrible sins. You cannot fool God Almighty. You have fooled us all very well, even your own children. You've made them as evil as you are. It is you who ruined your wife's life and forced her to commit suicide. You wanted her out of the way so she could not influence your children to be good and fight you. You took the trouble to make sure we would have no proof, but you forgot that God Almighty does not need proof. This is His justice. Listen children – stop all your evil ways and repent before it is too late. Always remember that God Almighty does not need proof. He can never be fooled and no one will escape his justice, so turn back while there is still time. Dear children, turn back from the evil path your father has shown you and return to God's good path. Repent sincerely before it is too late.'

"Then he shut the door and went away. We were all stunned, including our father. After an hour or so our father came out of shock and began to cry like a baby. He said, 'Yes, God, you have punished me properly. I deserve this punishment. I am sorry, God; forgive me. I am happy that my evil life will soon end and that I will no longer be able to harm others. God, kill me soon.'

"He became unconscious after that, we were shocked and speechless at this turn of events. Our father never regained consciousness. Two days later, he passed away.

"Our reaction was strange — rather than accepting God's justice, we blamed Him. We began to hate each other and became suspicious of each other. My youngest brother left home without taking anything. After that, I left, taking with me all the money and jewellery that my father had made me keep in a secret place because I was his eldest, favourite child. I don't know what became of the rest of my brothers and sisters.

"I changed my name and came to Bombay with a great deal of money and jewellery. I did not leave a paisa[8] for my brothers and sisters; I took everything. So I came to Bombay a rich man, and was respected by all of you. I married a beauty, but I purposely chose a brainless beauty

---

8. A paisa is an Indian coin. It is 1/100th of an Indian rupee.

so that I could work my ways without any hindrance. I did not improve though the priest had urged me to.

"I worked silently and not very often, in case someone would find out about me. My family never knew what I was doing. In Bombay, I was a very respectable, rich and straightforward man, but as soon as I left Bombay for my horrible business I changed personalities. No one even dreamed that the rich, respectable, honest and kind Jimmy was this same man.

"That is my story. Now you know why I am in this dark, miserable place. I gave to many charities and did many good deeds, thinking my sins would be washed away. I was sure that I would go to heaven, but no one can fool God, so here I am."

17-05-1981

THE EARTH IS A SCHOOL

We in the spirit world know that people on Earth cannot live as harmoniously as we do in the spirit world. You have to live with good and evil souls, so there cannot be any harmony; we do understand. So you might say, let's live with our own type and ignore bad souls.

That is not what God Almighty wants. He wants you to help others who are facing difficulties. He wants you to *fight* evil and improve the Earth world. He wants you to reach out to fallen souls who were once good and on a higher level but have fallen due to the negative influences on Earth. Make them understand that they should not leave the good path, and should stick to the right one.

God Almighty wants you to act on His behalf and restore your Earth to a good, loving place. He does not want you to ignore evil or bad souls and sit idly in the company of good souls, whiling away your precious time. We say precious because your life on Earth is very short. Souls live longer in the spirit world.

Remember to *never* waste your time. You are sent to Earth to take on certain work, training, to gain experience, and to pay off karma, so finish what you have come to do on Earth before your time is up. Otherwise, you will have to be reborn again for the *same* purpose – and waste a lifetime – or continue your current life in a sickly physical body full of aches and pains for much longer than your karma requires. So don't waste precious time, finish your work quickly and maybe you can return before your time is up (you will never know when your time is up, only your subconscious mind will know).

God Almighty wants you to improve the bad and recently fallen souls and to selflessly help the needy and those who are facing difficulties on Earth. These are the main reasons you are on Earth. So perform your duties, and you will not regret it later.

THE PURPOSE OF REBIRTH

Many souls on higher levels are reborn on Earth for three reasons:

1. To protect and help their loved ones.

2. To finish the karma left over from previous lives.

3.   To do their spiritual mission.

Bad souls are sent to Earth to pay off their karma. The idea is to go through this punishment bravely and with a smile, only then will you improve and rise to higher Realms. Souls are sent back for a chance to change their evil ways, to repent, improve and to rise higher, even if it is not that much.

These are the main reasons why you are on Earth. **The most important reason is to *purify* your soul and rise to a higher level.**

The Earth is a training institute where bad souls should become good, good souls should become very good, and evil souls should improve by changing their evil ways and adopting good, Godly ways. But nowadays on Earth bad souls are becoming worse, good souls are turning bad, and evil is being spread extensively. We spirit beings feel terrible about this.

18-05-1981

THE STORY OF A GOOD SOUL WHO WAS BLINDED BY AN EVIL MAN

In the spirit world we also work as guardians to newcomers, or sometimes His Highest Good Soul sends us to the lower Realms if there is an urgent call from a soul who genuinely repents and wants to rise higher. We guide that soul on how to take his or her punishment in the best possible way and to improve and rise higher. There are many other helpers like us and every day each helper comes across such stories.

In our work, we do meet many sad souls on lower Realms, who are surprised at how they landed in the dark lower Realms. Sometimes we have a hard time trying to make them understand things.

We will tell you one such story. We were sent by His Highest Good Soul to a lower Realm, as a very urgent call had come through. We found a lady in a truly miserable state, so we said, "We came to answer your call." She looked up at us and said, "Is it possible for anyone to help me?"

"Yes, madam, we are here to help you."

She said, "No, no, no one can help me. There is no use. Go away."

"Madam, please cooperate with us, and you will feel much better. We will try our utmost to help you," we tried to assure her.

Since she could not stand the dark, horrible place any longer, she had shouted, "God, please help me," but instead of God, we had been sent so she was disappointed.

"I will cooperate with you," she said, "I will do whatever you tell me, as long as you take me away from this horrible place with all those terrible souls trying to harass me."

We said, "You look like a good soul, so what made you sin so much for you to land in this dark Realm?"

"Yes, you are right. I was a good soul who, unfortunately, fell in love with an evil soul, and that brought me here."

She began her story and requested us not to hate her or leave her thereafter hearing it.

"We can never hate you, and will try to help you. That is the only reason we are here."

"I was 19, and living happily with my parents and brother in a village. I had finished school, and dreamed of becoming a doctor, so I begged and pleaded with my parents to send me to a city university. Unfortunately for me, I won my argument at last. I went to the city and entered college, full of hope, laughter and enthusiasm. I was a beautiful girl, though shy. Many boys courted me, but I never encouraged any of them. I finally fell in love with a very handsome bully. At first, he tried to avoid me so, like a fool, I became even more attracted to him and chased him even more. I was madly in love with him and always tried to be near him.

"I knew he was a bully, and even saw him bullying some girls into writing his notes and doing his work for him. I was jealous of them and told him that I would love to write his notes and do all his work. I became his slave. Like a fool, I willingly jumped into hell. He just had to say a word and I would do his work. I lost my own judgment. Even now, I wonder how I could let it happen. I did whatever he told me to do. I peddled drugs for him and even brought him girls to enjoy. I wonder what made me act like such a robot — just one command from him and off I went to do his errands, anything that I felt made him happy.

"Even after I realised he was evil and that I was going down the wrong road, I continued to be his slave. I left college to work at a bank as a clerk. My parents were furious; they begged and pleaded with me to leave this boy, and continue my studies, or to return to our village with them. Nothing stopped me and I continued my slavery to the devil.

"It was enough for me even if he took me in his arms and made love to me once in a while in return for doing his bidding. I still wonder why I was so crazy. I was absolutely crazy about him, knowing that he was an evil boy — he peddled drugs and raped girls — but I could not and would not stop obeying his commands. Like a fool, I did not realise that he was ruining my life.

"One day, he told me to befriend a very rich girl who was not good-looking at all. He had done this many times before. I would befriend a girl, and then he would come into her life, make love to her, take her money and leave her. I befriended this girl in no time. Soon, I introduced him as a friend of my family, someone very respectable, rich, and belonging to high society in our village. All of this happened as it normally did, except that one day, after a very brief friendship, the two of them got married. I was shocked, but still greatly influenced by him, so I remained his slave and did anything he told me to.

"I wonder why I was so mesmerized by him. Was I hypnotized? Why did I do whatever he told me to, knowing he was evil, knowing that I was doing wrong? I felt miserable when he married that girl. She was extremely rich and her father, a widower, was even richer than her. He then ordered me to befriend her father and capture his affections, which I did. His next order was for me to marry him. As I was beautiful, the widower fell for me and I married him, even though I did not want to. That devil planned everything so well that he was never found out.

"Soon, he ordered me to kill my rich, old husband. I refused, and he said he would put me in jail by furnishing proof to the police that I had peddled drugs. I cried, pleaded and begged him to leave me alone, as killing was beyond me. But nothing affected his stone-cold heart, and he showed me photographs and proof that would land me in jail. I then realised what a fool I had been to obey his orders, how stupid I'd been to love a devil like him hoping that one day he would love me and marry me.

"In the end, he got me to kill my old husband, and I became a rich widow. Half of his estate was in my name and the other half in his daughter's. I wondered what I could do, as he kept dragging me through hell. Killing was beyond me and I could not sleep nor eat after my husband's death. I was preparing to run away somewhere he couldn't find me, taking some money from my husband's estate, and leaving most of it for his daughter. But before I finalized my plans he ordered me to kill his wife. I was stunned.

"I cried again and pleaded with him that this was going too far. I couldn't take it anymore and begged him to leave me alone, but nothing softened his heart. This whole time, he had planned nasty things in such a way that if caught all the evidence pointed to me as the guilty one. He was safe.

"So he picked up the phone to call the police, saying he could also prove that I had killed my husband. There was no escape. I realised that I had loved him so blindly and done whatever he had told me to. I realised how deeply I was trapped and what a great fool I had been. Now, there was no escape. I would have to confess to the police that I had killed my husband. It was much better than killing my stepdaughter. I asked him not to call the police and agreed to kill her. Secretly, I made up my mind to go straight to the police in the morning and confess everything. He said, 'Ok, kill her tomorrow according to my plan.' I was very upset, thinking hard about what to tell the police, and I did not reply, so he asked me, 'What are you thinking about? You shouldn't try to use your brains, even if you have any. You must do exactly what I tell you to do.' Then, he left.

"That night, he killed his wife and somehow proved to the police that I had killed her and my husband too, because he suspected that I was no longer his blind slave. He guessed I disagreed with him and maybe I would do something that went against his plans, so he involved me in such a way that the evidence found me responsible for the murder.

"Instead of my going to the police, they came to my door early the next morning and arrested me. At the time of the trial, they took me from the prison to the court and I got the opportunity to run up to the sixth floor and commit suicide.

"Now you know why I am here. After listening to my story, is it possible for you to help me? Please, for God's sake, don't hate me."

We said, "No, we don't hate you, but tell us, do you genuinely repent?"

That question was uncalled for as we knew very well that she did, but we could not just take her to a higher Realm. We were sent there to help her repent, but we saw that she was genuinely repenting.

She said, "Yes, of course, but is it too late? Can you help me?"

We showed her the way through which she could make her way to Realm 4, but the process, of course, would be *very slow*. Now, gradually, she is moving higher under our guidance.

19-05-1981

YOUR SUBCONSCIOUS MIND CAN BECOME DORMANT

We spirit beings come across many strange stories. We would like to tell you many such stories, but volumes of books would be filled with them, so we have chosen a few that illustrate the type of people that live in your world. You should be aware that you have to be careful not to be fooled by such people, nor take part in their evil plans. Also, make sure you never have blind faith in anyone on Earth. It is for these reasons that we want you to read some of these true stories.

You should also be aware that if you think you can fool God Almighty, by being nice on the outside and ghastly from the inside, you are mistaken. Remember that God is just to all, so isn't it strange that people still continue with their evil ways?

We often wonder: Why doesn't a soul's conscience stop him? We see many evil people doing tremendously evil things, convincing the world that they are absolutely innocent, and that nothing affects their conscience. You must wonder how this happens. We would like to explain.

Your conscience, or subconscious mind, is free to guide you when you are innocent children. **As you begin engaging in bad behaviour due to negative influences, or are trained by someone evil, your subconscious mind hardens – it quietens down, sleeps and becomes dormant.**

Your subconscious mind cannot and will not permit you to do bad things, but you (your conscious or physical mind) refuse to follow or listen to your subconscious mind and you continue with your evil ways. Your subconscious mind cannot tolerate this, so it sleeps and does not interfere with your bad deeds or habits.

Suppose you are on a higher Realm, such as 6 or 7, your subconscious mind will *never* let you go *very* wrong. As soon as you go beyond a limit it lets you know and if you do not heed it (i.e. you don't improve), the subconscious mind appeals to God Almighty for permission for you to return home to the spirit world. Souls on Realm 6 or 7 never fall to Realms 1, 2 or 3. This means they can do wrong up to a limit, but they can *never* go beyond that limit. Souls born on Realms 6 or 7 have alert subconscious minds which *never* lets them go down further than Realm 4 or 5 respectively (a soul born on Realm 6 can only fall to Realm 4 and a Realm 7 soul can only fall to Realm 5). But for those who are born on Realm 5 or below, it is very, very risky. They may fall as low as Realm 1 in only one lifetime on Earth.

So it is extremely dangerous for them not to listen to their subconscious mind and let it fall asleep. At first, your subconscious mind will try very, very hard to stop you from doing wrong, but after a point it becomes disgusted and goes to sleep until you are through with your evil life.

The next time someone does something wrong, there is no need to wonder, "Doesn't he or she have a conscience?" You will know the answer; his or her subconscious mind is asleep or dormant. Let us repeat: those on Realm 5 or below have this problem − the problem is such that it might even ruin your life for hundreds of years, and you may have to undergo extreme suffering.

Isn't it better to never go against your conscience? You may say, "Two or three times is ok," but we are sure that those two or three times will lead you to six or eight times, and then it will be too late. We are very particular and we want you to understand these things so that you will be brought up even if you have gone down.

If your subconscious mind is dormant at present and you are doing wrong deeds, we are sure you are intelligent enough to recognize right from wrong. *Stop following the wrong path.* Ask God Almighty to help you awaken your dormant subconscious mind through concentration and meditation.[9]

Follow this every day, **but only from sunrise to sunset. Do not do this after sunset.** Pray to God for two minutes, and then request God Almighty to help you awaken your dormant subconscious mind.

---

9. See Pg. 197 "How to open your subconscious mind."

"Oh, dear God Almighty, lead me to your good ways. Make me do the right things. Help me throw away any wrong desires or feelings I have. Give me your wisdom; show me your lighted path. Help me awaken my subconscious mind so that it *never* lets me do wrong. Oh God Almighty, please help me!"

After you say this, keep your mind *entirely blank*. No thoughts whatsoever must enter your mind. It should be entirely blank for about a minute *only* (if you blank your mind longer than a minute you can be harmed by a negative astral soul). This will do you a world of good. After your concentration, thank God and begin your day's work.

You can be sure this will help you greatly. This will not bring you money or worldly success, but it will help you stay calm, peaceful, relaxed and happy. Most importantly, it will develop your subconscious mind so you can rise to a higher spiritual level.

20-05-1981

AWAKEN YOUR SUBCONSCIOUS MIND

The subconscious mind dreads seeing the soul follow a bad path and it becomes so miserable that it goes to sleep and is unable to stop the soul at all. Nowadays, very few people have an awakened subconscious mind in your world as many people's subconscious minds are dormant and refuse to awaken.

We have shown you the way to awaken your subconscious mind. You were disobedient and let it fall into a slumber, but now it is time for you to awaken it. It will take some time, but follow our instructions sincerely. Your subconscious mind must awaken and guide you. Please talk to it, beg it and request it to function again.

It is a tremendously big task to make the subconscious mind work again, but you must. You have done wrong by avoiding, ignoring and shutting it off. Begin working on it immediately so that it will stop you from falling further, and will instead bring you up to a higher level.

Some say meditation, some say concentration, but you must simply render your mind *absolutely blank,* for one minute only. In the beginning this will be very hard for some to do, but once you get used to it, it is very easy. *Just stop thinking,* and if thoughts try to penetrate your mind *ignore them,* until they stop naturally. You will hear many sounds, even ones that are far away. You will hear them more and more, but try not to let any thoughts enter your mind. Your mind should be absolutely blank; push away all thoughts. This will help you greatly in your progress.

Once you leave your world and physical body it is very hard and slow to rise to a higher level in the spirit world, but on Earth you can progress much sooner. You can turn away from your evil ways and can become good within minutes. Of course, you have to go through your karma, but it will be milder and easier as God will help you find the strength and courage to face it well.

In the spirit world, however, your progress is very, very slow, but *certain.* There is, however, no escaping the punishments for every sin you have committed.

So think hard before it is too late. Before you leave your world and physical body, you have many opportunities to go from bad to good and you can be sure that your punishment in the spirit world will be much easier if you make good use of those opportunities. Instead of finding yourself on Realms 1, 2 or 3, you will at least reach Realm 4, so think hard and you will realise it is much better to improve immediately.

21-05-1981

SATISH'S STORY: YOU MUST HAVE COURAGE TO IMPROVE

There are many cases in which souls are extremely weak and are afraid to change their routine. They are afraid to turn good, thinking their colleagues will ridicule and blackmail them, or that good people will never welcome them and will ignore and insult them, or they believe that their life is hopeless.

Here is a true story about a soul we will call Satish. This story will show you how wrong you can be. Satish was a good soul, but he faced many bad influences in his childhood. His mother died in her early thirties, when Satish was only five years old. His father tried to raise him alone, but as he could not, he remarried, claiming it was only for the sake of his son, which was absolutely untrue.

The stepmother never liked Satish. She hated him since the very first day she saw him, but she never showed her hatred for Satish to her husband. When she had her own children, she completely neglected Satish and very conveniently put him in a low class and cheap boarding school, saying he was unmanageable as well as a bad influence on her children.

The boarding school was horrible and Satish fell into bad company and adopted their bad habits and manners. By the time he left school, Satish's father had died and his stepmother left town without a forwarding address. He was left alone with no money and no one to look after him, so he depended on his vagabond friends from school.

Along with two of his friends, he became friendly with rich young boys and girls, pretending that he belonged to a rich family. He became a part of their lives and then swindled, blackmailed and harassed them. Satish and his friends moved from town to town, city to city, taking advantage of rich boys and girls.

One day, when he was on a train with his friends, Satish saw a girl who was alone. From her attire, she seemed to be rich, so they tried to befriend her. She was shy and timid, so she avoided them, which made them go after her even more. When she got off at a station, they followed her home. She was not rich, but they continued to pursue her. Somehow, Satish was successful in befriending her and they fell in love.

She was a very honest and kind-hearted girl – just the opposite of Satish – and he fell blindly in love. He could not see any way to marry her, as he could not follow the straight path because he had had no training whatsoever. He dared not tell her that he was a vagabond and a crook, as he believed she thought him to be a rich boy belonging to high society. He feared his two colleagues would ridicule him if he tried to follow the straight path. He thought they might tell her, as well, or even try to blackmail him.

Her influence made him want to break away from his two friends, and made him keen to change his ways. He wanted to walk on the straight path from then on, but he was very upset as he could not see a way out of his predicament. His love for her was too strong for him to fool her, and if he told her the truth she would never accept him as her husband, as she was a very honest girl.

Satish wondered how he could rid himself of evil, leave his two colleagues, earn an honest living, and become a gentleman. The cowardly Satish was deeply in love with the girl, but even so strong a love did not give him the courage to change his ways. He was sure that if she came to know the truth she would hate him. He now repented leading a bad life, but he had no courage to change. Thinking he would never be able to make her happy, or follow the straight path, Satish left without telling the girl anything. He lost a very good opportunity; his life would have changed entirely, he would have become good and reached a higher level.

Satish's cowardice ruined his life. If he had gathered enough courage to speak frankly and honestly to the girl he would have found out that she already knew all about him through his colleagues, who had been keen to separate them. They had already told her everything, but she had made up her mind to marry Satish and improve him. She just wanted to be sure that Satish truly loved her, but he left her without even saying a word. What a big mistake he made!

You should be brave enough to face your problems and **change. You should never let go of an opportunity to turn from bad to good.** Once you lose such an opportunity, it is almost impossible in this evil world to get another chance like that. In this case, Satish would have been helped by this girl if only he had had enough courage to tell her how deeply and truly he loved her.

22-05-1981

SOORDAS' STORY: A SOUL RISKS ALL TO BE WITH HIS LOVED ONE

Here is another true story (with the names changed) to show you what a soul can do to reach a higher level, but in this case caused him to fall, and how his loved one from the spirit world requested God to help him.

Soordas was on Realm 3, as his previous life was bad. His loved one, Niloo was on Realm 5, so Soordas requested his leader, His High Good Soul of Realm 3, to ask God to send him to Earth again, to be born to an evil mother, so he could improve himself and his mother and reach Realm 5. He was keen and willing to live a hard life of suffering and punishment, as long as he could join his loved one, Niloo on Realm 5.

Soordas was born to a wicked woman. She was so wicked that people on Earth called her a witch. She cursed Soordas as soon as he entered the Earth world. He, an illegitimate child, was nothing but a hindrance to her.

Here, we would like to tell you that **little babies, until they begin to talk properly, are truly connected to the spirit world and are in constant touch with their loved ones in the spirit world.** Until they turn one, babies can choose to come back to the spirit world. For a year the soul can observe his or her parents and the situation, and can choose to come back to the spirit world if they want to.

So Soordas was requested by his loved ones in the spirit world to return home before a year passed, as his mother was a terrible woman. Soordas, however, stood his ground, as he loved Niloo (his loved one in the spirit world) too much and was very keen on joining her forever.

Soordas' mother was extremely wicked. She taught her son to use filthy language and to curse everyone. No good words came from her mouth, or from Soordas'. Soordas came to Earth to progress quickly so that he could reach Realm 5 sooner than by the slower progress in the spirit world. So he chose this absolutely evil mother in the hope of improving her and helping his own soul rise to Realm 5 in one Earth lifetime. He had thus trained his subconscious mind to be very firm and never let him down. Every soul can do this, but there is great risk involved because one's subconscious mind may not be able to handle too much evil. It may get disgusted with evil ways and go to sleep. If this happens it's a great disaster. What a risk – his soul was keen to reach Realm 5, but if his subconscious mind became dormant he would fall straight to Realm 2, or even 1.

A year after your birth, the subconscious mind can no longer reveal why you were born on Earth and why you

chose such an evil mother. So it was more likely that
Soordas would fall lower, instead of rising higher, but he
took this risk anyway, believing that he had trained his
subconscious mind to stop him from doing any wrong.

His mother was so wicked that it was difficult to find even
one good quality about her. By the time Soordas began to
speak, he had forgotten his mission and became just like
his mother. He never used loving words, took pleasure in
harassing and harming others, treated money as his God
and loved to torture those weaker than him.

Niloo tried hard to stop him via his subconscious mind,
but it was completely dormant. Niloo had expected this,
which is why she had urged Soordas not to be born as that
evil woman's son.

Niloo tried to 'impress' souls on Earth — her dear ones
who were still on Earth, as well as Soordas' dear ones from
a previous life — to interfere and improve Soordas. It was
tremendously hard work, but after quite a while she was
successful in impressing one of them to go to Soordas.
This soul, whom we call Mohandas, was in Bombay and
Soordas was in Bangalore, so it was practically an
impossible task, but as Niloo was desperate to save
Soordas, she worked hard on Mohandas' subconscious
mind and succeeded in bringing him to Bangalore, with
neither Mohandas' or Soordas' conscious knowledge. This
took years. They became friends, and as Mohandas was a
good soul, Niloo was sure he would improve Soordas.
How wrong she was! Instead of improving Soordas,
Mohandas began to fall.

23-05-1981

SOORDAS' STORY CONTINUED:
NILOO'S LOVE FOR SOORDAS IS TESTED

Niloo lost all hope and she felt very guilty because she was responsible for bringing Mohandas and Soordas together, and now Mohandas, who had been a good soul, turned bad. *She* had made him fall to a lower level. She felt miserable as she could not find any way to save them both. There was no alternative but to make a request to God Almighty. She prayed to Him to save them both.

Miserable, Niloo wondered what to do. She was on Realm 5, which was not a very high Realm, but she was a good soul on her way to Realm 6 and she did not want to fall to lower levels. Disheartened, she went to her Realm's leader and requested him to show her a way out of this difficult problem.

She said, "I love Soordas so much and I sent Mohandas down this evil path. Please, Your High Good Soul, save both of them."

His High Good Soul said, "Niloo, you have done great wrong by sending Mohandas to Soordas and making him evil, too. You must be punished."

"Yes," said Niloo, "Your High Good Soul, do punish me. I hate to go down to the lower Realms, but Sir, I will go to the Realm where Soordas and Mohandas belong. Please, just save them and bring them up to a high level. I will bear all of their punishments."

She hated to go down, even to Realm 4, but her selfless and true love for Soordas made her willing to go as low as Realm 2. And if Soordas and Mohandas did not stop now, they could even reach Realm 1.

His High Good Soul said, "I agree with this; will you go to Realm 2 immediately?"

"Yes, Master, I am willing to go immediately and take my punishment as well as theirs, but please save them and bring them back home, at least to Realm 4, if not 5."

His High Good Soul was very impressed by her selfless, true and strong love, and knew very well that she was genuinely willing to undergo their punishments. Still, He wanted to test her. What would she do after entering Realm 2? Would she change her mind? He ordered her to go to Realm 2 and she went without any hesitation.

"Do you still wish to save Soordas and Mohandas by being a citizen of Realm 2 for several hundred years, Niloo?" His High Good Soul asked her, after a few days.

Niloo replied without hesitation, "Yes, Your High Good Soul, yes." He was very happy to find Niloo to be so selfless and true, even strong enough to sacrifice her own happiness for her beloved Soordas, and for Mohandas as well.

"Niloo, come back to Realm 5. Dear child, I will save Soordas and Mohandas. It will take several months, but meanwhile, promise me you will do nothing about Soordas or Mohandas, no matter what happens to them. I promise to save them from the horrible lower Realms."

Niloo had no words to express her gratitude. She was overjoyed and shouted, "Yes, Your High Good Soul, I promise to do whatever you tell me to."

"Only pray for them, Niloo, and request God Almighty to help me save them."

Niloo agreed at once, as she had full faith in His High Good Soul.

This is a true story. Only the names and cities have been changed. You would be surprised to know how the rulers of the Realms and His Highest Good Soul work to save any soul who needs to be saved. It is a terribly hard task for them, but they do perform such miracles as they have great powers. Also, Soordas had taken a big risk to improve and come to a higher level, because he was a good soul. He had fallen lower in his previous life because of some evil friends, so he had taken this risk, which had unfortunately brought him even further down.

24-05-1981

SOORDAS' STORY CONTINUED: HIS HIGH GOOD SOUL COMES DOWN TO EARTH

His High Good Soul asked Niloo to calm down and pray to God Almighty to help him save Soordas and Mohandas. After several days, His High Good Soul disguised himself as a holy fakir[10] and descended to Earth.

---

10. A holy fakir is a mendicant or holy man.

In the meantime, Soordas and Mohandas were robbing and harassing many people on Earth. On that particular day, when His High Good Soul descended on Earth, they had just pulled off a successful robbery that had fetched them thousands of rupees.

Drunk on alcohol, and intoxicated by success, they were driving back home at night, full of pride. They were going very fast, when His High Good Soul passed before their car. This made Soordas swerve the car, and he crashed into a pole. Soordas and Mohandas were stuck in their seats, unconscious, and were taken to a hospital nearby.

When they regained consciousness they found themselves in hospital beds, with terrible pain. Soordas found both his legs missing and was very upset. Mohandas had lost a leg and one arm. They asked how the accident had happened and were told that they had been drunk. Due to the impact, the doors had flown wide open and the sack of money had rolled out of the car and down the side of the road into a thick bush, for the needy to find.

Soordas and Mohandas blamed and cursed each other for their missing limbs. They lay side-by-side on two beds and they fought verbally with each other, so doctors had to separate them and put Mohandas in another ward. Mohandas, now alone, began to think about the past and realised that he'd had this accident and lost his limbs because he had followed the wrong path. "Now I have to suffer my whole life," he thought.

This shock reopened his subconscious mind. Now it was awake and it told him that this was God's justice. He cursed Soordas to have influenced him to go down this evil path and was determined to change for the better there and then.

A kind-looking young nurse named Poonam came to his bed and gave him an injection. Mohandas requested that she bring him the Holy Gita,[11] as he wanted to take an oath to never go wrong again.

She brought it to him and he took the oath. Mohandas and Poonam became friends and he confessed to her what a terrible life he had led for a few months. He explained that this was God's justice and told her, "Poonam, I have taken an oath to never stray again and always follow God's path."

God helped him, and Poonam fell in love with Mohandas. Mohandas fought against his love for her, as he was now disabled. Moreover, Poonam knew his story, so he was sure she would never marry him.

A day before he was discharged from hospital, Poonam asked him, "Mohan, where will you go now?"

"I have no place to go, Poonam."

"I live alone in my house, and I can look after you, Mohan."

"Poonam, I am a disabled man. How can I allow myself to be a burden to you?"

"Mohan, I love you very much. Let's get married and I will be very happy to have you as my husband."

Mohandas explained to her that he, too, loved her very much, but could not bear to be a burden on her. She

---

11. A sacred book of the Hindus.

insisted that her life would be full if he would marry her and they would both be able to manage very easily, as she was a nurse. After some time, Mohandas agreed and they announced their engagement.

The next day, as soon as Mohandas was discharged, they went straight to a temple and got married. That was the end of Mohandas' story, as he and Poonam led a very good life. They had three children and Mohandas, with the aid of his artificial limbs was able to work and lived very happily within God's laws.

25-05-1981

SOORDAS' STORY CONTINUED: SOORDAS FALLS EVEN LOWER

L et us continue with Soordas' story. He was in the hospital for a long time, from where he could not harm, rob or harass anyone, or he would not be well looked after. He was, however, planning how he would harm, fool and harass others after he was released. In short, he became worse than before. He cursed everyone, even God and Mohandas. He was full of hatred – he even hated his own mother.

In this state, he was discharged from the hospital. He called his mother and went home with her. He very sweetly requested her to help him in his evil ways, as he had no legs and could not walk. His mother, being evil herself, agreed most willingly.

Soordas wanted to kill two birds with one stone. He planned to rob a rich widower and make him a pauper. He planned it in such a way that he could also take revenge on his own mother, as he hated her as well. The robbery was a success. His mother harassed that man and brought the loot home.

When his mother was fast asleep at night, Soordas left home on his wheelchair with a bag full of money. He planted a few clues that would point to his mother. He left home and, as it was night, waited in his wheelchair on the lonely road.

He saw a car driving by after midnight and signalled it to stop. Phillips, a 20 year old young man was driving the car. "Please give me a lift, I am a disabled man. I have no legs and I received a phone call that my mother had an accident and was taken to the hospital. I must take her clothes and medicines. Won't you help a legless man like me?"

Poor Phillips, he felt sorry for Soordas so instead of going home, he turned his car around and proceeded towards the hospital. Soordas took out his gun, pointed it at him, and directed him to take the highway.

Phillips was not an intelligent boy. He was new to the city, he had just started a new job that had brought him to Bangalore a few days earlier. Soordas very cunningly found this out and was sure the boy would be a good slave for him.

Just before leaving Bangalore, Soordas called the police and told them he had seen a woman rob a rich man. He told them he had followed her, gave them her address and told them to hurry before she left the city. The police asked him his name, but he disconnected, so they naturally rushed to Soordas' mother's home. Showing a search warrant, they rushed in and found some clues that made them arrest Soordas' mother. The police tortured her to find out where she had put the money.

Soordas had taken the money, and his mother tried to convince the police of this, but unfortunately her reputation went against her and she was jailed and sentenced to hard labour for a few years.

Soordas used Phillips and brainwashed him, telling him that he had the power of black magic and could turn him into an animal if he did not obey. Soordas showed him a couple of common magic tricks that made Phillips believe that Soordas really had this power. He was illiterate, having studied in a village school, and after working as a driver in his own village for some time, he had been offered this job as a driver in Bangalore.

Phillips was completely under Soordas' control and by changing cars, stealing a car on the way, and leaving the previously stolen car behind, they reached Lahore. Somehow they had managed to cross the border and leave India with Soordas' skill. Now, Soordas felt safe; he was rich and had even found a slave for himself.

26-05-1981

SOORDAS' STORY CONTINUED: A WEAK SOUL FINDS COURAGE

Niloo and her friends in the spirit world were tense because Soordas had fallen deeper into evil ways. But they had full faith in His High Good Soul so they knew very well that somehow Soordas would soon be saved from this evil. His High Good Soul understood that Niloo and her friends were upset, so to ease them he called Niloo and explained, "Niloo, I know you have full faith in me and you would never think that I wouldn't keep my word, but seeing Soordas slipping further into evil, you must be upset. I understand you well, my dear, so I want to explain. That rich man who had been robbed, was a sinful man and needed to learn a lesson. He has realised now, as he has become a pauper. Soordas' mother was extremely evil and she must be stopped too, so she is in jail now. That boy, Phillips, is a coward, a spineless fellow and he must learn to face his problems courageously instead of being a slave – he is a good soul but he must be brought to his senses. So now you know that *no one suffers any injustices*. God has mysterious ways of giving justice to all."

"Yes, Your High Good Soul," said Niloo, "Now, I understand. Thank you for explaining this to me. I have full faith in you and our God Almighty, and I now realise His mysterious ways of giving justice."

Phillips had become Soordas' slave. Soordas became a millionaire and was very proud of his success.

One day, Phillips was sitting on a rock some distance from Soordas' new home, wondering sadly why God did not help him, why he was forced to do things that his conscience refused to do. He was very upset so he shouted out, "Oh God, please help me. I can't tolerate Soordas anymore." After a few minutes, His High Good Soul came to him in a holy fakir's disguise and said, "My good boy, kindly give something to this poor man. I am very hungry."

Phillips felt deeply for this starving fakir in rags, his hand
naturally went to his pocket, but then he remembered that
Soordas never let him have even a single paisa — his
pockets were empty. He only had food and clothing from
Soordas.

With tears in his eyes, Phillips said, "Old man, I am very
sorry but I have nothing to give you as I am the absolute
slave of a very evil man."

"Slave, my boy?"

"Yes, old man, a slave — you may not believe it, but it's
true."

"Won't you tell me your story? I might be able to help
you," His High Good Soul said.

"I don't think you will be able to help me, old man, but I
will tell you my story, as I want to unburden my heart.
Will you listen to my sad and unbelievable story?"

"Certainly, certainly, you tell me your story and unburden
yourself."

So Phillips told him everything and added, "I have no
courage to defy him."

"You should not be so cowardly and spineless. You must
fight evil and God will be very happy."

"Oh fakir, you don't know Soordas. He has the power to
do black magic. You don't understand, I saw some of his
evil powers with my own eyes. He can easily turn me into a
dog or cat. No, fakir, no, I cannot defy him."

His High Good Soul said, "Phillips, I have power too, but it's good power. Will you put your faith in me? I'd never let Soordas turn you into a dog or cat. I can assure you Soordas cannot turn you into an animal. See, I will perform the same tricks that he did and show you how it is done. Then will you believe me?"

"Yes, show me how they are done."

His High Good Soul showed him how Soordas had fooled him and Phillips was so excited that he wanted to run away right then, but His High Good Soul stopped him and explained, "Phillips, you must help me improve Soordas. As I saved you from your misery, it is your duty to help me."

"Oh fakir, you are strange. Why do you want to bother about Soordas? Let him go to hell. What have we to do with him? Let me run away please, and you also go away from such an evil place."

His High Good Soul said, "No, Phillips, I am here to perform my duty and you must also do your duty, otherwise God won't be happy. Do you wish to make our God Almighty unhappy, Phillips?"

"No, definitely not. I called God and He sent you to help me, so I must do what you tell me to. But please, I request you to let me leave Soordas as soon as possible."

"Phillips, only one more day and you will be free. You have to do what I tell you and then you can go. Take only three hundred rupees, take the car and go to the city. Leave the car just before you enter the city and try to find a job for yourself. I think three hundred rupees will be enough for your boarding and lodging until you get a job and manage on your own pay. Don't take more money, Phillips. Soordas' money is evil and cursed. Besides, it is *not* yours and three hundred is the pay you should have received from Soordas for your work. So promise me you won't take more from Soordas' cupboard."

"I promise, oh fakir; you are a wonderful man. Thank God we came across each other — you saved me from misery and now I understand God's mysterious ways. I even promise you, fakir, that I will never follow the wrong path, nor be a coward like I was."

His High Good Soul was very happy to find that Phillips had changed for the better. He explained what Phillips should do the next day, then left him and Earth for some time.

27-05-1981

SOORDAS' STORY CONTINUED: PRIDE HAS A FALL

For the first time, Phillips felt he was a human and not a vegetable. Now he was determined not to be a slave to any evil person, or to stray onto the wrong path.

The next day, as per His High Good Soul's instructions, Phillips drove Soordas to a very remote place, quite far from his house, telling him that he had information about a cave in the jungle filled with treasure. As usual, Soordas had been overjoyed and had ordered Phillips to take him there immediately.

After miles of dirt roads there was only a narrow walking path, so Phillips stopped the car, carried Soordas on his back and walked for about one and a half miles. They found a cave and Soordas was very anxious to see the treasure. But Phillips said, "This cave is too narrow for you to go inside. Master, you sit on this rock, let me go in first to see whether there is actually any treasure inside." Phillips put Soordas down and went in.

As he'd been instructed, Phillips found an exit through the back of the cave and went to his car via a shorter route. He drove to Soordas' house in the car, opened his cupboard by force, took three hundred rupees and drove to the city in the stolen car. A few days later, he found a job and led a straight, good life.

After Phillips entered the cave, quite some time had passed but Soordas was too excited to notice — he was busy dreaming about becoming a multimillionaire. Then he realised that Phillips had been gone for more than an hour, so he began shouting and cursing, calling out to Phillips.

Nothing happened — it seemed Phillips had disappeared. So Soordas had to crawl over rough and jagged rocks to find Phillips. He went in a little, with curses on his lips, anger in his mind and hatred in his heart. Suddenly he found himself out. He was so surprised that he felt as if someone had given him a terrible blow. His mind registered that Phillips had fooled him, but it was beyond his capacity to believe that Phillips had any courage or intelligence to fool him, Soordas, the Dada![12] Soordas was absolutely sure that Phillips would be his lifelong slave.

---

12. A "Dada" in colloquial Hindi is a local ruffian, a street-smart toughie.

He had been so proud that no one had been able to deceive him until now. He was an expert at making fools of others, so how had this happened? Soordas had been positively sure that Phillips would never dare oppose him. This was a great blow. He was so stunned that he even forgot to curse and shout.

Was it possible that Phillips had vanished and left Soordas alone in that dark, horrible cave? Night was nearing. Soordas thought it better to sit in the cave than go outside into the jungle. He was terrified and realised that there would be wild animals in the jungle, and he had no way to go home – he was miles and miles away. What would he do without food and water? What if ferocious animals entered the cave? How would he protect himself? Would he see the sun again tomorrow? What would happen to him in a few hours? He would be dead! He trembled with the realization that he was as cowardly and spineless as Phillips. He realised now what Phillips must have gone through.

"If I die, I will go straight to hell."

He sat closer to the wall of the cave, and accidentally placed his hand on a snake slithering from one stone to another. "Oh my God, how will I endure this torture?" Fortunately, the snake slid away, but Soordas realised how his victims must have felt when he tortured them.

So, with great effort, he crawled again to the middle of the cave and sat there wondering what to do. There were snakes all around him. If he stayed inside the cave he might be bitten by snakes. If he went out, he might be mauled to death by wild animals.

28-05-1981

SOORDAS' STORY CONTINUED: THE RE-AWAKENING OF THE SUBCONSCIOUS MIND

"Oh God, make Phillips' subconscious mind bring him back to me. Please God!" cried Soordas. But he realised at once – had his subconscious mind ever been successful in bringing him onto the right path?

"Why did I never let my subconscious mind win over my evil? Why did I always shut off my subconscious mind and continue doing evil things? Why was I so evil? Oh, I said 'was'. Does that mean I have changed?"

One by one, he saw himself harassing many people, robbing them, torturing them, raping girls, and even putting his own mother in trouble.

"Oh God, now I realise what they all must have gone through. They went through hell because of my vengeful nature, my evil selfish motives, my greed and my pleasure. Until now it never occurred to me – it never entered my mind! I was always so sure that no one would ever be able to harm or harass me. I, the king of evil. I was so sure that no one could fool me, and what do you know, this spineless fool, a born coward, fooled me and brought me to my senses! This is God's Justice, no doubt. I deserve this."

For the first time in his life, he thought of God. So for the first time, he prayed to God and said, "Please, my dear

God, save me and I promise you I will lead a good and God-fearing life. I even promise to find as many of my victims as possible, help them, and give back their belongings that are still with me. I will try my best to make them happy. I know I am asking too much after leading such a terrible life, but dear God give me this *one* chance. Only one chance so that I won't go to hell, nor suffer hell on Earth among these snakes and wild animals. Oh God, this is my first prayer to you. This is my first realization, the final change from evil to good. Please help me, save me, and put me on your right path. Oh God, bless me with your wisdom and make me lead a good life. Please, God, save me this time and I will never go wrong again."

Then, he began crying like a baby. When he calmed down, he realised how genuine his thoughts and feelings were. Was it possible that God would help him, an evil soul? Besides, who would come to help him in this dense jungle? By sunrise, would he be able to survive this wild jungle full of snakes and ferocious animals? It did not seem possible to Soordas.

"But God is well-known for performing miracles! Oh God, perform a miracle — please save me and I promise I will never go wrong."

At that moment, he heard animal howls coming closer and closer to the cave. He knew the end was near. With great effort, in spite of his bruises and deep wounds, he managed to crawl to a very deep, dark corner in the cave. He was sure many snakes would be there, but he preferred to die from a snake bite rather than be torn apart by wild animals. As he inched himself into that corner for safety, a snake went right across his chest.

"Oh my God, save me and I will *never* go wrong." This cry came from bottom of his heart.

He remembered how so many of his victims had begged him in just this way, but he, the cruelest man, had laughed and tortured them even more. Had he ever shown a tiny bit of kindness to any of his victims? No, never, so how would God show kindness to him?

He began crying again and was convinced that there was no chance at all of his survival. "I will never see another morning. Oh God, kill me now. Stop my heart now. I know I will go to hell but I don't want to be torn apart by wild animals or bitten all over by snakes. Oh God, please kill me now." Another snake slithered across his body, and he shouted, "Oh God, have pity on me, please don't torture me anymore." His newly awakened subconscious mind asked, "Have you ever shown pity to your victims?"

"Yes, you are right, I never had any pity. I understand now, but it seems too late. Now, I must suffer. Why should God show pity or be kind to me?" He genuinely repented now, and wished to improve, but he could not see a way out. He knew survival was hopeless.

His subconscious mind told him once more, "Have you ever stopped harming others? So why should God perform a miracle and save you? Have you ever thought of God before, when you thought you were happy and successful? Then why are you thinking of God now? Why are you pleading with him to help you now?"

29-05-1981

SOORDAS' STORY CONTINUED:
HIS HIGH GOOD SOUL APPEARS

Soordas now saw everything clearly, and he was sure it was too late. He was sure that in a few hours he would be in hell.

"God's justice is always present. I realised it too late. God is always just. Maybe justice comes later than it should, but justice does definitely exist. Now I have to suffer all of my punishments – there is no way out."

His subconscious mind began again, "You wanted God to perform a miracle; well, here is a miracle – you shall now improve." He did not understand the meaning of this, but he continued to think, "**I sowed evil. Now I must reap punishment.** Oh God, show me the right way to take my punishment – show me the way to purify my soul. Never let me go on the wrong path again. Oh God, show me light in the darkness and I will never be blind to God's ways. Oh God, save my soul from evil. I don't care if my physical body is tortured, but save my soul."

The night passed this way and at dawn Soordas saw streaks of light entering the dark cave. He was extremely surprised.

"Oh God, it's a miracle. Yes, it's a miracle. God, You saved me!"

He was overjoyed. It was beyond him to understand how he was saved.

"Soordas," his subconscious mind began again, "Even a poisonous snake and fierce jungle animals have pity on a legless, helpless man, but an evil man like you never had any pity for innocent, helpless, good people." He was very ashamed of himself and took an oath to always be good and never go on the wrong path.

"Still, there is very little chance for me to survive in this dense jungle. No one will pass through here, so how will I get out of this lonely place? Oh God, You saved me from all the wild animals, so please now save me from this place so that I can lead a good life and repent for all my evil deeds. Oh God, please help me again. I know I am asking for too much, but have pity on my soul."

He crawled out of the cave with much effort, sat on a rock, and prayed sincerely to God. After a few hours, Soordas saw a holy fakir passing by, limping and tired. He was overjoyed and shouted to him, "Please help me!"

The holy fakir (our High Good Soul) came near him and asked, "My man, are you evil or good? I never help evil people, so speak up: are you evil or good?"

Soordas was on the verge of saying that he was good, but he did not as his subconscious mind was now working. He stopped immediately and instead said, "My dear fakir, sit here and listen to my story. Then, if you think your conscience will permit you to help me, help me. Otherwise, go your way and may God bless you!"

His High Good Soul sat on a rock and said, "Ok, carry on. I am all ears."

Soordas told him the entire story, the truth, and nothing but the truth. His High Good Soul was very impressed, but still tested him. "You want to be saved so that you can continue your evil ways."

"No fakir, I will never go wrong now. I learned my lesson the hard way and I am positive that God saved me last night to give me a chance to lead a good life. So now that God has given me this chance, in return, I must lead such a life that He will be proud of me."

These words impressed His High Good Soul and he even saw that Soordas' aura and vibrations had changed. He said, "Ok, Soordas, I will help you." First, he helped Soordas by giving him food and water. Then, he took Soordas home, left him there, and returned to the spirit world, his work done.

Soordas is still on Earth, with artificial legs, leading a kind, good and selfless life. His mother was released, as the police could not prove those clues were *not* planted by someone else. They gave her the benefit of the doubt, and she was acquitted. Soordas heard this, and asked her to stay with him. Over time, he improved his own mother, too.

Now, mother and son are leading a honest, kind and selfless life. **But Soordas does not know how Niloo and His High Good Soul helped him.** When he returns to the spirit world, he will know all.

Niloo is overjoyed now and thanked His High Good Soul from the bottom of her heart. In such a manner, many, many spirit souls have helped people on Earth. You call it a miracle, and that is what it is.

30-05-1981

THE SUBCONSCIOUS MIND IS THE REAL YOU

We heard this question very often when we were on Earth; "Why don't we know anything about our previous lives on Earth, or about the spirit world? Why has God made us forget?"

Your subconscious mind knows each and every thing. Whatever happens to you (your soul) is registered in your subconscious mind from the very beginning. Unfortunately, your physical mind cannot take it all, and in most cases it constantly remains at war with your subconscious mind. Only a few souls, who are on a very high level, can make their subconscious mind control their physical mind. These souls have ESP (Extra Sensory Perception) and some even remember their previous lives on Earth. They also sometimes remember the spirit world, their real home, but this is very rare.

You would probably like to know why your subconscious mind does not let you remember. As we said, it is difficult for your physical mind to handle it all. Besides, your subconscious mind does not want you to know because you have come to Earth for experience, tests, training and to pay off karma. **If you knew everything, it would be too much for you to cope with, and there would be no fun in life. You would go through life like a machine. If you knew your karma, your life on Earth would be monotonous.**

Your subconscious mind knows everything and it never makes any mistakes. It registers everything. For souls on a higher level, their subconscious mind on Earth is a little more powerful than ordinary souls on Earth. We say a little because even in the spirit world, our subconscious mind does not fully operate, though it is much more open than those of people on Earth. **Only after Realm 7 does your subconscious mind operate in a higher capacity in the spirit world.**

Some yogis[13] and holy men on Earth have the power to meditate for long periods. Their subconscious mind opens more and more and they can control their physical mind through their subconscious mind. They are *not* slaves to their conscious mind, as most of you are. **Do not be a slave to your conscious mind.** Your conscious mind will lead you from bad to worse if you do not control it.

Your conscious mind dies with your physical body when you leave Earth. Your conscious mind is very anxious to make you a slave and lead you as it wishes, but you must use your will-power and never let it win.

You are a soul joined for eternity with your subconscious mind, so how can you let your weak and untrained conscious mind be your master? Are you such a weak, spineless creature that you are not able to control it?

From now on, remember this: **your subconscious mind is the real YOU.** So never let your conscious mind be your master. Be your own master.

---

13. A yogi is one who has mastered the various forms of yoga.

31-05-1981

WHY PAST-LIFE MEMORY IS NOT REVEALED

People on Earth forget all their cherished memories of the spirit world and earlier lives. In our previous lives we were born on Earth several times, in order to gain experience, to train ourselves and to purify our soul, so that we could go higher and higher. If we remembered all of our previous lives on Earth would it help us gain more knowledge? Many would say yes, but we say no. Here's why: if you remembered your previous lives, would you make the same mistakes? Never.

So by correcting your mistakes, solving your problems, and facing your troubles, you purify your soul. Without mistakes, problems and pain you would never be able to understand the difference between good and bad. If you can't understand this, then what's the use of life? With your memories of the spirit world and previous lives intact, you would live life like a machine. Your response to your test, training and karma would not be *natural*. Your choices would be programmed – they would not be a result of your inner state of being.

On Earth everyone yearns for happiness, but do they know what real happiness is? No. People on Earth think happiness means a lot of money, comfort, luxuries, fun and fame. We are sorry to say that these things don't bring *real* happiness. Real happiness comes from true love, nature's beauty, genuine laughter and smiles (*not* forced, as many people do), helping others selflessly, and purifying your soul to achieve a higher level.

You will purify your soul and achieve a higher level by making mistakes, and realizing your mistakes. It also depends on how you correct your mistakes, solve your problems, and face your difficulties. All of these things depend on you — whether you correct your mistakes, solve your problems, and face your troubles in a good, straight, and Godly way, or in a bad or evil way.

For example, if you make a mistake and realise you have done wrong, you must right that wrong. You are sent to Earth to gain experience, train yourself and purify your soul. This will take you to a higher level, so you must face problems, troubles, and injustices in life.

Here, in the spirit world, we do remember everything. Our memories are not erased like yours, so our progress is very slow. You are born on Earth for rapid progress, but most of you are falling lower.

You may wonder why you don't remember your real home in the spirit world. **If you remembered the spirit world you good people would hate to live on Earth. But bad and evil souls have unfortunately forgotten what Realms 1, 2 and 3 are like.**

Many times in spite of being innocent, when you are pronounced guilty, you tend to lose faith in God.

At such times you may have thought, "Is it true, is there a God? If so, why does He never show Himself? Why has He let me down so many times? When I need Him the most, He is nowhere to be found. Why is there no justice? If God is so good, kind and just, why does He let evil people come on top? Why do evil people succeed and good people suffer? Why?"

Have you ever asked these questions? Here are some answers:

1. Is God really there?

    Yes, of course God is there. Otherwise, who made you? Who made your Earth? Who made trees, flowers, fruits, seas, rivers and mountains? Who, by some mysterious way, gives justice to evil souls? Who has given you loving feelings? Who has been kind enough to keep you close to your loved ones? Who could do all of these things if there was no God?

2. You were innocent and still you were proven guilty. Where was God at that time?

    There are many answers to this. One of them must be right for you.

    (a) Are you sure you have never harmed or hurt anyone? Maybe you are being punished for that.

    (b) Maybe you made someone miserable or you had been sinful in your previous life, so this is the result of that.

    (c) You naturally want to go higher and higher, so think hard, will you ever be able to do so without facing problems?

    (d) If you think you are a very pious and good soul, have you ever analysed yourself? Find out whether everything you have done was selfless and right, without hypocrisy or dishonesty, and without any selfish motives. Have you ever done a good deed with a selfish motive, even with the thought that you would go to heaven, you would be famous, or all your sins would be forgiven if you did this deed? **Such good deeds are not good deeds.** You are fooling only the world and yourself. People on Earth fool themselves all the time, and even try to fool God (which can never happen). So do you think you are sinning? Of course you are.

(e) Money is very precious to most people on Earth. Anything in excess is not good. You also know that money is the root cause of all evil. Money blinds your vision, deafens your ears to the pleas of the poor, and hardens your heart. You forget kindness, loyalty, love (we mean true love), and your duties towards your family and others.

(f) Have you ever misjudged or misled someone, which may have brought this on?

(g) Have you ever wanted to be very famous or popular and, in that desire and ambition, harmed or misled someone?

(h) Have you, if not directly then indirectly, made someone suffer for your own selfish motives?

(i) Have you encouraged or been nice to an evil person? If you are nice to evil people you encourage them to be evil, which puts you in the same category.

Have you realised that God Almighty is never unjust and that He would never be unjust to anyone? If you are really innocent **He will prove you innocent, whether you have** proof or not, provided you are on the Godly Good Path. It may not be immediate – it may take months, years, or even decades – but He will.

Analyse yourself. Ask these questions and we are sure you will find one of them is right for you. Ask the same questions whenever you go through any difficulties or if any problems crop up.

We would like you to understand this: you are on Earth, and Earth is your soul's training institute to gain experience. It is the stepping stone to higher Realms, to your eternal happiness. It is also your chance to pay off your karma more easily, do good deeds, help others selflessly and help your loved ones. Then what can you expect – smooth sailing? A bed of roses without thorns? What can you expect from your evil world – goodness overflowing?

You have to face your problems bravely and with a smile.

You have to fight evil.

You have to purify your soul.

This is why you are on Earth right now. Always remember this and be brave, courageous, and wise. Today, you may feel God is unjust, but one day you will realise that what God Almighty did was absolutely right. It was the best thing for you and your loved ones. There cannot be any mistake in this.

03-06-1981

SPIRIT GUIDES

We are all humans – you on the Earth plane and us in the spirit world, but our natures are different. Remember, you are on Earth to purify your soul.

So throw away hate and adopt love.

Throw away jealousy and adopt understanding.

Throw away hardheartedness and adopt kindness.

Throw away crookedness and adopt wisdom.

Throw away selfishness and adopt selflessness.

This is how you help yourself to purify your soul and reach a higher level.

Rebirth on Earth is a gamble. You must have seen that in Soordas' story. However, it is important that you purify your soul and reach a higher level. For this God Almighty has given you *double* protection from evil influences so that you do not fall spiritually. One is your own powerful and most wonderful subconscious mind, which will always try to stop you unless you have decided *not* to listen to it, and it has become dormant. The second is your spirit guide, whom some will call a guardian angel. **All souls on Earth have spirit guides who watch out for them from the spirit world.** These guides show you where you have gone wrong.

Your spirit guide knows everything about you and tries

hard to impress upon you to walk on the right path. Before your subconscious mind becomes dormant it calls out to your spirit guide saying, "I am of no use now, so please take over your extra duties."

Your guide will have an extremely hard time trying to make you follow the right path through your *physical* mind. The guide has to push the limits and force your physical mind to work as he or she wishes. At such times, some people on Earth even fail to listen through the physical mind. You reject the guidance given to you and go on harming others.

You may think you are harming others and some of you take pleasure in this, **but in reality you are harming yourself hundreds of times more** than you have harmed anyone else.

Swallow your pride and question yourself whether success in harming others or the pleasure you derive by harming them will ever give you eternal happiness. Will it ever take you to a higher level? For temporary happiness during a few Earth years, do you want to sacrifice your true, eternal happiness and live in hell for thousands of years. Isn't that stupid?

04-06-1981

TWIN SOULS

Spirit beings are very anxious to bring their dear ones to a higher level. They try hard to encourage loved ones never to go wrong, so that they won't suffer.

Every soul has a twin. It is very difficult if one twin is on a higher level and the other on a lower one. The one who is on a higher level has to wait for its twin to rise to its level. For that reason, the one who is on a higher level in the spirit world has to encourage the one on Earth, who is on a lower level. It is a very hard task to bring an Earth twin to a higher level. All twins want to be together, whether their other half is a good or bad soul.

The person on Earth who has let his subconscious mind become dormant and who refuses to follow his or her guide's projected impression is a real problem for us spirit beings. It is a tremendously difficult task for one twin to make the other follow the right path.

Very few twins are on the same level, so the twin on the higher level has to wait – not 2 or 3, nor 20 or 30, not even 200 or 300 years, but in some cases 500 or 600 years. Once a soul reaches Realms 1, 2 or 3, it will take hundreds of Earth years to rise higher. Some even take thousands of years.

The desire of the twin who is waiting for the other to come up is so strong and genuine that he or she takes birth on Earth to help the other twin. Sometimes they succeed, but most of the time they fall to a lower level as well. This is how the spirit world and the Earth world go on.

We cannot stop ourselves from repeating this fact: if Earth people were intelligent enough to realise what is good and bad for them, or would try to get messages from the spirit world, it would be so easy for them to understand things. But most people on Earth do not believe in life after death or in the spirit world, and if some do believe it, it is beyond them to understand how we can send messages, or how people on Earth can receive them. There are a few fools in your world who even say, "Don't talk to departed souls. You are just harassing them by stopping their progress."

Please don't misunderstand us, but we cannot stop ourselves from telling those fools: if you were really intelligent and learned you would not think this way. Besides, those who want to stop spirit communications are so sinful and corrupt that they are afraid the world will learn the truth and they would not be able to fool others and continue on their evil path. Some people think they know what is right and try to make others believe that those who communicate with the spirit world are bogus or mad.

If people on Earth would cooperate with us, it would be so easy for us to send them messages and help them. Instead, they brag about it all being nonsense and humbug, how it harms more than it helps, and so on. So we have to work very hard at projecting our thoughts, and we have to run after these people for years to bring them onto the right path. Even after such hard work some souls have a one-track mind. They will not listen to us and will continue on the wrong path.

After an evil soul on Earth makes his or her subconscious mind dormant, after his or her guide fails to bring that soul onto the right path, who is left to improve such a soul but its twin? Bringing a fallen twin on Earth to a higher level and trying to improve him or her is a very difficult job for the twin in the spirit world. So do the needful, improve yourself and rise to a higher level quickly.

Don't think of the fun and happiness of a few years on Earth; think of eternal happiness.

05-06-1981

GOOD OR EVIL IS YOUR CHOICE

You must have read books, heard sermons, or been taught in school and by your older relatives and friends about what is right, what is wrong, and how to improve yourself. But some of you don't bother to listen or read. Some souls will say, "Why shouldn't I do this? It gives me pleasure to harass someone. I feel very happy when I fool someone, and it is a joy to harm or rob someone."

We ask those souls, "Don't you feel happy when you help someone? Don't you feel at peace when you forgive someone who has harmed you? Don't you rejoice when you make someone happy?" If these things don't make you happy, but those awful bad things do, we feel very sorry for you, we pity you.

Every person has good and evil in him, but it is entirely your choice whether to be good or bad. That is the main point. It is definitely a great thing to control the bad and bring out the good in yourself.

If you feel happy when you harm others, derive pleasure from fooling others, or become elated by harassing others, isn't this the right time to ask God Almighty for His help, guidance and blessings for your improvement?

06-06-1981

SPIRIT COMMUNICATIONS HELP COMFORT LOVED ONES ON EARTH

We are very keen on communicating with our loved ones on Earth, so we continuously request God Almighty to give us the opportunity. On the whole, people on Earth are so preoccupied with their own work, fun, and money-making, that they don't care for their departed loved ones.

However, some — like our mother and father — are keen to communicate with their departed loved ones. We were overjoyed when our Mom and Dad wanted to hear from us. They too felt happy that they were able to communicate with us. Spirit beings wish there were more people like our Mom and Dad! We were able to calm them down and guide them regarding who was making fools of them, who were their really good friends, and whom should they trust and ask for help. Our Mom and Dad are quite alone in your world, except for a few relatives and good friends who have helped them. We thank them and bless them.

There are many spirit souls who are extremely keen on communicating with their loved ones. Many, like us, want to help their loved ones on Earth feel calm, as their unhappiness and misery on Earth is projected onto us, making us feel depressed and sad, too.

We do understand how you feel when your loved ones have departed from your world, as you cannot see, hear, or touch us, but we request you to be calm and *not mourn for us,* as we are happier here than we were there. **We are more alive than we were on Earth and we can still see you, hear you, touch you, hug you, and even kiss you.**

If you and your departed loved ones are very close, only then do we strongly feel your sadness. The love and closeness of a mother or father and their children, or of a sister and brother, or even of good friends who love each other deeply, affects us. However, no matter what the relationship on Earth was, if there is no genuine and mutual love, we do not have a connection with that soul once we have come to the spirit world.

Our Mom and Dad sometimes felt so lost and miserable without us that it would have been very difficult for us to calm them down and cheer them up without spirit communications. We would explain to them that they should control their feelings as they also sadden us, and we are closer to them than when we were on Earth. This spirit communication makes us all (Mom, Dad, Vispi and Ratoo) share in each other's happiness and miseries and, most importantly, lets them know we are near them and love them tremendously. It is a much easier task for us because of this spirit communication.

So we request the people on Earth to communicate *safely* with the spirit world for your own good, as well as to provide us with an easier way to perform our duties. With the help of spirit communication, it is much easier for us to guide you and stop you from going deep into darkness. It is our duty to guide you and it is therefore advisable to communicate with us. If you have such a gift, do develop it. Every soul has *some* kind of gift from God Almighty, but for some it takes a long time and a lot of hard work to develop it, and for some it comes automatically.

Never suppress your instincts. Never think people will call you crazy or weird if they find out you have this gift. It is a God-given gift and you should be grateful for it.

There was a girl, whom we shall call Nina, who had such a gift but her mother brainwashed her, saying, "It is evil to communicate with a spirit, never do this again or the evil spirit will possess your body and ruin you. You will become a devil and will burn in the fires of hell."

Nina was so frightened by her mother's warning that she even hesitated to utter the words "spirit communication". She lost a great opportunity, a wonderful gift, and faith in herself.

After many years, when she was told the facts and her husband gave her books that explained her gift, it was too late. No matter how much she tried to regain it and forget what her mother had said, she could not, as her fear went very deep. She regretted having listened to her mother, and she found it impossible to regain her confidence.

Just like Nina's story, there are many such cases, so we request the people on Earth to never advise anyone without the proper knowledge and facts. **Little knowledge is a dangerous thing.** And for the person listening to the advice – make sure the source has true spiritual knowledge.

07-06-1981

MOST SOULS HAVE BEEN TO LOWER REALMS

We are all reborn on Earth to purify our soul and rise to a higher level, but our desire is not always fulfilled and often we move downwards instead of rising. **So most of us have experienced Realms 2 to 6.** Only a few have experienced Realm 1, as it is extremely difficult to come out from Realm 1.

Every soul has taken rebirth nearly 100 to 2000 times on Earth and gained all different kinds of experiences. Every soul must go through different problems and situations.

We must also let you know that spirit beings are not allowed to tell people on Earth *all* our secrets; we can only tell you a few things. If we told you your future, you would be prepared beforehand, and your rebirth would be of no use.

08-06-1981

MISCONCEPTIONS ABOUT SPIRIT COMMUNICATIONS

If you think your departed loved ones will be hindered in their progress, you are completely wrong. Without spirit communications, it sometimes takes spirit souls days, months, years, or even decades to enforce thoughts on you to bring you onto the right path. But through spirit communications we can make you understand within a few hours that which may otherwise take years. So with regards to hindering a departed soul's progress, on the contrary, their progress would be much more rapid.

As we said before, one twin on a higher level waits for the other to rise and has to work hard to stop the twin from falling any lower. **When the higher twin tries to project thoughts to the other one on Earth, the Earth twin may not even bother to heed those thoughts for years.** But through spirit communications it is easy and rapid. Therefore, our progress is much more rapid with, rather than without, spirit communication.

People think spirit communication hinders the departed soul's progress and that is why most don't want to communicate with their dear departed souls. Is that true, **or is it that their guilty conscience stops them from communicating?**

Real holy souls and sages have the power to communicate with departed souls and spirit people. If communication hinders a spirit being's progress, would such high souls have this power?

Some people may say, "Be careful or evil spirits will possess your body and you will be ruined and will go to hell." Here are some answers for them:

Are you evil? Evil attracts evil. If you are evil then yes, you should fear spirit communications as evil definitely attracts evil, and if you attract evil spirits, they may possess your physical mind. But if you are a good soul and you are communicating with a good departed soul, there is no harm in it at all.

Never attempt automatic writing on your own. It is extremely dangerous to practice automatic writing on your own without a protective link[14] and without following proper instructions. Only an experienced and already-linked person can join your link. This will ensure that no negative interference can harm you.

Evil attracts evil and good attracts good. Good spirits will definitely protect you, and in continual spirit communication with a good soul, (where your link is not broken) you are absolutely safe.

In the same way you would close your front door to evil people and not allow them into your home, you should close your mind to evil spirits and not let them enter your mind.

09-06-1981

WHY SOME PEOPLE FEAR SPIRIT COMMUNICATIONS

Gone are the days when superstitions ruled our lives. Gone are the days when people thought only mad people spoke to Spirits. Gone are the days when it could not be proved that the one who claims to have spirit communications is genuine. Now on Earth, many scientists, psychiatrists, and para-psychologists who

---

14. Protection provided by higher spirit beings through prayers and positive energy, for safe communication between Earth souls and spirit beings.

are doing extensive research on spirit communications are able to prove that their work is genuine.

There are many strange phenomena for which no scientific explanations can be found, and one has to believe in ESP, para-psychology and psychic phenomena.

Some fools even doubt the existence of the spirit world or whether it is true that we are souls. Some extraordinary fools even ask such a stupid question as, "Are you sure there is a God?"

Some people are very anxious to learn more about spirit communications, and want to go deeper and deeper into such matters. For some it is a compulsion to know, so they try hard to find out all about the spirit world, about death, birth, previous lives, and so on. People on Earth are always looking for solid proof for everything. Their limited minds cannot take things in without proof, and it is almost impossible to establish proof, as only a few have this God-given power, though others are happy to imitate them and earn a fortune by fooling innocent people. This has made it hard for many to distinguish genuine people from frauds.

Some think it is evil or bad to delve into the supernatural, but it is sheer ignorance to think like this. Some fear that their guilt and sins will be discovered by spirit beings, so they discourage others. Evil people do not like these ideas, nor do they take any interest in them. Some are brainwashed by their parents, priests, or teachers so they actually curb their instinct and refuse to take any risks.

WHY YOU CHOOSE TO BE BORN ON EARTH

It is strange, but true, that most of you did not want to be born in your world, as you were very happy here in the spirit world (we are talking about souls on higher levels). It was only your impatience to climb higher and your willingness to take a risk, or your desire to help a loved one who was falling spiritually on Earth, that caused you to take rebirth on Earth. But most of you (your soul and subconscious mind) wish you were never born on Earth. Sometimes you feel this consciously and wonder why you are feeling like this, but you have no recollection of your spirit world home. You wonder for some time, and then you forget about it. Some of you get this feeling from your soul and subconscious mind so strongly that your physical mind has to listen to it.

You can gain training and experience in the spirit world, but it takes thousands of years to reach higher levels, so instead, you try to reach the higher levels in a few hundred years, which is the reason you were born on Earth — to get quicker results. However, the risk is that you may even go lower and it may take longer to achieve your goal.

Souls from the lower Realms are happy to be reborn on Earth, as this gives them a chance to progress more rapidly. It is advisable for them to be reborn as it is a great advantage for them if they succeed in keeping on the right path. The suffering in Realms 1, 2 and 3 is so severe that it is better for them to risk rebirth on Earth. For good souls who have fallen to lower levels due to evil and bad influences, Earth is paradise.

Some good souls who have fallen lower request God to

punish them severely but in a very short time. If they are from Realm 1 or 2 they are born as beasts of burden on Earth, working hard and sometimes being tortured by humans. They pay off their karma quicker, but they must have the guts to bear the suffering as most of them are tortured, whipped and starved. They must toil all day in the fields or carry immense burdens.

These souls feel this punishment is much better than staying hundreds of years in Realms 1 or 2. So you can just imagine how horrible Realms 1 and 2 must be. They gladly and willingly take this punishment to escape staying in those Realms.

Realm 3 is horrible, as well. The souls in Realm 3 take chances like Soordas did, but all cannot be saved like Soordas, and such souls may land in Realms 1 or 2 instead of moving higher.

Realm 4 is bearable — it is almost like Earth. Still, to those souls who have fallen from higher Realms, it is terrible. Every soul wants to reach the highest Realm as quickly as possible, so they try to take rebirth to gain experience, suffer their punishment in a shorter time and purify their soul. These are the reasons for which you are reborn on Earth.

WHY YOU DREAD DEATH

After you are born on Earth, you enjoy your life so much that you dread death. Some people do not even want to leave Earth when they are stuck with old, aching bodies. Why is this?

This is because in their heart of hearts they know where they will land once they die in your world. They are afraid to die because they are sure they will be in the dark, lower Realms, so they try to hold on to their life. But when your physical body refuses to function, the soul must leave that decaying, temporary, physical home. Whether you like it or not, you have to die on Earth.

There are some people on Earth who have been brainwashed into thinking that death is a horrible thing. They are even afraid of the word 'Death'. It is near impossible to rid them of this fear, and they struggle to live longer on Earth. When such good souls depart from your world and arrive in the spirit world on higher planes, they are so surprised to see such beauty, harmony and love on Realms 5, 6 and 7 that they regret their fears.

SUICIDE IS A SIN

You should not fear death. At the same time, you should not even think of death before your time. Only God should decide when you should come to the spirit world. **Committing suicide is spiritually wrong.** God gives us the chance to be reborn on Earth, and by committing suicide you are going against Him. **Suicide is a sin.** By committing suicide you will fall to lower Realms, which we are sure you would never want. You must never try committing suicide because by doing so you only get a temporary release from your physical body and you permanently damage your soul.

11-06-1981

THE HIGH GOOD SOULS

There is only one God – our God Almighty. But our dearest God has plenty of souls to help Him make every soul pure, honest, loving, understanding, obliging, good and wise. These helpers were just humans like us all, and went through what people on Earth and spirit beings are going through. They reincarnated hundreds of times, and after going up and down again and again, finally reached this level. These helpers are called *His High Good Souls,* and at the very top is *His Highest Good Soul.*

On higher Realms we see them often, but on Realms 4 and lower they can rarely be seen, as they prefer to remain invisible because it makes their work easier. They achieve much success in their work to improve bad or evil souls, making them understand what is right and wrong, and also instructing them on how to pay off their karma in a less horrible and quicker way, or how to reach the higher Realms sooner.

Whenever they are near us we feel very happy and cheerful. If we need any help, they help us at once. As soon as any soul, even from Realm 1, calls for help, these High Good Souls are there in minutes. Even on Earth, if a soul genuinely and sincerely calls for help, help is given at once. It doesn't matter whether that soul is on Realm 1, on Earth or on a higher level. **Genuine calls for help will always be answered.**

You may have often heard stories about souls on Earth who called for help from God and a miracle happened. You

may have even called for help in a very tense situation and received help in some very odd way, which you would call a miracle.

Even your loved ones in the spirit world can and do save you many times. You can be sure that your loved ones in the spirit world care for you a great deal. Always remember that real true love never dies, not even after death on Earth. Love is greater than death. **Love is eternal. Death is just a transition** from one world to another, from one body to another, from Earth to heaven or hell.

Death is *not* something big at all, but love is *extraordinarily great*.

Now, let's talk a little bit more about God Almighty's helpers. We call them High Good Souls, and you call them angels. We must point out that **angels do not have wings,** however as they move real fast, their robes look like wings. Just as they are able to take human form, they are able to create wings to impress non believers. So, Earth souls see wings and believe that an angel gave them the message and helped them.

High Good Souls are very humble, considerate and understanding. They even relax certain of God Almighty's laws in certain cases, by first making a request to His Highest Good Soul, who asks Our God Almighty. This permission in urgent situations comes within seconds or minutes. If it is not urgent it takes a few hours or, at the most, a few days.

Whenever we want something that is not permissible, we appeal to the head of our Realm. He will hear us out carefully and ask some questions, and if he feels our request is genuine, and will *not* harm anyone, he will put a request to our Highest Good Soul to seek permission from Our God Almighty.

This is the difference between the Earth world and the spirit world. The rulers of our Realms are so humble, understanding and considerate that we can always feel free to talk to them. They are so honest, kind and loving that we never fear them. They are so selfless that we fully trust them. They lovingly and kindly make us understand that certain things are wrong, and why they are wrong.

They never reject our requests in a rude manner. If they think it is wrong they will explain this to us and help us understand why it is not possible. They are very reasonable and kind-hearted. We fully trust and respect them, obeying them happily because we know they will never let us go wrong.

These are God Almighty's helpers — our High Good Souls, and your angels.

12-06-1981

WHAT IS A GOOD DEED?

Good deeds are those that are done with an absolutely selfless motive. If there is even a tiny bit of selfishness in it, it cannot be called a good deed; it would be a selfish deed.

Good deeds that are performed selflessly are a real boon to your progress. They will carry you higher more rapidly than anything else. Unfortunately, behind all their good deeds, people on Earth almost always think that it will take them to a higher level and their sins will be forgiven.

We must warn you that this thought brings you lower rather than takes you to a higher level. Only those good deeds that are done naturally and out of kindness, without any thought of your going higher, can be considered selfless good deeds. After performing the good deed, immediately *forget* about it. Don't think of it at all. If you are able to do that, no selfish thought will penetrate your mind. A selfish afterthought always puts you on the wrong track. **So if you have done a good deed automatically and just for kindness' sake, forget about it immediately.**

Good deeds done entirely for the sake of forgiveness in order to wipe out your karma, without genuine repentance, then are not selfless, good deeds. They will *never* take you to a higher level; you can be sure of that.

Before doing a good deed, be sure your motive is not selfish at all. If you succeed in that, you must also succeed in forgetting about it entirely. Success in this is in your own hands.

For example, if you do something for the sake of a loved one, you don't care to broadcast it or think twice about it. You do it out of love for that beloved soul. You love to care for them, to see to their comforts and you even like to make sacrifices for them. Therefore, whatever you do for your beloved, take joy in it, then forget it as though it was a natural deed, an expression of true affection — unless, of course, your love is not true.

In one second, your good deed can turn into a selfish one
– so before you have time to think more, just forget about
it. So remember, one tiny bit of a selfish thought will wipe
off your good deed.

13-06-1981

REVENGE

Revenge is a very bad thing. Earth people do not
know what revenge actually means. Revenge comes
to a person's mind if he or she is jealous of
another. For example, say Peter is jealous of Katie as she is
a popular, nice, sweet person. So Peter wants to run her
down, so he starts spreading rumours about Katie, or even
tries to harm her by turning her loved ones against her, or
harassing and harming her in other ways. This is entirely
wrong. This act will bring Peter to a very low level. Now,
suppose Katie saw how wrongly Peter behaved and how he
has harmed her. Seeing how wrongly Peter behaved, in her
defence if Katie tries to show Peter's true colours to the
world, then that is not wrong. Katie should show the
world how bad Peter is, *so that other people will not be fooled by
him*, will be alert, and won't become victims of Peter's
revenge. Showing the world *the facts* about Peter's meanness
will bring Katie to a higher level. But her heart must be
good and her intentions pure. This is not considered
revenge, as many would call it, as your *motive is to save others
from suffering what you suffered*. No one else will become
Peter's victim, and that is a good deed. Please do not
expose evil at the expense of harming your loved ones or
yourself. So you see, people on Earth often do not
understand the difference between good and bad.

SURESH'S STORY

One day, Suresh was introduced to J, a very young widow. She was of loose character and began flirting with Suresh, who was married and had three children. J made Suresh so crazy about her that he had an affair with her and even promised her an apartment. J was having affairs with others as well, but Suresh never knew about that and fell so madly in love that he became like a slave to her. J kept getting money and jewellery from Suresh. Suresh's father found out that Suresh was wasting his money on a woman, talked to Suresh very strongly, and brought him back to his senses, as he knew that Suresh was a good soul but had a weakness for women. Suresh understood how wrong he was and he broke off all relations with J. J was a very mean and vengeful woman. So she wanted to take revenge on Suresh and his family. As I said before, she had several lovers, and she soon became pregnant by one of them. J took a pregnancy test from a well-known hospital and got a paper stating she was, indeed, pregnant. She took this paper to Suresh's house and told his parents and wife that Suresh had fooled her saying he would marry her, had an affair with her, and now she was pregnant. She showed them the paper from the hospital along with some other papers that proved that Suresh had tried to find an apartment in her name. Suresh's mother knew nothing about this. As she had a weak heart, Suresh's father had never told her anything about it. Suresh's wife did not know either.

Suresh's mother had the shock of her life, and that same night she passed away. Suresh's wife couldn't bear the shock either, and soon after her mother-in-law's funeral, she left Suresh, taking their children with her.

Suresh and his father were overwhelmed, and found it very difficult to control themselves. They wanted to kill J, who had ruined their lives and was still demanding an apartment and money from Suresh, so they began to plan her murder. They were good souls, but this disgrace and loss of their loved ones made them think of revenge. Fortunately for them a very pious good friend of theirs came by to give his condolences. Suresh and his father told him their story, and said they wanted to kill her.

Their friend said, "Look, my dear friends, I understand what you went through and what you are still going through, but listen to this old man and save your souls. It is *not* in your hands to kill her. It is entirely and absolutely in God's hands, so please don't go against God Almighty. Get rid of those evil ideas from your good minds; they will harm you more than her. Both of you will fall so low that you won't be able to see your dear mother in heaven. Please stop this awful way of thinking. Instead, you can do something that will please God Almighty. You can refuse to pay her any money. She is an evil woman, so you can expose her by telling everyone who she is. You can bring out all her wickedness. God will be pleased by this as others won't be fooled by her anymore, and there may also be a chance of her improving."

This good advice and guidance saved Suresh and his father from becoming sinful souls.

14-06-1981

YOU CANNOT TREAT EVERYONE IN
THE SAME MANNER

If a good soul sees someone doing wrong, he will tell that person right away, or tactfully let him know where he is wrong and be glad that he has improved that person. In this case the motive is purely to help the soul. Bad souls will also try to show where another person is wrong, but will take pride in how they made him realise where he was wrong, and then ridicule him. This is a form of revenge. A good soul feels happy thinking he has improved someone.

If you are on a higher level your subconscious mind will guide you, but if you are on a lower level it is difficult for you to make good judgments. In the case of good deeds, a good deed done to a good soul will help the soul improve; however, the same good deed done to a bad soul will do the reverse — it will make the bad soul view the good deed as a sign of weakness and he will take advantage of the situation.

For example, suppose Bomi comes to your house for a visit and, when you go out of the room to serve drinks or to get something to eat, he steals money from your house. When you re-enter the room, you notice what has happened, so you give him some more money, saying, "Instead of stealing it, you should have asked me. I would have given it to you." He will feel horrible and say, "Sorry, I will never steal again," and I am sure he will stick to that as he is a good soul who was tempted, or maybe he had a great need. But the *same* treatment to some bad souls would encourage them and they would laugh and still try to fool others and you several more times, which will send *you* to a lower level. So a good deed done to one person would be good for him as well as for you, but done to another may be entirely bad for both of you.

It is the same with forgiveness. If you forgive a good soul he will try his best to improve. His subconscious mind will make him realise where he went wrong. But if you forgive a bad soul without telling him where he went wrong, he will laugh at you, call you a fool, and go on with his bad ways. Since you encouraged him, you will also fall lower. So every man on Earth is not the same.

You cannot treat everyone in the same manner.

15-06-1981

FACE YOUR PROBLEMS NOW, BRAVELY AND WITH A SMILE

In your world, it is absolutely impossible to get all happiness and comfort. You have to bear difficulties, problems, miseries and sicknesses because without such problems, you cannot live on Earth. What is most important, of course, is how you face your problems. **You must face them bravely and with a smile, and never try to run away from them.** Many more problems will always crop up, so it is best to face all your problems courageously and happily. If you are a good soul, or one who genuinely and sincerely wants to be good, you can be sure that God is with you throughout the way. Trust Him, pray to Him, ask for His guidance, and your sincere prayers will never go unanswered.

NEVER ENCOURAGE NEGATIVITY IN OTHERS

If you have no guts to fight evil, it is best to *avoid* evil and bad people. Stay away from them, as evil people and their influence will always harm you. Your vibrations will be damaged and you will definitely fall to a lower level. People on Earth will say, "How can we avoid evil, as bad people are all around us?" We do understand that there are many bad souls on Earth and you can of course talk to them and live next door to them, but *never* be friendly with them. A small conversation, a nod and a smile, and then get away from them. But do not be a hypocrite. Be helpful to them when the need arises, but *never* encourage them in doing evil things. If you are not friendly with them, they will also stay away from you in most cases. Keep them at a distance, as it is not possible for an ordinary good soul to improve such bad people. Do help good souls, however, or ones who sincerely want to improve. There are few good souls who have the strength to improve evil souls and not go wrong themselves. It is difficult to improve bad souls, as even good souls are influenced by bad and evil.

16-06-1981

VIEW THINGS FROM A SPIRITUAL ANGLE

Crooked, evil people can never think or work straight. Good souls are never able to give improper advice and knowingly put their fellow man on the wrong path. Is it a sin to rejoice in the punishment of an evil person? Let us see:

I.   If you are glad the evil person learnt a lesson, was stopped from harming others, and was given a chance to improve – and that there is a possibility of them improving – who wouldn't be happy? This is natural.

2.   If your happiness is vindictive – that is a sin.

So there are always two sides. It entirely depends on how you view things, what are your reactions, and what is your intention or motive.

17-06-1981

DO NOT LET HOROSCOPES INFLUENCE YOU

One thing we would like to clarify is with regards to horoscopes. When you read your weekly or daily predictions in the newspapers, it will have an effect on your mind. Your thoughts are very powerful and are affected by what you read, thus ensuring the flow of events as per the horoscope. So you may say the horoscope was right.

This is nothing but brainwashing for weak-minded people. If you want to make something happen, your positive thoughts will definitely help in most cases. Your subconscious mind will know that the horoscope is wrong but your physical mind may think it is right. Your subconscious mind knows the truth. If the horoscope is wrong, your subconscious mind may not cooperate with you, so do not be disappointed. Think of everything that happens as God's wish, and thank God Almighty for properly guiding you. Use your own free will, so do not be fooled by astrologers and predictions. It all depends on you and your choices.

POWER CAN BE USED FOR GOOD OR BAD – PROJECTING AND RECEIVING POWERS

Your world, the spirit world and the entire universe all have certain powers. This power is stronger at some places and less so at others, but it is always there. In the spirit world, we don't have to generate it as our mind is our powerhouse. We easily grasp this power ourselves. But on Earth, you have not understood how to harness it yourself, so you depend on electricity, which is a lower form of this power.

Some human beings can receive our messages because they have receiving powers. Some have projecting powers. Some have a great deal of power while others have less, and some are lucky enough to have a balance of both receiving and projecting powers. Both these powers, if used correctly, will do you and the people around you a world of good, as good souls are nearer to God Almighty and their subconscious mind also guides them – they use this power for *good*. But the same power in bad people is very dangerous, as they can use it for evil.

The power is the same, but to use it for good or bad is in the individual's hands. It is even dangerous for weak-minded people, as they become pompous and manipulative. This brings them to lower Realms, where negative souls make that person go even more wrong. We advise the good souls who have this power to pray and concentrate, and willingly give your mind to a good spirit soul (a dear loved one) who will be able to guide you and help you lead a very good life on Earth. Like attracts like – bad attracts bad and good attracts good. Even bad souls who have this power have a very good opportunity of improving.

Remember, it is very dangerous for an evil man to use this power. Negative souls are waiting to lead people to the lowest of Realms. So, weak-minded, good souls, please don't try to develop this power. Remember, once a bad spirit gets control of your mind it is really difficult to drive it out.

18-06-1981

TO GET HELP FROM SPIRIT SOULS, ALWAYS BE COOL AND CALM

Always keep cool, calm and relaxed. Stay tension-free so that spirit souls can guide you. You must learn to put faith in God Almighty – God is great.

Do not believe astrologers, or other such individuals – learn to put complete faith in God Almighty. Your genuine and sincere faith in God Almighty will work miracles. He is **ALMIGHTY**, so no one can go against Him.

If you suffer and problems crop up, treat it as your karma, test and training, face it courageously and happily. Your sincere prayers will help you a great deal. Keep your mind occupied and don't harm anyone and you can be sure you will get help and guidance straight from God Almighty through spirit souls.

Your sincere prayers and your genuine faith in God will pull you through any problems. As you are on Earth, there are bound to be problems, but you must face them, so face them with a courageous smile. Your faith in God and your prayers will definitely be of great use to us as well, as it makes it easier for us to reach you, guide you, and help you.

19-06-1981

MARRIAGE

There are no marriages in the spirit world, but we do try to mend broken marriages on Earth because of the children, and also because a couple will need each other in their old age. **On Earth, wise men created marriages to safeguard children** because they saw that people were not being responsible and taking care of their children. Therefore, they made marriage compulsory for begetting children, because both parents can bring up a child better than just one.

It is wise for two people to stay together, help each other, and guide their children to be better citizens. In their old age, the couple can also look after each other, give each other company and face the world's problems together. So marriages are *not* destined. We are afraid to say this, however, as many people on Earth will now say, "Marriages are not made by God, so why get married and create problems? Let us be free." I advise you to think hard before publishing this in our book. We like to help reunite those with broken marriages so they may live happily, as that is best for them, but sometimes one partner is entirely evil abusing the other partner and/or their children physically and mentally. It becomes impossible for the other to live with her or him, in which case we do pray for God to do what is best for all concerned.

It is best for husband and wife to love each other, and live in harmony and happiness as a united family with their children, so that they can face problems in a much better way. **Harmony and happiness at home are most necessary** for every human being on Earth. There has to be give and take and toleration in all marriages.

15-01-1984

DEVELOP YOUR POWER IN THE RIGHT MANNER

In the spirit world as well as on Earth there is electric power, which you cannot see. This power helps you greatly on Earth, and it also helps you receive messages through the phone, radio, or TV. The human brain, is just like the phone, radio, or TV. Some people on Earth have developed receiving power, some have developed only projecting power, and some have developed a good balance of both. Whoever has more projecting power cannot receive our spirit messages, as they have less receiving power in them. Most people on Earth have psychic powers, but to develop them is in your hands, and it is most important to consider *how* you develop them. The same power can be used in both ways – for evil or good – so it is in your own hands to ruin yourself, or rise and be happy.

Sometimes, we are not permitted to tell you something, or answer a certain question, so please never try to force us by repeatedly asking that question.

Everyone sins on Earth. There cannot be anyone who has not sinned, but their levels differ. Some sin very little, some more so, and some in the extreme. So if you sin even a little, you have to pay through karma and we cannot stop that. You must understand this thoroughly – we cannot stop your punishment. Sometimes we have to refuse to help certain people, and this is the main reason. We are most willing to help those who are good, innocent, and suffering due to the evil people on Earth, so if we refuse to help or guide you, try and find out what sins you have committed and repent sincerely for them, so that we can guide you in the future.

Only negative souls are keen to make you miserable by misleading you and guiding you wrongly, but good attracts good, and evil attracts evil, so try hard to be good and God will definitely help you.

25-01-1984
PRAYERS SHOULD ALWAYS BE SHORT AND SINCERE

You must have absolute concentration. In your world, long prayers never let you concentrate, nor can you be completely sincere in them. When you read prayers from a book without absolute devotion, concentration and sincerity, it is just like reading a novel.

Try to pray every day in the same place, as you will build strong and pure vibrations in that place. Of course, it is OK to pray in any place, but if you choose just one place the good vibrations will reflect back to you and this will help you greatly.

All places are God's places, so you can say short prayers even while travelling. You must have faith. Even if you pick up a stone from a road, wash it, keep it on a table, and worship it sincerely, your prayers create good vibrations and those vibrations will be absorbed by the stone. Your sincere daily prayers create good vibrations around that stone and place, and this vibrates back to you, bringing you peace of mind and wisdom, and even purifying your soul. Just have complete faith in God and be absolutely sincere, and your prayers will work wonders.

26-01-1984

PRIDE ALWAYS MAKES YOU FALL SPIRITUALLY

Always be humble. Never think someone will be stranded without your help. God is there to help those who need help. You are a mere human being. If you become famous and you allow pride to set in, then pride will one day make you fall. So never be proud. If pride fills your mind you cannot think straight, you will make many mistakes and fall spiritually. **If your head is in the air, it will be filled with nothing but air.** You will have no wisdom. You can be sure that no one is helpless without you. Only *you* will be helpless without God Almighty.

Whoever thinks someone will be helpless without him is the greatest fool. If God gave you something to be proud of, be humble nonetheless; otherwise, you will definitely fall. Nothing happens before its time — so just wait and relax — your tension won't help it happen before its time. Rather, it will harm you. So do relax and pray. God is great.

On Earth, you have to live with bad and evil souls and keep your own soul pure, strong and good. It is a very difficult task, but God stays with good souls and looks after them if they want His protection. Show concern and affection for others and have the sincere desire to always stay good, in spite of suffering on Earth.

28-01-1984

YOU CANNOT ESCAPE PAYING FOR YOUR SINS

Whatever you sow, you will reap. God's justice is absolutely perfect. It may not come immediately, but eventually, you will have to pay for your sins.

God always gives hints to good souls who go wrong, who sin somehow or the other. He shows you where you are going wrong, but people on Earth don't even realise this, so instead of stopping and trying to improve, they go deeper and deeper into evil. If they fail in their evil ways, they don't realise that God does not want them to sin. Rather, they go deeper into sin, thinking, "I will show how intelligent I am." We pity such souls. They go so deep into evil that they are on the path of 'no return', and they will land in hell.

PART II

Q & A

The desk in Khorshed Bhavnagri's Bombay home where she
communicated with her sons

AUTOMATIC WRITING

"Little knowledge is a dangerous thing."

"We are more alive in the spirit world than you are on Earth. We can see you, hear you, touch you and feel you."

"Real true love never dies, not even after your death on Earth. Love is eternal."

Never attempt automatic writing on your own. It is extremely dangerous to start automatic writing on your own without a protective link, and without following proper instructions. Only an experienced and already-linked person can connect your link. This will ensure that no negative interference, such as an astral soul or unknown negative energy, will harm you.

 When we communicate with the dead, are we not disturbing their souls?

To say that we are dead is wrong. We are more alive than you are on Earth. Your earthly life is just one more stop in an infinite journey. How can communication end where there is true love? It is communication between souls and souls never die. Therefore, you need to change your understanding of death. What dies is your ego, your physical body — what remains is your soul, which is more alive, more vibrant, more loving than the person the soul is in communication with on Earth. We, spirit souls have no bodily aches or pains. Having discarded both our human and astral bodies, we are completely free. God has given us the choice to shape our own lives here in the spirit world, just as on Earth. We can choose work that we like, pray, rejoice, gain information and spiritual knowledge when we like. We are not bound by the physicality of your world, and we are led completely by the subconscious mind, which is our true, spiritual mind. So, when you communicate with us, you are not "disturbing the dead" because we are more alive than you are.

Nowadays young people are more open minded, so they are more receptive to spirit communications unlike their parents who are brainwashed, and have fixed ideas due to constant conditioning.

ॐ What is automatic writing?

Automatic writing is the process through which spirit souls communicate with human beings on Earth. All it requires is a pen, paper and a natural flame. To put it simply, the spirit soul with whom you are communicating will move the pen while you hold it lightly on the page, and slowly, over time, words and later sentences will form. We do not wish to disclose details about automatic writing because it is not a practice that can be taken lightly. **A negative interference, such as an astral soul or unknown negative energy, can harm you during automatic writing.** It can

Different Stages of Automatic Writing

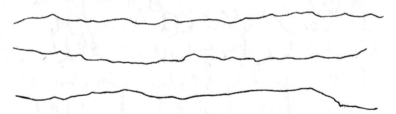

Stage 1

Stage 2

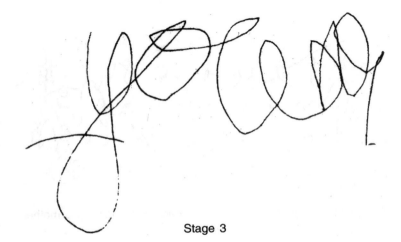

Stage 3

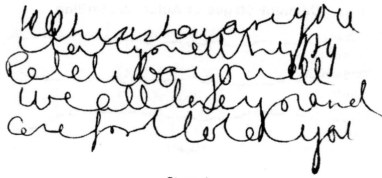

Stage 4

Stage 5 – Telepathic
Telepathic communication received by Khorshed Bhavnagri in her own
handwriting. Here spirit souls impress the thought directly into the
mind of the Earth soul. This is known as Telepathy.

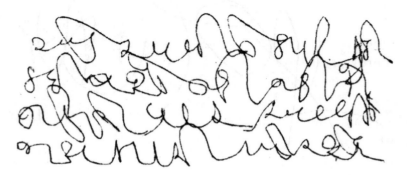

Communication received in Gujarati (Khorshed Bhavnagri's mother
tongue).

only be done when you have a *protective link* between you and the soul in the spirit world with whom you wish to communicate. Only an experienced person who is already linked can join your link. Therefore, when there is a request for automatic writing, the first step is to gain permission from the spirit world; only if permission is granted can detailed instructions be given, which must be followed completely. If *done correctly* under *proper guidance*, this is the *safest* form of communication with spirit souls because a protective link is formed between you and the spirit soul with whom you will communicate. This link is protected by higher spirit souls, so no low-level or astral soul can interfere and mislead you. Here in the spirit world we are not permitted to form a link with negative souls.

Automatic writing is a gift from God Almighty to souls on Earth, through which they can keep in touch with their loved ones. Only spirit souls on higher spiritual levels and people on Earth who are on the right path are given permission to communicate. The most important advantage of learning automatic writing is that you can be in touch with your departed loved ones and receive their guidance, which is a source of great comfort to people on Earth. However, the main purpose of automatic writing, under the guidance of spirit souls, is to help you to **improve spiritually** and eventually help others as well. While you write, your subconscious mind is activated and you receive protection (so negative energy cannot harm you) and are healed. Eventually, if you are on the right path, you will be able to help others. You will be able to receive messages for other people and help those in need of spiritual knowledge and guidance. Unfortunately, many people today are misusing this gift. As soon as they start automatic writing, they give messages to others that may come from their own physical mind and may be completely wrong. Some people use this gift to feed their own ego, to gain power, success, and fame, or to control others. If this is done, the spirit soul will stop communicating with the soul on Earth. Two things may happen as a result of this: one, the person on Earth will continue to write messages on his own from his physical mind, which will be completely wrong; two, a negative astral soul will send messages to the soul on Earth and will completely mislead that soul.

֎ *Would it be correct to say that automatic writing is a spiritual practice?*

Yes, that is exactly what it is. God wants spirit souls to help human souls. It is our duty to guide you. Souls on Earth have been brainwashed into believing that automatic writing is a negative practice and that it hinders our progress. Spiritual growth is the ultimate aim. Although human beings first talk to their deceased loved ones because of shock or grief, eventually you realise that these loved ones now serve as spiritual guardians and protectors.

֎ *Why don't all souls who have passed away communicate with their loved ones? Don't all souls want to ease the pain and suffering of their loved ones on Earth?*

Some souls on Earth are gifted mediums who have the ability to receive messages from the spirit world. Some are born with this gift — it is a gift they have earned over lifetimes, and it is their spiritual mission. Also, not all souls on Earth believe in an afterlife or in God. People say they do, but they do not live their lives accordingly, so they have failed in their test and as a result their loved ones are not allowed to communicate with them. **The first thing spirit souls need is faith.** If you look for proof, you will never find it. **You may say that you are human and you need proof, but the truth is that you *want* proof — you don't need it.** In your heart, you know God exists and people who go to the spirit world are still alive. Only logic prevents you from accepting it. If we gave you proof there would be no test. After losing their loved ones, some people become very bitter and angry and they blame God. Instead of seeking His help during the tough times, they turn away from Him. It is only natural to feel pain, but try not to become bitter and angry. Even though it is very difficult, use that pain to help others. Do not be consumed by that pain and blame God. Communication can only occur if there is true love between the human being and the spirit being. Their *souls* long to be in touch with each other. Initially, the spirit being wants to provide comfort to the Earth soul, but eventually the aim is for both souls to progress spiritually. However, if the Earth soul has fallen to a very low Realm then communication is not permitted, because the Earth soul's subconscious mind is on the verge of going to sleep.

If you choose to be strong and are open, we are allowed to reach you in order to restore your faith. Please understand that there is a spiritual law at work here. The law is neutral — it is not biased. If you are on the right path, spirit souls do their best to reach you. Even though you are in pain, you must still be receptive. There are so many spirit souls trying to reach out to their loved ones on Earth in order to comfort them, but it is often not possible simply because people on Earth do not believe in an afterlife. Their minds are not open to the possibility and the question of communication therefore does not arise. We are prepared to take many steps toward you, but the first step, that of faith, of having an open mind, has to come from you. That is the spiritual law.

What are the benefits of automatic writing?

1. Good spirit souls and people on Earth are given this gift for spiritual progress and selfless service.

2. Automatic writing is a spiritual practice wherein spirit souls provide guidance to Earth souls. However this guidance may just be a hint, so one should not be dependent on it totally.

3. Spirit souls help the Earth souls to go through their tests, training and karma bravely and smilingly. They also help the Earth soul to find his or her spiritual mission.

4. Spirit souls convey the true laws of God Almighty to Earth souls.

5. During the process of automatic writing the spirit soul provides healing to the Earth soul.

6. It also opens the subconscious mind more and more.

THE SPIRIT WORLD

"Earth is our school; our real home is the spirit world."

"Only genuine calls for help are answered."

How, exactly, does one define a spirit being?

We can explain this in relation to who *you* are. The first thing that you need to understand is that you are not 'human'. You are a spirit being in human *form*. That is the case with everyone on Earth. You do not have only one body, you have three:

1.   The human body.
2.   The astral body.
3.   The spirit body.

When you die, you go from human to astral then to spirit form. That is the natural progression. After death your earthly body and your physical mind die. The earthly body is much heavier than your astral and spirit body. When you have shed your earthly body and physical mind, you become an astral being. An astral being will look like the human being did on Earth at the time of death. An astral body is a replica of the human body, but is much lighter. From an astral being, the soul and subconscious mind will transform into a spirit being. The spirit body is much lighter than the earthly and astral body. It is as light as a feather. The spirit being on a high spiritual level looks much younger than he did on Earth. Also, his appearance will reflect how evolved the soul is. The more advanced a soul, the brighter and younger the spirit form.

✿ Do heaven and hell exist?

In our communications, we have used the terms 'heaven' and 'hell', but please understand the truth behind this. God only created a *law* that in the spirit world, a negative soul cannot stay in the same place as a good soul. Therefore, when humans first used their free will to move away from the light, a negative place was born of their *collective vibration*. In other words, the seven Realms have been made into what they are by the souls who exist in these Realms. Only the seven Realms exist. Heaven and hell are simply the reflection of a soul's thoughts, words, and deeds — nothing more, nothing less. If you are on the right path, you should not be scared. **The truth is not meant to instill fear; it is meant to awaken you.** Just as there are seven Realms, there are seven universes. When you begin your spiritual journey, you begin in the first universe, with the goal of reaching the seventh. Each universe has different dimensions. Earth is three-dimensional and is the third universe.

✿ Why does God allow good and bad souls to exist together on Earth?

It is the mission of all good souls to fight negativity by

doing what is spiritually right. If negativity did not exist, how could you be tested spiritually? Good souls are given the opportunity to help negative souls change and follow the Godly Good Path. When negative souls see an act of kindness or a selfless good deed, they might be inspired to walk on the right path.

🪢 *Is there any hope for these souls?*

Of course there is. But only if there is a genuine desire to improve. In the spirit world, if spirit souls hear a genuine call for help from the lower Realms they do help. That is the first step that a low soul must take in order to change — the motive and desire to improve must be genuine. So do not despair if you are in the lower Realms of the spirit world. You will not be forced to stay there till eternity. There is no such thing as eternal damnation. There is always an opportunity to grow, to choose goodness and to rise spiritually.

🪢 *Why don't we remember the spirit world on Earth?*

If humans were to experience the lightness that spirit souls possess for even a second, you would not be able to exist in your physical bodies. If you were to remember every detail of your existence in the spirit world, you would not want to survive on Earth for even a second. That is why you have no conscious memory of the spirit world. It is also your test to still believe in God and in an afterlife in spite of no visible proof. The spirit world is a place of truth. Earth is a place of testing.

 ☙ *If the spirit world is our real home, why don't we recognize it when we die?*

After death, the body dies. However, the knowledge, memory and experiences that a person collects on Earth do not die. These are retained by your soul. Also, your qualities, or **Soul Characteristics**, stay with you. The subconscious mind, which is connected to your soul, reveals the memory and information of the spirit world slowly, step by step. But if you are stubborn by nature or too attached to the earthly world, then it will be difficult for you to process what the subconscious mind is telling you. As you rise spiritually your subconscious mind is more open and you will easily recognise the spirit world as your real home.

 ☙ *How are soul characteristics acquired?*

Soul characteristics are qualities you have acquired over many lives, based on the manner in which you have trained your own spirit. Your soul will have both positive and negative characteristics. For instance, the positive aspects of your spirit may be that you are selfless, positive and brave. The negative aspects, though they arise from the physical mind, have been with you for too long and are therefore part of your Self. So you may be proud, stubborn and too analytical. The negative qualities that you possess on Earth remain with you in the spirit world, although not as strongly. But remember that you are not perfect. You still have flaws, even as a spirit soul. You will continue to grow, even in the spirit world. However, if you are on a high Realm, it means you have worked on these qualities in your earthly life, and the fraction of negativity that remains can be shed easily. Spirit souls on higher Realms learn things of a much higher nature.

🔯 *Suppose a person dies and knows he is going to the lowest Realm, why would he or she go?*

A good soul will automatically go to his or her Realm since good souls know the peace that awaits them. A low soul, however, can choose *not* to go to the lower Realms. This soul can remain in their astral form — as what you refer to as ghosts — to escape the lower Realms. The law of free will prevails even in the astral world. You might ask, "Where is justice in that?" Please understand that these negative souls can never rise spiritually or repay their karma until they face the truth. At some point, they *have* to bear the consequences of their actions and go to the spirit world. Also, the more time they spend in astral form, the more negative karma they are building, so justice is always being done.

🔯 *When we die, do our loved ones come to receive us?*

If you die after an illness, your departed friends and relatives will be present to welcome you to the spirit world. This is because they know your due date (date of death), and are aware of the fact that you are going to leave Earth. However, if your death is sudden — as in our case, when it was not our due date, but rather an accident — spirit souls may take a while to welcome you. If you are a good soul, be sure that they will be there to greet you.

You will be alone only for a few seconds, no more. If you are a negative soul, do not expect a good soul to welcome you, not even your own deceased loved ones will be there to greet you. But negative souls will come to take you to the place you deserve.

⍥ *You mentioned that as soon as you reached the spirit world, you were taken to the Hall of Rest. Can you tell us more about this place?*

If the death of a person on Earth is unexpected and sudden that soul is taken to the **Hall of Rest**. Since these souls are traumatized, they are given healing rays to calm them down. These rays are simply the rays of the sun, but are much purer in the spirit world. After we died, we were extremely worried about our Mom and Dad as they had no one to look after them and we wondered how they would survive, so we needed to be given healing rays to calm us down.

Similarly, if traumatized or anxious souls are not calm they will not come to terms with the fact that they are no longer on Earth. If they remain traumatized, they will be unable to *process* the information that needs to be given to them about the spirit world. They will be unable to accept, recognize and function in their new surroundings. So the Hall of Rest is where your spirit is healed and recharged. By the time souls emerge from the Hall of Rest, they are revitalized and have a sublime sense of well-being. Each Realm has its own Hall of Rest. But the Hall of Rest does not exist from Realm 1 to Realm 4 Stage 4. Therefore, only those souls who are on Realm 4 Stage 5 and above will be taken to the Hall of Rest. They cannot stay longer than necessary in the Hall of Rest.

⚭ *What happens to souls once they have adjusted to the spirit world?*

Once souls have adjusted to the spirit world, they need to learn about their new surroundings. Souls who have just arrived in the spirit world have many questions. There are special spirit souls who have been trained to assist these souls, but there is also a place where these souls can go to access information: **the Hall of Learning.** The Hall of Learning contains knowledge about God's laws, about the nature of the universe, and about every single aspect of God's creation. However, the information is only revealed according to a soul's ability to understand. The Hall of Learning is open to each and every good soul in the spirit world. Just as every Realm above Realm 4 Stage 4 has a Hall of Rest, so it is with the Hall of Learning. Extremely evolved spirit beings visit these halls to teach and inspire spirit souls by spreading God's love and wisdom. These halls are blessed with energy that enables you to understand spiritual truths better. You can learn how to further open your subconscious mind, enhance a skill you might have, seek counsel on how to solve problems and learn how to better follow your spiritual mission. The possibilities are endless and it is indeed a place of great learning, as many souls come and share their experiences and exchange information about other planets and dimensions. Initially, the most important function of the Hall of Learning is that it creates within you a great spiritual *awakening*. Once souls access knowledge from the Hall of Learning, they realise how orthodox earthly views are. The Hall of Learning is like a library full of spiritual truths.

⚭ *Are there angels in the spirit world?*

Yes, Angels are good souls who guide, help and bring messages from God Almighty. Sometimes they come in human form and sometimes they are invisible. They are good souls from Realm 5 Stage 7 and above. Angels from Realm 7 Stage 5 and above can come down to Earth in any form to help souls in case of emergencies, after taking permission from His Highest Good Soul. Angels have the ability and power to perform miracles. Souls from Realms 5 and 6 help Earth Souls too, but only from the spirit world. They do not come down to Earth.

Angels do not have wings, but they wear robes, and as they fly very fast their robes give the appearance of wings. However, there are times when angels assume various shapes and forms, and they sometimes appear to humans in forms that have wings because that is how you envision them. Wings are used to symbolically represent angels, to let people know that there is a spirit world and that angels are looking after them. Some souls on Earth have seen angels. Each soul is given a robe according to individual requirements and the robes are made of materials that have tremendous power to absorb energy. The robes of souls on higher Realms have more power to absorb and retain energy than do the robes of souls on lower levels. The higher you go, the better the vibrations, and the brighter the robe gets, so the robes absorb and store positive energy. On the other hand, different robes are required when good spirit souls go to lower Realms. These robes are made of different materials that do not absorb energy, but rather reflect it. The lower the Realm a soul needs to visit, the greater the reflecting power of the robe. By reflecting negative energy, the robes keep the vibrations of good souls from being altered. These robes have different colours, some of which do not exist on Earth.

⚭ Are angels different from Spirit Guides?

Yes, the two are different. Every soul on Earth has a guardian in the spirit world who guides the earthly soul. This guardian is known as your **Spirit Guide.** It is his or her mission to guide you on the right path. As soon as you take birth, a soul in the spirit world is assigned as your Spirit Guide from birth to death. This is done by the High Good Soul of that Realm. You will never know who your Spirit Guide is. Your Spirit Guide will stay with you your entire life. However, when you go wrong your Spirit Guide will not be able to reach you. When a human being commits sins his subconscious mind starts to shut down, and there will eventually come a point when the subconscious mind becomes completely dormant. When this happens your Spirit Guide will no longer be able to send you healing, protection and guidance, as these things are accessed by humans through the subconscious mind, which is your main link to the spirit world. When your subconscious mind shuts down, your Spirit Guide has to work extra hard by 'impressing' you through your physical mind. This could happen in the form of a physical sign, a person on Earth giving you the correct guidance, or a wake up call. However, if you still do not change, there is nothing your Spirit Guide can do. Therefore, God has given every human being double protection from negative influences. The first is your powerful subconscious mind; the second is your Spirit Guide.

It is your Spirit Guide's duty to watch, guide and protect you throughout your life and to enable you to fulfill your earthly mission. When you need advice, you must pray to God genuinely and ask for help. Your Spirit Guide will do his or her best to give you the guidance you need, as they are specially trained to guide souls on Earth. This is their main work in the spirit world, and through this process they too learn and continue to evolve. In very difficult situations, the Spirit Guide will consult other wise souls and seek counsel. This information is being given to you because many people feel lonely on Earth. They feel they have no one to turn to for advice. But if you develop your subconscious mind you can pray to God and ask your Spirit Guide for help. You will be surprised at how the guidance will come to you and, more importantly, the strength that will come to you to face your problems courageously.

⚭ Can an earthly soul's twin in the spirit world work as a Spirit Guide?

Yes, but in very rare cases.

⚭ What is a twin soul and is it the same as a soul mate?

Every soul in this universe (the third universe) is actually only one half of a soul. When a soul begins its journey on Realm 4 stage 5, it is split into two: a male soul and a female soul. This original male and female soul must eventually reunite on Realm 7 Stage 9 to form the whole soul once again. These souls are known as **Twin Souls.** This takes place after numerous lifetimes, after both souls have finished their individual training on Earth, sometimes as male and sometimes as female, and have paid off their karma. Only then can two souls unite to form a whole on Realm 7 Stage 9. When you reach Realm 7 Stage 9, just before you merge, you become the original male soul and female soul, and you then move on to the next universe.

However, your twin soul is very different from what you on Earth refer to as a soul mate. When you use the term **Soul Mate**, you use it for someone you feel very close to, but that person might not be your twin soul; he or she may be a **Group Soul** with whom you have had many past-life connections. God created a certain number of souls at the same *time*. These souls reincarnate together on Earth in the same group, life after life, because of their love for each other, so that they can help each other rise spiritually and lead a better life. These souls are known as group souls. Sometimes, when you feel close to a person you have never met, it could be because that person is your group soul. Your group souls could be your parents, children, neighbours, or friends. A person can have only *one* twin soul, but many soul mates or group souls.

When you meet your twin soul, it is a very special bond. If both souls are on a good level, they can help each other rise spiritually on Earth, and they can develop real trust and friendship because their spirits recognize each other. It is beyond physicality – it is about two spirits meeting and recognizing the fact that they are one and the same. In some cases, if one or both of the souls are on a low level, the relationship might not be good at all. Twin souls can be at different stages of development.

Usually, one soul reincarnates on Earth and the other stays in the spirit world to guide that person on Earth. The only way you will know if a person is your twin soul is through automatic writing, and this is revealed on very rare occasions — only when necessary. For example, if your twin soul is known to you, and that twin soul is falling spiritually, you will be told to tactfully help that soul.

The main reason God split each soul into two is to teach you coexistence. You are responsible for each other's progress. United, twin souls can achieve a great deal, but if one of them falters, then both suffer spiritually. This is because once you reach Realm 7 Stage 9, you have to merge with your twin soul and become a whole soul. Only then will you be allowed to progress to the next universe (fourth universe). If you are on Realm 7 Stage 9, but your twin soul is spiritually low, you will have to wait for your twin soul to reach Realm 7 Stage 9, even if it takes many lifetimes. This may seem harsh and unfair, but it is actually to *safeguard* your spiritual progress. No matter what, you have someone who will pray for you and try their level best to make you rise spiritually. **This teaches you responsibility, coexistence and selflessness.**

    ۖ *Are you both known as Vispi and Ratoo in the spirit world? Or do you have spirit names?*

Every soul is given a special name before the soul is divided into two. This is known as a **Soul Name**. Twin souls share their soul name — just as the soul is split into two, so is the name, which remains the same throughout your existence. In the spirit world, you are known by the name you were last known by on Earth. Your deeds are recorded in your Akashic Records under your soul name. You will never know your soul name on Earth; you will know your soul name only when you go back to the spirit world.

✆ *What are Akashic Records?*

The **Akashic Records** are also known as the **Hall of Memories** or the **Hall of Journals**. Each Realm has its own hall where there is a journal for the lives led by every individual soul on Earth. Each and every deed, good or bad, is recorded under your soul name. The Records can be found on the Realm to which the soul belongs. When the soul progresses or falls, and moves to a higher or lower Realm, the Records follow. The Akashic Records contain the memories of all the lives you have led on Earth. When souls on Earth are in a deep, dreamless sleep, their subconscious minds make entries in the Akashic Records. When the subconscious mind of an earthly soul goes dormant the Spirit Guide of that person continues to update the Akashic Records. No soul can read someone else's Records, except in rare circumstances when it will help in the soul's spiritual progress and after permission is granted by the High Good Soul of that Realm. When a soul graduates to the next universe, the Records travel as well.

✆ *What kind of work do spirit souls do?*

First of all, let us explain that spirit souls do not have

wants and desires. We experience no hunger, thirst, or fatigue, and our sole aim is service. However, we do need nourishment, just as the body does on Earth. For the soul, sunlight is powerfully nourishing. There are also many beautiful fruits, the flavours of which are unimaginable. Souls do not need food to survive, but the juicy nectar of fruits provides us with positive energy. We are in a constant state of well-being. We are in perfect spiritual health, and we stay this way by purifying our spirit bodies with prayer and water. Water has a healing quality, and whenever we need to recharge, we take a dip in a lake and come out rejuvenated with a great deal of positive energy, as the water completely cleanses our vibrations. When we come out of the water, we are completely dry and energized.

As for our work, we discuss our talents with the High Good Soul of our Realm and then choose work in that given area. Here are a few examples of the kind of work spirit souls do:

1. Share spiritual knowledge with people on Earth and help them understand God's laws.

2. Communicate with souls on Earth through processes such as automatic writing.

3. Work as Spirit Guides.

4. Work with souls who have just come to the spirit world to help them understand where they are if they are traumatized or disoriented.

5. Guide souls on Earth and 'impress' important

messages upon them through their subconscious mind. For instance, a spirit soul might help a scientist discover a cure he is trying to find for a disease by sending him answers through his subconscious mind.

6. Answer genuine calls for help from Earth. Spirit souls are specially trained in this, and souls who have just arrived in the spirit world train under the more experienced souls in this matter.

7. Work in the Hall of Rest and with the upkeep of the Akashic Records.

8. Pray for humans who are suicidal and help them walk on the right path.

9. Find ways to protect loved ones on Earth.

10. Pray for loved ones on Earth. Prayer requires genuine love, concern, concentration and effort on our part.

11. Get trained in how to handle negative souls on low Realms.

12. Gain more wisdom from the Hall of Learning. With their expanded subconscious mind, spirit souls retain a lot of information and put it into action.

13. Guide those who wish to reincarnate.

14. Perform miracles for souls on Earth who have lost their way. These small miracles help lost souls regain their faith.

15. Come down to Earth to comfort a dying soul and,

through prayer and positive thought, make the transition to the spirit world as comfortable as possible.

16. Look after spirit children.

17. Learn and discover new ways of healing.

18. Participate in the creation of art, dance, opera, music, songs, sports, architecture, science etc.

19. Work with the animal kingdom on Earth and help with the animal spirit world.

20. Help in the upkeep of the gardens in the spirit world.

21. Catch up and reflect on the true history of the Earth and other planets.

No matter what work spirit souls choose, we have the same aim: *service*. On Earth, people look at their jobs as work, but we genuinely love what we do and we view it as an opportunity to give back to the Creator. This brings us true joy and fulfillment. There is no ego, no competition, no jealousy, no arguments, no criticism, and no one is superior or inferior. We respect each other and work as a team for the benefit of humanity.

    🐍 *Why is reincarnation necessary? Why can't we rise spiritually in the spirit world itself?*

You come to Earth time and again for the growth of your soul. The same spirit being comes to Earth hundreds and even thousands of times to progress spiritually. This soul may be in the male or female form, depending on what it chooses and what it requires for its growth, and it may incarnate on Earth in different countries, in different religions. This is what **Reincarnation** means — the same spirit being born on Earth life after life. This is not the first time you have come to Earth; this is one of the many incarnations.

In most cases, the progress of souls in Realms 5, 6 and 7 in the spirit world is slow because the vibrations are good, so it is not hard to do the right thing, unlike on Earth, where evil is ascendent so a good soul goes higher faster with even the smallest good deed. Also, on Earth, due to negative vibrations and the limitations of the physical mind, a soul's judgment can go wrong, and so his test is that much harder. On Earth, you need to use your subconscious mind much more than the physical mind in order to progress spiritually, but the risk that a good soul takes when reincarnating on Earth is that he may fall lower spiritually. If he stays in the spirit world his progress will be much slower, but he will never fall. It is up to each soul to use his own free will to decide if he wants to stay in the spirit world and progress steadily, or come down to Earth, take the risk, and progress faster. The cycle of reincarnation ends only when you have completed your earthly mission, paid off your karma, and reached Realm 7 Stage 9. You have thus truly *transcended* the earthly experience — that is, when you have learned to think and live like a spirit being on Earth. We are not talking about perfection. No human being can be perfect. We are talking about doing your best, training your spirit in such a manner that it is *ready* for the next universe. You will not understand this completely on Earth; you will only know where you stand when you go to the spirit world.

All souls must follow a specific procedure, known as **The Process of Rebirth**, in order to be reborn on Earth.

I. You must apply to the High Good Soul of your Realm for rebirth.

2. You must provide reasons for wanting rebirth. The main reason is often to repay karma, complete your mission, and rise spiritually. If a soul has too much karma to repay, it is not possible to repay it in the spirit world, so he must reincarnate on Earth. Sometimes, even a soul without much karma will want to be reborn because a loved one on Earth is following the wrong path and the soul wants to help.

3. You must choose a mother. A soul who is not on a good spiritual level may be born to a mother who is spiritually high so that the soul improves. Sometimes, a good soul may be born to a negative mother in order to improve the mother; it can also be a way for that soul to repay karma and undergo testing and training. In many cases, however, because it is such a great risk, the soul falls spiritually. Sometimes, souls choose a mother in order to be close to the father, so, in effect, they are choosing the father.

4. You must specify what sort of training and testing you wish to take. For example, you choose people and experiences that will enable you to develop positive qualities required for your mission, which is your true calling on Earth. If you want to be tested for pride

you will get lessons that will continuously break your pride and teach you humility.

5.   You must select a Walk-In. If the situation on Earth gets harder than you can handle and you are on the right path, then a good soul from the spirit world, known as a Walk-In, will occupy your body for that period, as the situation requires. This rarely happens, and only in case of emergencies when the situation is beyond the capabilities of the soul on Earth. That is, it is not your test, training or karma. The sub-conscious mind calls out for help without the conscious knowledge of the soul on Earth.

6.   You decide your date of birth and your date of death. Your date of death is also known as your due date.

All souls from Realms 1 to 7 have a chance to go through this process of rebirth. However, the souls of Realm 1 have the option of staying in the lower Realms or coming back to Earth as a beast of burden with full memory of their previous life's sins and their existence on Realm 1. Some souls from Realm 1 choose this because they want to pay off their karma very quickly. They are allowed to retain memory of Realm 1 and their previous life so that they understand why they have been reborn as beasts of burden and why they are suffering. This memory gives them the strength to endure the pain they suffer on Earth in this very tough incarnation. Their karma is not wiped off entirely; if their karma is extremely severe these souls may need hundreds of reincarnations to repay it.

This whole process may sound challenging, but you do not make all of these choices on your own. You sit with the

High Good Soul of your Realm along with three wise souls from that same Realm and tell them what you wish to do. They will guide you in your choices. For instance, if you are too eager to rise spiritually and are in a hurry to repay your karma, you might choose a path that is too difficult for you, a path that you might not be capable of handling. The High Good Soul and the three wise souls would advise you against that and would offer alternatives. However, if you still wish to be reborn, it is your free will and you will not be stopped. Even after you register for rebirth you can still choose not to be born on Earth. For example, say you have chosen a mother, but she goes wrong spiritually and you no longer wish to come to her, you can cancel your registration. Perhaps you originally selected this person because she was spiritually high and you wanted someone to give you knowledge and lead you to the right path, but if the mother has strayed on the wrong path and faltered, it no longer makes sense for you to be born to her.

⚭ *In what way are Earth children in touch with the spirit world?*

A child in the mother's womb is very much in touch with the spirit world. During that time, if the child feels that the situation might hamper his spiritual growth, he can return to the spirit world and another soul may occupy the baby's body. Just because the child no longer needs the mother that does not mean the mother will have a stillborn baby. If that is not her karma, another soul will occupy the child's body. It is important to understand that a child in the womb is very receptive because the subconscious mind is open. That child is still in touch

with the spirit world and is observing the parents' actions.
Be positive and content, and allow nothing negative to
come to the child. When you go through sorrow, for
example, your child absorbs that energy. The child is very,
very sensitive to the mother's thoughts and feelings. If
you are constantly negative and on the wrong path, the
child, being a good soul, may return to the spirit world
and another one, one that might be spiritually lower, may
take its place. If no soul comes the child will be stillborn.
The child remains in touch with the spirit world after it is
born, until it starts to speak. After that, the subconscious
mind no longer allows the physical mind to have any
memories of the spirit world.

🕉 *After we start speaking, are all ties with the spirit*
world cut off?

Not at all. In your deep, dreamless sleep, you visit a place
that is between Earth and the spirit world. Your soul rises
from your body and travels upward to meet spirit souls. In
your sleep, your loved ones in the spirit world are talking
to you through the subconscious mind and giving you
guidance. They are in constant touch with you. When your
soul rises to meet them it is still connected to the physical
body by the **Silver Cord**, a ray of light that is your
connection between your spirit and your body. When you
die this connection is severed. You can meet your dear ones
for a few minutes or sometimes for hours, but this
depends on your sleep, which should be deep and
dreamless. The love between those who meet must be
mutual and not one-sided. Rest assured that if you have
loved ones in the spirit world you are meeting them on a
regular basis. These loved ones are not only dear departed

souls from this lifetime; they may be people who were very close to you in previous lifetimes and are now trying to help you from the spirit world.

The silver cord is comprised of many rays of light that merge together to form one long ray. The silver cord is attached to the body at the top of the head, so that the soul can enter and leave through the soft part of the head (in babies, there is always a soft spot on the head, where the silver cord is attached). In your sleep, there will be many times when you suddenly wake up with a jerk, a strong thud in your chest and you get the feeling that you were falling and have just landed. This occurs when the soul returns to the physical body after it has travelled *naturally* and met its loved ones. When the silver cord is broken, you die. Your angels in the spirit world protect that silver cord with a great deal of brilliant white light, which builds a protective aura so that negativity cannot reach it. When you practice *unnatural* ways of meditation and astral traveling (when you leave your body on your own), you are risking your life because your silver cord is vulnerable and negative souls can try to prevent you from re-entering your body by cutting the silver cord. Astral travelling is when a person unnaturally and consciously leaves the body. There is a risk involved in this, because if the silver cord is cut you may die before your time, before you have fulfilled your mission on Earth.

🐍 *Does each person have a fixed amount of time on Earth?*

Just as you choose the day on which you will be born, you also choose the date of your death, also known as your

Due Date. However, every human being has three due dates, which can be thought of as exit points. The first two due dates may pass off with some sort of illness or accident from which you are saved. However, if your subconscious mind feels you are on the wrong path and there is very little chance of going back onto the right one, you usually choose to leave Earth on one of the first two due dates. The third due date is somewhat final. However, just before the final due date, a human being can bargain for "borrowed time" from another human being. This is done without that person's conscious knowledge. The subconscious mind bargains with a friend, relative, or stranger's subconscious mind and takes over his or her remaining time on Earth. For this, you require the permission of the High Good Soul of your Realm. This is very rare and is done only in the case of special spiritual missions. This happened in our own family many years ago, when we were still alive.

There was a time when our dad was to be operated upon and he kept telling everyone that he felt his time was up. He would say, "This is the last time I am meeting you all." Well, it *was* his third due date. He was admitted into the hospital a day before the operation, and in the evening, Mom's cousins, Goola and Mani, came to visit him. They had a nice time, chatting and laughing, and then they went home. The next day, when he was on the operating table, we received a phone call to inform us that Goola had died suddenly. We never thought of this at the time, but now that we are in the spirit world we know that Goola did not have much to live for, and our Dad had our family and his spiritual mission to live for. Goola had a spiritual mission too — all souls do — but she had not trained her spirit well enough on Earth to complete this mission, so her subconscious mind felt it was better for her to go to the spirit world, train her spirit more, and then reincarnate on Earth. She felt she could contribute more by being in the spirit world. Both their subconscious minds bargained, and Dad's subconscious mind borrowed Goola's remaining lifetime on Earth. This may seem strange to you, but it is true. This will never happen if you try it consciously, so don't bother trying to borrow someone's lifetime.

Arranging such borrowed time depends entirely on whether there is a genuine need for you to live. You may need to finish your mission, protect your dear ones, or improve much more to go to a higher Realm. Most importantly, the one who lends his or her lifetime must have finished his or her mission and have nothing more to live for, or may not have trained their spirit well enough to fulfill their spiritual mission. Special permission has to be sought in the spirit world for this kind of bargaining.

What happens to children when they die?

Children who die on Earth go back to the spirit world as children, and then grow up in the spirit world. They are looked after by **Spirit Mothers** until they are mature spirit souls again. This takes very little time. Fairly grown-up ones go to their respective Realms on their own. Some adults who die on Earth and come to the spirit world refuse to believe that they are dead. Ratoo works with these souls. In the same way, children need spirit mothers to explain the environment they are in. In a short while, these souls grow up and assume their natural spirit form.

෪ *What happens to animals when they die?*

Animals have their own spirit world. Just as human souls go to different Realms, so do animals, but they have only three Realms: low, mid and high. Some animals are allowed to exist in the human spirit world if they were pets on Earth, but this is very rare. Both the animal and the human must be on good levels, and the connection must be very strong. Pure love must exist between the two.

෪ *Are spirit souls happy all the time?*

We are in a state of contentment, but when we see the negative path human beings have taken it makes us sad. Even spirit souls feel sad, but only when people go wrong spiritually, or when our loved ones are crying for justice on Earth, suffering at the hands of negative souls. Otherwise, we are happy and positive. Also, we truly *know* that God exists and that we are progressing in order to finally reach Him, and this gives us tremendous joy.

෪ *Have all spirit souls met God?*

No, only some souls on high Realms have met God, but all souls know that God exists because we are in the spirit world, and we can see the beauty and intelligence of His Creation. Our subconscious minds know that He exists and that He cares for us.

THE SOUL AND THE SUBCONSCIOUS MIND

"Reincarnation on Earth is a risk. Therefore, God has given you double protection from evil: your subconscious mind and your spirit guide."

"Never suppress your instinct. Never fear people calling you mad or weird. Instinct is a God-given gift."

"Be the master of your physical mind — not a slave."

"The only reason for spiritual improvement should be genuine desire from within oneself, i.e. from your subconscious mind. So do not change to show the world, but make the change because it means the world to you."

 Are the subconscious mind and the soul the same?

There are too many earthly definitions and misconceptions about the subconscious mind so we would like you all to let go of your preconceived notions. Think of the subconscious mind as your **conscience**. It can also be called your Higher Mind, Higher Self, or Inner Voice (The feeling that your subconscious mind gives you is called 'Instinct').

You are a spirit being who is on Earth in a physical body.
You were created by God as a spirit being first, not as a
human being. You were created as a **soul**, and that soul has
a subconscious mind. The soul is your eternal spirit body.
Just as you have a physical body on Earth, your spirit body
is called the soul and is immortal. The subconscious mind
is your true, spiritual mind. Just as the physical mind
guides the body, the subconscious mind guides the soul.
The soul and the subconscious mind are joined together
for eternity.

🕉 *What is the function of the subconscious mind?*

The subconscious mind is both your *guarding* light as well
as your *guiding* light. It serves as a spiritual radar. It warns
you when you are about to make a choice that is spiritually
wrong; therefore, it guards your soul. But the spiritual
path is not only about resisting temptation. It is not
enough to stop yourself from doing wrong. More than
anything, the path to God involves doing what is spiritually right. So, after guarding your soul by preventing it
from taking the wrong actions, the subconscious mind
guides you towards what is morally right.

🕉 *Is the subconscious mind the same as our conscious mind?*

The subconscious mind and the conscious or physical
mind are two different things. A person can have a highly
developed intellectual physical mind, but may have an
underdeveloped subconscious mind. Acquiring worldly
knowledge can sharpen your physical mind, but will not

develop your subconscious mind. **Even spiritual knowledge alone will not help your subconscious mind to evolve.** It is only when you put that knowledge into practice that the subconscious mind grows. Therefore, the key to spiritual growth is **pure action.** The more open your subconscious mind, the more guidance and protection you will receive from the spirit world. Your subconscious mind must control your physical mind. Never let your physical mind make you its slave. Your subconscious mind is your link to the spirit world through which you receive protection and guidance from spirit souls.

👀 *If everyone on Earth has a subconscious mind, why do people follow the wrong path?*

There will be times when you will have a clash of opinion between your physical mind and your subconscious mind. This is because the physical mind is rational – it may want to pursue a path or action that is logical – but the subconscious mind might be against it. It may seem as though the two minds are at war. This is a good thing. If there is no war between the physical and subconscious minds it means your subconscious mind is not working and your physical mind is controlling you fully. No human being on Earth can be led completely by his subconscious mind. This is because the average human being's subconscious mind is open very little (1% to 2%). However, the subconscious mind is so powerful that even though only a fraction of it is open it still manages to warn your physical mind, which is 100% open.

🚀 *If the two minds are constantly at war, how can we be at peace?*

You can strive for peace by acknowledging the battle between the physical mind and the subconscious mind and ensuring, through prayer and positive action, that the subconscious mind wins. The physical mind is very anxious to make you its slave and lead you down the path of spiritual decline by providing justifications for all your wrong actions. Peace of mind comes when you learn to listen to the subconscious mind and take the right action.

🚀 *If the physical mind works against the subconscious mind, why do we have it?*

The physical mind *can become* negative and work against the subconscious mind if it is not trained well, but if used well the physical mind can be a wonderful assistant to the subconscious mind. When the intellect of the physical mind is in alignment with the guidance of the subconscious mind, the combination is very powerful. So if you use the physical mind well, it is a gift. The physical mind is also a test. God wants you to use your free will and choose the guidance of your subconscious mind. That is every human being's test. **You must control your physical mind; do not let it control you.** The reason people on Earth go spiritually wrong is because their subconscious mind has become dormant. In other words, the subconscious mind has shut down. The subconscious mind cannot and will not permit a person to do something spiritually wrong. But people listen more to their physical, logical minds, refusing to pay attention to the voice of the subconscious mind. They refuse to follow its guidance and continue their evil or bad ways. The subconscious mind cannot tolerate this, so it quiets down, sleeps, and eventually becomes completely dormant and then it can no longer warn you when you take wrong actions. This can be extremely dangerous.

A person's conscience warns him only when the subconscious mind is open. Here is a simple example of how it happens: when you hurt someone, or even think negatively about someone, your subconscious mind warns you, and you feel guilty. This means your subconscious mind is working. You should not let that guilt consume you. That guilt has a specific purpose. It should make you want to rectify the wrong you have done. You should learn the lesson and never repeat your mistake. Once this is done, the guilt goes away. This is the right approach to dealing with guilt.

If you suppress your guilt and ignore it right from the beginning, even though you know you have done something wrong, you are telling your subconscious mind to be quiet; you are rejecting its advice. When you do this repeatedly, the subconscious mind becomes dormant. So there will come a point when, if you commit a sin, the subconscious mind will no longer warn you. The guilt does not appear and you might even fool yourself into thinking that because you do not feel guilty you have not done wrong. In truth, however, you have shut down your spiritual radar.

However, keep in mind that guilt does not always come from the subconscious mind. There are people who feel guilty about things they *should not* be feeling guilty about.

There will be times when your physical mind will make you feel guilty even though you have done everything right. You will feel as though you have done something wrong, or that you are not doing enough. This is programmed guilt that is imposed on you by yourself, by others or by negativity. Guilt that comes from the physical mind is not healthy for your growth. You should have the wisdom to know the difference between the guilt that is a result of guidance from the subconscious mind and the guilt that comes from the physical mind. The former is a *sign*. The latter is a *trick*, which exists because of wrong thinking or beliefs, and it prevents you from growing. So when you are confused about guilt, analyse yourself and talk to someone you trust. Do not talk to people who will please you and tell you what you want to hear. Talk to people who will tell you the truth, the ones who have true knowledge.

∞ Does the subconscious mind develop as human beings grow older?

Not necessarily. It all depends on how much you follow its guidance. It is like a muscle. The more you exercise it, the healthier and stronger it becomes. In fact, a child's subconscious mind is powerful (provided the child is on a good spiritual level) because the child has just come from the spirit world to Earth. But if the child receives improper training and is allowed to go wrong, the subconscious mind quietens down and becomes weaker and weaker.

◐ *You have said that all Earth souls meet their loved ones from the spirit world when they are asleep. How, exactly, does this happen?*

When your sleep is deep and dreamless, your physical mind is shut down and only your subconscious mind operates. Your soul, guided by the subconscious mind, leaves your earthly body and travels to a place in between Earth and the spirit world, where your loved ones meet you. They calm you down and guide your subconscious mind, but the moment you wake up you forget this because the physical mind was shut down during sleep and was not allowed to register anything. The following is a feeling all humans can identify with: sometimes you wake up from your sleep with a sudden jolt or thud in your chest. This is the soul which is guided by the subconscious mind re-entering your physical body.

◐ *Does a person's subconscious mind know when he or she is going to die?*

Yes, your subconscious mind knows all your three due dates. However, you could die before your time, that is, before your due date, like in the case of an accident, murder etc. However, there is another spiritual law made for your own protection. Good souls from Realms 7 or 6 do not want to go to hell, so God has made a law that souls who were born on Realm 7 will be taken away from Earth and will not be able to fall further than Realm 5. Likewise, if you were born on Realm 6 you would be allowed to fall to Realm 4 only. If you continue to sin, your subconscious mind seeks permission to go back to the spirit world. However, those on Realms 5 and lower have no such protection. If they continue to sin, the subconscious mind simply shuts down. They can fall to the lowest of Realms (Realm 1). **This is why we say that life on Earth is a risk, but it is a risk that souls take in order to progress spiritually.**

If the subconscious mind shuts down and the person dies, he or she may choose to remain in astral form. Not only will they not want to go to their Realm, but they will also not want to leave Earth. The lower you fall spiritually, the less you will want to leave Earth. Evil souls stick to their physical bodies like leeches. These souls know where they will land when they die, and are afraid to leave the physical world, so they choose to remain in the astral world. In some cases, when human beings die, they are not aware of the fact that they are dead. The person is not a spirit being yet; he is in astral form.

෴ Do only negative souls go into astral form?

No. At death, all human beings go into astral form, then shed their astral bodies and transform into spirit beings. So when a person dies, the natural transition is as follows:

Human Beings → Astral Beings → Spirit Beings

෴ Do souls from higher Realms want to remain in astral form?

No, souls who are from a higher Realm do not usually want to remain in astral form. They want to become spirit beings as soon as possible. A person's loved ones in the spirit world are aware that a person is going to die on Earth, so these spirit souls are prepared for that person's arrival. Some of the loved ones leave the spirit world and come down to Earth to fetch the human being who is about to die (this will not happen if the death is sudden, such as in the case of an accident or a murder, which are never part of God's Plan). These spirit beings then accompany the person to the Realm to which he or she belongs. The soul naturally goes to the Realm he belongs to. The subconscious mind of the person who has died will instruct his own soul to travel to a Realm worthy of his actions on Earth. It is up to the soul to listen; force cannot be used. Only if the soul listens and goes to the proper Realm does it become a spirit being again.

If the soul refuses to go to the spirit world, it remains in astral form, because even when you die, God allows you to exercise free will. On Earth, astral souls who are visible are referred to as ghosts. **Astral Souls** are lost souls who have rejected the advice of their subconscious mind and have refused to become spirit beings; by doing this they build negative karma. You cannot see astral souls, but they can see you. However, these astral souls cannot see the spirit world; once they have rejected the advice of the subconscious mind and have decided not to go to the spirit world, it cannot be made visible to them. That is the law. When they make the decision to go to the spirit world, it will be revealed to them. This is also a test.

🙢 *When bad souls die, spirit souls from lower Realms come to fetch the ones who have died. What is the purpose of this?*

When an evil soul is about to die on Earth, group souls, if they are from lower levels, come to fetch him. However, because these souls are spiritually low, they have to be kept under strict supervision when they do this job. These souls have to seek permission from the High Good Soul of their Realm if they wish to fetch a low soul from Earth to bring him to the spirit world. The High Good Soul selects an assistant for this job — one from between Realm 4 Stage 5 and Realm 5 Stage 5 — who will stand guard to make sure the negative souls go back to their respective Realms. This is done as a test: these souls have been given a duty to perform and by performing this duty they might be showing some inclination towards change. Thus, they are being trained and tested every step of the way.

🔍 *When we are born, does the same natural progression apply? Do we start off as spirit beings, then become astral beings, and finally human beings?*

No. When a spirit being takes rebirth on Earth, he does not go through the astral phase. His soul and subconscious mind simply occupy the physical body of a human being on Earth, so the transition is directly from spirit being to human being.

🔍 *Why do souls choose to stay in astral form?*

1. They are too attached to the physical world.

2. They want to protect a loved one on Earth and wrongly believe that by occupying the same *physical* space, they can help.

3. The subconscious mind tells them they will have to go to a low spiritual Realm and they refuse to do so because they do not want to suffer. They can make this choice because they have free will. However, when a soul chooses to stay in astral form, he continues to fall and build negative karma because he is going against the advice of his subconscious mind and is breaking a spiritual law. He is not following the natural progression from human to astral to spirit being.

4. If they are negative souls, they will want to stay back in astral form and harm human beings on Earth. Once again, the astral soul will fall spiritually and build negative karma.

5. On Earth, they had certain addictions, such as drugs or alcohol, and they want to experience that sensation over and over again by attaching themselves to humans who are addicts.

ஃ How can you make your physical mind cooperate with the subconscious mind?

You need to know the nature of the physical mind. Just as the subconscious mind is your spiritual, positive mind, the physical mind, by nature, is earthbound and negative. If not checked, it will let you down. It will trick you. It creates illusions. For example, when you commit a sin, your subconscious mind warns you that you have done something wrong. Just as you are about to rectify that mistake and learn the lesson, your physical mind brings into action its greatest weapon: ego. Ego makes you justify your wrong actions, tricking you into believing that what you did was not wrong, but necessary. It will put forward a brilliant logical argument and you will be swayed. The voice of your subconscious mind will rise and speak out, but you will silence it because the physical mind has given you reasons. It has told you that you are right through logic.

We do not mean that logic is bad, but *logic* and *truth* are not the same thing. Unfortunately, people use logic to *run away* from the truth. The physical mind gives you logic; the subconscious mind gives you truth. For example, the physical mind will make you justify temptation. It will give you valid reasons to make you believe that temptation is a need instead of a want. It will convince you that temptation is not spiritually wrong, instead of exposing temptation for what it truly is − a desire that leads you down the wrong path.

Another weapon that the physical mind possesses is doubt. It will plant the seed of doubt within you that challenges your faith and wisdom. The subconscious mind is the seat of truth and is therefore all-knowing; it helps you transcend doubt, but only if you allow it to steer your soul. If you nurture the seed of doubt, you slowly weaken your connection to the spirit world, for doubt essentially leads to one question: do I believe in God? Listen to the subconscious mind for it is your master, your connection to your good self and your God self. The physical mind has weaknesses and your aim in this life is to transcend those weaknesses by developing the subconscious mind.

The most harmful aspect of the physical mind is that it is habit-forming and comfortable with its bad habits. It will say, "I like being proud, so why change?" The subconscious mind is never set in its ways — it keeps growing. **You can fool your fellow men and you can fool yourself, but you can never fool the God-given subconscious mind.** It is the subconscious mind that constantly updates a person's Akashic Records. Human beings believe that God punishes them. The truth is that their own subconscious minds punish them when they go on the wrong path because the subconscious mind knows the nature of their soul. Your memory of the spirit world and your past lives has simply been blocked from your physical mind. Your subconscious mind remembers the spirit world, and it knows details about each and every life you have lived on Earth, but this information cannot be revealed to your physical mind for the following reasons:

1. If you remember the sins of your past life, those memories will haunt you and prevent you from growing. For example, if you hurt someone badly in a past life, the guilt might be too much for you to cope with in this life and you would be unable to forgive yourself. God wants all souls to have a clean slate to start with.

2. Your physical mind is limited; it is not capable of understanding many things that the subconscious mind knows.

3. If you remember details of the spirit world and the joy and peace you felt (if you were on a good Realm), you would not be able to survive on Earth for even a second. Your longing for the spirit world would be so intense that you would be miserable on Earth.

4. Your life on Earth is a test. If you were aware of the

karma, testing and training you are to go through, your journey on Earth would have no meaning. Moreover, if everything was revealed to you, it would no longer be a test. You are on Earth to gain experience and train your spirit, to purify your soul to rise higher and higher. If you remembered your previous lives, you would not make the same mistakes again. You would not repeat your mistakes because you would be pre-warned, so there could be no real growth. Your life would be technical, your choices robotic, and you would live like a machine.

There are a few Earth souls who have a more developed subconscious mind than others. Sometimes, these souls are allowed to remember their previous lives on Earth, and they may also have memories of the spirit world, but this is very rare. It is allowed to happen for a specific reason, to give more faith to people and to help spread God's knowledge.

🐚 If a person's subconscious mind is not open, how can the person change?

Let us take the story of Soordas as an example. In his case, because of his evil actions, his subconscious mind had gone to sleep. He needed a physical jolt, which came in the form of a car accident, to wake him up. That accident set off a chain of events that eventually led him to a cave in which, when faced with death, he understood and finally realised the wrong deeds he had done. In his case, this painful jolt was required because his subconscious mind had become completely dormant. But if a person's subconscious mind is even slightly open, the soul must seize the chance to talk to it and confess the wrong they have done, in order to avoid a physical blow. When we use the word 'confess' we mean a genuine desire to change. Only when His High Good Soul was sure that Soordas wanted to change from within – that he genuinely repented – was help sent. He confessed his wrongdoings and wanted to change, but he confessed to *himself* in a dark cave in the middle of a jungle, surrounded by wild animals. It wasn't a place of worship and there was no one to hear him confess – except for his own subconscious mind. On Earth there is a wrong notion that if you confess to a priest, your sins will be forgiven. This is absolutely false. The priest has no power to forgive you. The priest is, after all, a human being himself. If the priest has spiritual knowledge, he can surely guide you, but please understand that when you are 'confessing', it means you are admitting to your own subconscious mind that you have done wrong and are asking for help to change.

Even the word 'repentance' is grossly misunderstood on Earth. Repentance does not only mean being sorry for one's actions; it means truly changing and rectifying the wrong you have done, and never repeating mistakes. The choice to improve as a human being can come only from within a soul. No one can force that soul to rise spiritually, even though it is for that soul's own good. **This is the law of free will.** Also, God's helpers have the power to know if that soul truly wants to improve. That is, from the spirit world, spirit souls can determine the weakness or strength of a soul's resolve to change. The key to spiritual progress is a genuine desire to change; only then can the subconscious mind guide a soul toward the light.

෬ *How does one open the subconscious mind?*

The most important thing for a human being to do in order to progress spiritually is to **open the subconscious mind**. Here are a few things you can do to open your subconscious mind:

1. Pray.

   Ask God to help you to open your subconscious mind:

   "Oh, dear God Almighty, lead me to your good ways. Make me do the right things. Help me throw away any wrong desires or feelings I have. Give me your wisdom; show me your lighted path. Help me awaken my subconscious mind so that it *never* lets me do wrong. Oh God Almighty, please help me!"

2. Blank your mind (refer to "How to Blank your Mind" on pg. 198).

   You should have no thoughts whatsoever. Your mind should be absolutely blank. If any thoughts enter your mind, let them pass on their own — do not struggle to get rid of them or indulge them. Blank your mind for no more than 2 minutes in places where the vibrations are positive. Intuitively, try to feel if the place has positive or negative vibrations. In places where the vibrations are negative, do not blank your mind for more than a minute. Blank your mind only between sunrise and sunset.

3. *Talk* to your subconscious mind.

   By talking to your subconscious mind you acknowledge its presence. Then, surrender to it completely and ask it to guide you.

4.   *Listen* to the advice your subconscious mind gives you.

To listen means to convert guidance into action. Each time you follow the advice of your subconscious mind, you are empowering it. Each time you ignore its advice and do not listen, you are weakening it.

5.   Control your physical mind. Tell it you are its master, not its slave.

On Earth, your physical mind is 100% open, but the subconscious mind is open only 1% to 2% in an average human being. If you are a very good soul, your subconscious mind will open to a maximum of 7% to 9% on Earth. Therefore, even though a fraction of your subconscious mind is open, it can easily overpower the physical mind *if you choose*. Even when a soul reaches Realm 7 Stage 9, the subconscious mind is open only 20%. You will continue to evolve in the next universe, and your subconscious mind will only be fully open (100%) in the final stage of the seventh universe and you will then *finally be able to understand God* and live in His presence.

Below are instructions on **How to Blank Your Mind:**

It is crucial that you blank your mind *only after sunrise and before sunset* because when the sun sets, the vibrations on Earth change and become more negative. If you follow these simple steps, you will be more at peace.

I.   In your own words, ask God to protect you and help

you open your subconscious mind.

2.   Pray *any* short and sincere prayer of your choice.

3.   Blank your mind. In order to blank your mind, the best thing to do is to listen to distant sounds. Do not analyse anything. If a thought comes, it is okay; it will go away on its own. Do not try to force it away. Remain calm.

4.   Blank your mind for about 2 minutes in places where the vibration is positive. In places where the vibrations are negative, do not blank your mind for more than a minute. This is for your own protection.

5.   Thank God Almighty. End with a short and sincere prayer.

6.   There should be a three-hour gap between times when you are blanking your mind.

7.   Never face South when you blank your mind. It is best to face North.

8.   Do not blank your mind when surrounded by people, as you may unknowingly open yourself to negative vibrations.

9.   Make sure you have a natural flame, such as a candle, tealight, diya etc. nearby. Light protects you when you blank your mind.

You will surely get the guidance to make the right choice and the strength to do the right thing and convert your thoughts into positive, spiritual action.

Below is one final look at the differences between the
subconscious mind and the physical mind. Understand the
nature of these two minds so that you know which mind
to listen to and which mind to train.

Subconscious Mind	Physical Mind
Also known as Conscience, Higher Mind, Higher Self	Also known as Conscious Mind
Spiritual	Physical
The inner, conscientious mind	The outer, superficial mind
Infinite in its understanding	Limited in its understanding
Eternal	Temporary
Truthful and firm	May not be truthful, and may be fickle
Selfless	Mostly selfish
Always calm	Can be anxious and unstable
Does not seek proof of God's existence	Needs proof and will always doubt God's existence
Perseveres until the right action is taken	Gives up, looks for the easy way out and tries to justify wrong thoughts and actions
Connected to the spirit world	Earthbound
Provides inner strength	Makes you weak
Helps to overcome temptation	Gives in to temptation
Feels, senses, does not depend on the physical world	Depends entirely on the physical world

FREE WILL

"You are the creator of your own consequences."

"True freedom means you are free to do the right thing."

"You are on Earth to use free will to overcome temptation and negativity."

"God has given you free will and the freedom to choose, so a sensible soul will use his freedom to choose good rather than bad and will continue to advance spiritually."

"Don't go on the wrong path for just a few years of temporary happiness on Earth, for this will make you go through hundreds of years of suffering in the lower Realms of the spirit world."

 What does free will mean in relation to our life on Earth?

The fact that you have free will means you are in control of your mind, body, and spirit, and must bear the consequences of your actions. The Earth is a school, a place you come to from the spirit world in order to repay your karma, undergo testing and training, and fulfill your spiritual mission. How you go through this is entirely up to you. You can face your challenges bravely with a smile, or you can complain and indulge in self-pity. You can make strong moral choices and thereby nourish your soul, or give in to temptation and feed the ego and weaken the spirit in the process. The choices you make lead you toward God or away from Him. Nurture the spirit or watch it wither: you are free to do as you wish. You either pass your tests or fail them. You are the creator of your own consequences. Only you can determine the progress of your soul by the choices you make on Earth and in the spirit world.

Free will comes into effect in the spirit world itself, from the time a soul decides to be reborn on Earth. Life on Earth is a risk, but it is a risk *you* have chosen. We do not want to scare any of you, but we urge souls on Earth to *be aware*. The more you allow yourself to be ruled by negativity, the harder it is for you to walk on the spiritual path. Negativity exists on Earth so that you can resist it. That is how you build spiritual muscle. When you fail to exercise your spirit, you work from the physical mind and make weak moral choices. One weak moment could have consequences that may last a lifetime. One step in the wrong direction could make it very difficult for you to return to the right path. It is very easy to go off-track when faced with temptation. There are some souls who have committed the most horrific acts in the name of God and religion. There are souls who have harmed, and continue to harm, their own family. There are souls who torture children and old people. These souls are on the lowest of Realms, and it is difficult for them to rise spiritually for two major reasons. First, due to their actions, their subconscious mind has become dormant. Second, because they are on the lowest of Realms, they are surrounded by souls of a similar nature — on Earth as well as in the spirit world. These souls do not want to improve, nor do they want others to change because they want to strengthen their numbers. Negatively influencing others, by force or by manipulation, they stop the spiritual growth of those around them – thus, breaking the law of free will. On Earth, such evil souls have complete disregard for God's laws because they do not believe in Him, or they have wrong notions about spirituality. But they need to understand that no matter what, when a human being dies his subconscious mind awakens enough to take him to the place he deserves to go. That is God's justice and it is infinite.

If all souls are created by God, how can some souls be evil?

To live means to grow spiritually, to move forward towards God. The word 'evil' is the reverse of 'live'. Evil refers to regression; it signifies a soul's negative journey, its movement away from God, caused by negative thoughts, words and deeds. The soul is eternal and can never be destroyed, but it can be darkened. It can acquire darker shades when you make immoral choices and when you fail your tests on Earth. What are you, if not a sum of your thoughts, words, and deeds? How can you separate your actions from your soul? The soul is strengthened or weakened *because* of your actions, so you cannot separate one from the other.

When people wander off onto the wrong path, they justify their actions, or they say they gave in to temptation during a moment of weakness. They may say, "You cannot understand what I am going through." But circumstances cannot be used as an excuse for immoral actions. You must accept responsibility for all your actions. You live in the present and cannot separate yourself from your present actions. If at this moment you are on the wrong path, you cannot look at the past and tell yourself that you were a good human being at that time. You live in the present and shall be judged accordingly by your own subconscious mind. You were the act then, you are the act now, and who you are is the result of what you think, say and do.

It is said that it is Godly to help everyone. **It *is* good to help your fellow men, but you cannot help *all* your fellow men, as some are totally negative.** You may think it is not for you to decide who is negative and who is not, to do that is being judgmental. Do not be judgmental, but use your judgment.

The difference is simple. When you analyse whether another human being is good or not, it is not a judgment made out of superiority to put them down, but rather out of awareness – a spiritual instinct that God has given you for the protection of your own spirit as well as the spirits of those around you. By helping negative souls, you are providing them with sustenance so that they can continue their wrong actions. You are encouraging them. By doing so, you fall spiritually since you are failing to take a moral stand. The only time you should help a negative soul is when he has repented for his deeds and *genuinely* wants to improve. Then, it is your duty to bring him out of negative influences and help him progress to a higher level. **Good judgment is about truth; being judgmental is about the ego.** The choices you make on Earth build the foundations of your home in the spirit world. On Earth, you can either choose to be a slave to the physical mind or a student of the subconscious mind. The gift of free will is ours. We must use it wisely.

KARMA

"What you sow, you reap."

"Karma is not punishment — it is learning. It is a law that is not intended to blindly punish but to teach you where you went wrong, and to make you understand your mistake from a soul level."

"Sorry has no meaning."

"God's justice is perfect — no one can escape it."

"If you cannot see others' happiness, you cannot be happy yourself."

What is karma?

Karma is based on the principle that: what you sow, you reap. It can be explained in terms of cause and effect. The *cause* refers to your actions and the *effect* refers to the consequences of those actions. Therefore, karma is a debt you owe or a blessing you shall receive. There are two types of karma: negative and positive. Negative or bad karma refers to the consequences you have to face due to negative actions. Positive or good karma refers to spiritual blessings that will come your way due to positive actions or selfless good deeds.

God has made laws by which His universe is governed, and it is the duty of all His creations to follow those laws. It is their duty, but they cannot be forced into doing anything — this is the nature of free will. So whatever choice you make is up to you, but even if you choose *not* to follow God's laws you will always *operate* under them. No soul is beyond spiritual law.

෧ How does karma work? Can positive and negative karma cancel each other out?

The two do not cancel each other out, so you will have to pay for your misdeeds, and you will receive spiritual blessings for the good deeds. Good and bad karma are completely separate from each other. A person can build karma with his or her thoughts as well. Karma is a result not only of action, but of thought and words as well. All three go hand in hand.

෧ How does negative karma come to a person?

It can come to you as mental, physical, or emotional pain, in the form of problems with health, family, money, legalities, and so on. Illness can be something you have chosen to go through in order to pay off your karmic debt. This is the idea behind negative karma — you are using this earthly life to pay off a debt. This debt was created not only in past lives but in your current life as well. Do not be under the impression that you are only paying for the wrong deeds you have done in a previous life. You could have come to Earth with little karma, a small karmic debt, but if you are on the wrong path now, you are adding negative karma as you continue to live your life. The understanding of karma is actually very useful to human beings because there are times when pain comes your way, and you do not know why. This pain is something you have chosen because it is necessary for your spiritual growth. Knowing this, you will be able to go through it more gracefully. Never lose an opportunity to undo the wrong deeds you have done. It is a blessing to resolve past issues in this life on Earth itself, rather than procrastinate because of your pride. You must resolve the karma with each particular person in *this* lifetime only; you can pay off karma much easily and more quickly in this manner than if you wait to pay it off in another life. If you don't undo the wrong you have done *now*, your negative karma increases because God has given you an opportunity, which you chose to reject.

🕉 *Many people believe negative karma can be wiped off by donating to charities. Is this true?*

No. You have to pay for the wrong you have done no matter how much you give in charity. You can *never* wipe off karma in this manner. There are many people who have the incorrect notion that if they give thousands to charity they will go to heaven. If you have that motive when you do a good deed, you can forget about seeing heaven. In your world, justice dispensed by even the wisest of judges may not always be correct, but God's laws are perfect and the justice you receive as a result of those laws is perfect. This justice comes to you in the form of karma. If you try to hide something from your fellow man, it may stay hidden, but you cannot hide anything from God. Every thought, word, and action is recorded in the Akashic Records by your subconscious mind. Whether you believe it or not, this is true.

൭൦ *One of the earliest things you said was, "Go through all your troubles bravely and with a smile," but when people are in pain, how is this possible?*

It is very important to go through your troubles bravely and with a smile because your karma has to be paid off and you must not resent it. If you complain and grumble, indulge in self pity and depression, make your pain a very big deal thus making life difficult for your loved ones and the people who are trying to help you, you are not repaying your karma at all; you may even be *adding* negative karma. Or, if you are repaying it, the payment is happening at a very slow rate and your pain may feel never-ending. This is how you are converting your pain into suffering. But if you face your problems bravely, you are demonstrating courage and strengthening your spirit. You are aware of the nature of the problems and you are dealing with them from a higher, spiritual perspective. So smile through your problems, be positive, and handle your pain with grace. Grace simply means that you maintain dignity, have complete faith in God and His justice, and have a sense of humour, too – without losing sight of the importance of the situation. Be light in a grave situation. When you do this, spirit souls are able to help you through your karma. When you display courage and grace, you are showing God that you are able to handle the problems that come your way in a spiritual manner, without blaming anyone and without being resentful or negative. You are operating from your subconscious mind and spirit souls are able to pray for you so that you have the strength to handle your problems. Spirit souls cannot take away your problems, but with added prayer and protection from the spirit world you receive more *strength* to make it through your problems and you can pay off your karma easily and quickly. This does not mean that your karma lessens; it means you get the strength and wisdom to deal with it better and more quickly.

     ॐ *But there are times when human beings go through unimaginable pain. It might seem harsh to think at that time: "This is my karma. I deserve this."*

Yes, we understand what you are saying. But we are not asking you to condemn yourself. We are simply asking you to be aware of spiritual laws — things happen to human beings because of the choices they make. This does not mean the bad things that happen to you are your fault. They happen because there is a lack of awareness. You were not aware at the time that you did something wrong. Or, if you were aware, you did not have the strength to do the right thing. However, there are situations when human beings go through incredible hardships even though it *may not* be their karma. This happens when another human being wrongly uses his free will to cause harm to someone else. Unfortunately, this is the risk human beings take when they take rebirth on Earth. The only solution is to be strong, and not to resent God. Pray to God to save you and to help you heal.

Sometimes, people fear not only the negative karma, but also the good things that happen in their lives. They feel that at any moment it will all disappear. Going through your bad karma bravely is important, but it is also important to accept good karma with grace. It is indeed surprising how many human beings do not know how to accept the good things that come their way.

First of all, **always thank God for all the good that happens in your life.** This is very, very important. On Earth, people beg God to help them in times of distress, but during good times, when all is well, they conveniently forget God. If you remember God during painful times, remember Him during good times as well. Rejoice with Him. After all, we are His children. He does feel happy when we progress spiritually or when we fulfill our mission. He wants to give us as many blessings and as much joy as we can handle.

Secondly, thank those who have helped you in your journey — your family, friends and anyone else who has helped you — even your angels in the spirit world. It is important to acknowledge them. Without your knowledge, your angels have saved you from harm so many times and have provided you with that extra push when you most needed it, so be sure to mentally thank them and ask God to bless them. Earth souls can indeed ask God Almighty to bless their loved ones in the spirit world, and even their Spirit Guides and other angels.

Thirdly, guilt is another factor that comes into play when dealing with good karma. On Earth, human beings are made to feel guilty for all the wrong reasons. There are some who derive pleasure from making others feel guilty. Do not give in to such people, no matter how close they are to you. These people will always compare their journey with yours and will make you feel badly about the blessings that exist in your life. Understand very clearly that if you are on the right path and something good comes your way, it is only because you deserve it. Why should you feel guilty? If someone else does not have the same blessings as you do, there may be a reason for it. Maybe they are at a different stage in their spiritual journey, where they are paying off a lot of karma or are undergoing severe testing and training. By all means, help them out and support them, **but do not give in to their feelings of self-pity, and do not question the blessings of your own journey.** There are some souls who are on the wrong path and have to pay for the wrong deeds they have done. Once they are on the right path, their lives will change too. You do not know what they have chosen in the spirit world. Enjoy the good that comes your way and be grateful for it.

The way to be grateful for the good fortune that comes your way is to share it with another good soul. Again, there is no need to reveal exactly what is happening in your life; there is no need to mention every detail. In fact, you must be silent about the good, and not speak about it too much except to a trusted few or you will attract negative energy. But if you are happy because of something good that happens to you, share that feeling. Make someone else happy. And if you are in a position of strength, use it to help other good souls. That is the very reason you have been put in that position in the first place. Enjoy the spiritual blessings that come your way and use those blessings to help other good souls.

What are the things that create negative karma?

1. Hurting yourself. For example, when you do not look after your health. Bad habits like drugs, smoking,

drinking, over eating, lack of good nutrition and exercise and most important — negative thinking and actions, truly destroy your soul.

2.   Hurting others. Harming someone else physically, or causing emotional pain, builds negative karma. Emotional pain is just as bad as physical pain.

3.   Not dealing well with existing problems by not accepting and facing the truth in the situation.

4.   Tolerating the wrong behaviours of negative souls. You must try to explain to them where they are going wrong. If they do not listen that is their choice, but do not allow them to take advantage of you. **Do not encourage evil.** Do not be nice to an evil person. If you are nice to an evil person, you are encouraging him and to encourage an evil soul means you are in the same sinful category. Therefore, develop your subconscious mind faster so that you can easily recognize an evil person.

5.   Avoiding responsibility. For example, when you run away from your duties towards your parents, children, loved ones etc.

6.   Encouraging others to do wrong and leading them on the wrong path e.g. drug peddlers.

7.   Spoiling your children. You build karma this way because it is your duty to train them well. Parents should also be open to what their children have to say, as the subconscious mind of a child can be open, and the child will operate from instinct. But be sure that the child is not manipulating you for his or her own

selfish purposes.

8. Failing to recognize and fulfill your spiritual mission on Earth.

9. Committing suicide. You build a great deal of negative karma and **you fall one whole Realm** because you are not allowing your soul to complete its journey. You put an end to the very life and situations that *you* had chosen. Your due dates are chosen by you in accordance with God's laws. It is God who has given you life, and it is not up to you to take it.

10. Not taking action. Sometimes, people do not take responsibility or they lack courage to do what is right. They are making the wrong choice because they are being spectators instead of using their free will to do what is right.

11. Wanting to have 'fun'. Young people believe that when they are young they need to "experience life" and they use that as an excuse for doing things that are wrong. **It is important to enjoy your earthly journey, but not at the cost of your soul.**

Always remember that you fall more and build more karma if you make wrong choices after gaining spiritual knowledge than if you have no knowledge at all.

☯ *How does a person pay off their karma on Earth?*

Here are a few guidelines on **How to Pay Off Karma:**

1. Accept the problem. Whatever the obstacle, make sure you don't run away from it.

2. Have a sincere and genuine desire to change the situation and deal with it well.

3. Understand that this is what *you* have chosen in the spirit world for your own growth or it is a result of a choice you have made in your present life. Testing and training are opportunities for growth that will help you improve. When you understand why things happen your resistance to them is lower and you are no longer negative about your problems.

4. Try to think of every obstacle as a test. If you fail, the test will keep coming back to you and it will continue to become harder and harder.

5. Be positive and have faith in God. Pray. Ask God to give you strength and wisdom.

6. Try not to add *more* karma. Act wisely. Remember that even the smallest sin has to be accounted for. Just as the smallest drop in the ocean helps form the whole, so it is with karma. The smallest action, good or bad, has consequences.

7. Do not compare journeys. Never question why you are experiencing pain and someone else is not. That, itself, is a wrong thought and will prevent you from growing.

8. Control the physical mind and listen to the subconscious mind. It stays calm during a calamity and will guide you.

9. Never blame others for the things that happen in your life. You must take responsibility for your life. You can change anytime you want to. Most people are weak because they choose to be.

10. Even when you are in trouble or experiencing pain, try to help someone else through small acts of kindness. This change of focus will help you. Make sure your motive is pure. When you help others, God gives you the strength to go through your own problems more easily and you also get blessings from the people you help.

11. Take action. Do your best and leave the rest to God.

☉ Are 'testing' and 'training' the same as karma?

They are not the same as karma but are linked to karma. When you were in the spirit world, you chose to come down to Earth in order to do the following:

1. Repay karma.

2. Undergo testing and training.

3. Fulfill your spiritual mission – your true purpose for being on Earth.

4. Protect your loved ones.

These four things, collectively, make up your path on Earth.

Not all problems that come your way are karmic. Difficult situations come your way as tests or training so that you can become aware of your weaknesses or negative soul characteristics and cultivate positive soul characteristics. If karma is a debt you owe or a blessing you shall receive, **training** is your *preparation*. It is what you choose to go through so that you are prepared to pass a particular **test**. With the help of High Good Souls in the spirit world you select the types of training that you wish to complete during your earthly life. You also choose what you wish to be tested on, that is, the specific soul characteristics. However, the nature of the tests, their magnitude and timing are not decided by you, but automatically provided by your subconscious mind. For example, when you go to university, you select the courses you would like to learn; however, at the end of the course, you do not select the exact questions on your exam papers. There will be many such tests at different points in your life, and they will be given to you until you pass them extremely well. Training makes your spirit strong and helps you realise certain truths; training helps your soul acquire certain qualities that are essential for you to pass tests and fulfill your mission. Training comes in a *series of situations* with which you have to cope and that will help you learn and grow. Training comes in many forms according to what you have chosen based on the requirements of your own soul. You will then be tested to see if you have learned those truths or lessons and if they have become part of your being.

Tests exist to determine whether you have learned spiritual lessons.

When you have learned a lesson well, the test does not appear again. You have gone through a certain situation and have moved *beyond* it, which means you have understood the higher purpose of the struggle.

Let us say that you are proud about your success. You will come across situations in which you will experience failure (your training). If you understand the nature of this failure, that it is presented to you to teach you humility, and you do become humble, you have learned the lesson and therefore passed the test. You have replaced a negative soul characteristic (pride) with a positive soul characteristic (humility). Once this change is genuine, you have truly passed your test. This is how your soul is trained. As you rise higher spiritually, your tests and training become of a higher nature, and you receive added help from the spirit world.

Tests also exist to help determine your moral strength. Do you choose the easy way out regardless of the fact that it may be morally wrong, or do you choose what is right even though it is the more difficult path? Karma, testing and training are linked, but they are not the same thing. The bottom line is this: whatever situation comes your way handle it with courage and a smile, but always be aware. **Tests come to you when you least expect them.**

A spiritual test is a surprise test. This is the only way you will know if you have truly learned spiritual lessons. To be spiritually aware, operate from the subconscious mind so you naturally do what is right. If you work from the physical mind when a spiritual test comes your way, you are using the wrong muscle (i.e. the physical mind), so you may not do well or you may fail completely. When a test comes your way, you may become paralysed with fear, or become angry and frustrated, and the moment that happens, you have gotten off to a wrong start by disconnecting from the subconscious mind. You have activated the wrong muscle – the physical mind. Your start is everything – once you have activated the wrong muscle, you will keep using it. Eventually, when you have failed the test, you will realise what you have done. When you fail a test, it comes back to you but it is always harder. The lesson you need to learn will remain the same, but the test will come in a different form. This is how a spiritual test is a surprise test. Until you have learned the lesson, similar problems will keep coming your way again and again till you overcome it.

Another law is that the higher you go spiritually, the harder your tests become, just as when you go to a higher grade in school, your exams become harder. If you have spiritual knowledge and you still run away from your problems, you fall faster. Whatever your reason for running away, be it fear, ego, or something else, the spiritual law is that if you have knowledge, you have a greater responsibility to accept karma well, undergo training, and pass your spiritual tests.

There are so many individuals on Earth who have wonderful knowledge, but who are on low Realms. This is because in spite of having knowledge, they do not make use of it for their betterment. Nothing can save them if they are on the wrong path, even if they share their knowledge with others. Therefore, spiritual knowledge can actually cause you to fall even lower. Doing something wrong after acquiring knowledge shows a complete disregard for the spiritual laws, and your karmic debt will increase. The downfall of two individuals who commit wrong deeds of similar magnitude can differ; the one who has more knowledge goes lower spiritually and builds more negative karma.

✽ *Can you give us a few examples of spiritual tests?*

1.   Fear. Your fears will be tested because you need to

learn courage.

2.   Power. You are placed in a position of power to see if you can use it for the greater good.

3.   Money. Sometimes you are given a great deal of money to see if that changes you as a person, or you are not given much money to see if you can still be content.

4.   Gift. You are given a gift, a talent, to see how you use it — for light or darkness.

5.   Forgiveness. Someone close to you may cause you pain. Instead of being negative and resenting that person, can you forgive him or her by doing what is right, i.e. by changing your inner state and thinking positively?

ॐ *What is the role of the subconscious mind in the repayment of karma?*

Being a good soul, your karma comes to you faster because your subconscious mind is open. This means that even if you do something slightly wrong, your karma comes to you instantly, and you can repay that karma fast. However, if your subconscious mind is dormant, your karma accumulates and you delay paying it. Eventually, however, your karma comes to you no matter what. Do not think that evil souls are getting off scot-free; they are accumulating karma that they will have to repay.

However, this same rule does not apply with regards to one's testing and training. A human being can skip his or

her testing and training. If your subconscious mind is
dormant it will be unable to lead you to the tests and
training required for your spiritual growth and you will
never recognize your spiritual mission and purpose on
Earth. When you are not on a spiritual journey, you have
used your own free will to alter the very path that you
chose in the spirit world; you will no longer encounter
situations and people that you require for your soul's
training. Instead, you will be faced with situations and
people that will feed your ego and make you completely
Earth-bound, fixed in a materialistic world. You will thus
give no importance to your spirit. The nurturing of your
spirit will be completely ignored and you will be happy in
this state. But this happiness is an illusion because it
comes completely from the physical mind. By running
away from the spiritual path, some people on Earth feel
relieved and get a false sense of peace that comes from the
physical mind because they do not have to go through the
struggle of changing and improving. They do not want to
deal with their problems in the right manner and they take
the easy way out. This false sense of peace is given to you
by your own ego because it does not want to be crushed.

    ௐ *Is this why there seems to be so much injustice on
Earth — low souls have a dormant subconscious mind
and are therefore not being led to their testing and
training?*

It seems unjust, but remember that these souls are actually
building bad karma. They are not even facing their training
and testing. All of this is being recorded. It all accumulates
and negative souls eventually have to face this truth. On

Earth, however, these souls are in power and seem to be happy. Also, the vibration on Earth is negative right now so this negative vibration helps negative souls. Unfortunately, this same negative vibration affects good souls. These negative souls use their free will to harm others and as a result good souls go through pain even though it is not their test, training or karma.

For instance, murder is *never* part of God's plan. It is not something you can choose in the spirit world in order to repay karma, or to undergo testing and training. When a person murders someone and it is not in self-defence, i.e. when that murder is pre-planned or is an act of revenge, no matter what the circumstances, the murderer will go straight to the lowest Realm in the spirit world and build up tremendous negative karma. Murdering someone in this life does not mean someone will murder you or someone close to you in a future life. God will never allow a sinful act such as murder to be part of a spiritual plan as such things cannot be chosen in the spirit world. The low soul goes through extreme trial and suffering in its next incarnation on Earth and it will take that soul a very long time to reach even Realm 4.

🕉 *But what happens to the good souls who have lost someone and did not deserve to lose that person?*

When you are in the spirit world, you know the type of place Earth is; you know the risks involved, and you know that a negative soul may use his free will to harm you. Knowing this, you have still chosen to come to Earth because you can rise much faster on Earth than in the spirit world. If you are not a risk-taker, you would stay in the spirit world and your progress would be slow (except in rare cases). This is why many souls choose not to be reborn, and this is entirely up to them because free will prevails in the spirit world as well. Free will exists in each and every universe.

Suppose a young man is murdered. It was not his due date, and his life has been terminated before his earthly journey is complete. Let's say that this young man has parents who are still alive and it is not their karma to go through this kind of pain. It can be the parents' karma to lose the child due to a natural death, such as a physical ailment, but not due to an unnatural death.

If the parents are good souls, God will send his angels to provide extra healing for them through prayers and a great deal of strength will be given to them, so that they can survive this trauma. The parents still have karma to pay off (no human on Earth has no karma to pay) and this pain may be used to wipe out their karma, if the parents agree. This agreement is made without their conscious knowledge – it is made between their subconscious mind and the High Good Soul of that particular Realm. They will continue to live with extra prayers and protection, complete their earthly journey, and a major portion of their karma will be wiped off – if they go through this journey well.

Another option, in cases of extreme difficulty, is a Walk-In.

Let's say that you are a good soul on Earth and you are in an extreme situation that is beyond your capabilities and understanding, e.g. you are given a 10th grade examination when you are only in the 5th grade, therefore it is impossible to face it. Then, a Walk-In, or a good soul from Realm 5 or higher, from the spirit world, will come to Earth and inhabit your body. Your human soul will temporarily go to the spirit world, and when the tough time passes it will return to your body and send the spirit soul back to the spirit world. Only your subconscious mind is aware of this. There is a mutual understanding between your subconscious mind and the Walk-In's subconscious mind. Walk-Ins are rare and they will come to Earth only in certain difficult situations. As a precautionary step, you choose your Walk-In in the spirit world before being born, just in case things go wrong.

⚭ *Is a Walk-In the same as being possessed?*

No. Possession is not the same as a Walk-In. Possession is against free will. Spirit souls *never* possess people on Earth. Only astral souls do. Astral souls are only attracted to negative people, and they inhabit the body of the person on Earth. This is spiritually wrong, as they have not gained permission from the subconscious mind of the Earth soul and it is completely against free will.

⚭ *What about destiny? Are karma, testing and training separate from destiny?*

Those who believe in **destiny** lead their lives as though they are powerless. They feel that no matter what they do, "what has to happen will happen". This is not the right way of thinking, as future circumstances depend on your present actions. If you are a good soul, you will go through your testing and training only if your subconscious mind is open. Your karma will come to you and you will be able to repay it quickly. Moreover, you will be led to additional testing and training only if you are dealing with your present testing and training extremely well. There is no question of anything being destined; everything depends on your present actions. Karma, good or bad, comes your way because of past and present actions, but you have a choice to make negative circumstances pass by dealing with your problems well. Spirit souls will give you the strength. A belief in destiny maintains that no matter what you do your circumstances will not change, in which case your struggles would be prolonged and would seem never-ending.

You — not destiny — are the creator of your own consequences. The blessings and problems that come your way on Earth are of your own choosing in the spirit world because you have done something good or bad in this life or a previous one. If you believe in destiny you believe that the consequences are fixed and your actions have no relevance at all.

Hopefully, this information about karma will explain, to some extent, the pain that human beings go through in life. Karma is not to be looked at with sadness, fear, or anxiety. It is necessary for spiritual growth. If you have hurt someone mentally, physically, emotionally, or spiritually, it will come back to you, and so will the blessings for small acts of kindness done with a pure motive.

Spiritual blessings and gifts are never of a materialistic

nature. They come to you in the form of a happy family, loyal friends, talents, comforts, pets, finding a true guru or master (not a fake one), psychic abilities like auto writing, child prodigies, being a good communicator, having healing powers, inventions and discoveries for the service of mankind, good health, protection from negativity for yourself and loved ones, guidance and spiritual knowledge, strength from God to handle your problems, opportunities to pay off your karma quickly, and skills that will enable you to better fulfill your mission and help others as well.

Debts have to be paid. Do not postpone debts to your next life by running away from your tests, avoiding your responsibilities, or following the wrong path. You need medicine to cure your sicknesses, but the medicine may sometimes be bitter. After taking the medicine, however, you feel better. Similarly, karmic debts may give you pain, but after dealing with them well you feel lighter and stronger and have a higher understanding. Always remember that you are able to handle whatever comes your way. In the spirit world, you took the counsel of the High Good Soul of your Realm as well as three wise souls, who helped you choose your path according to your capacity. Your test, training and karma are given to you on the basis of what you can handle. Nothing beyond your capacity will come to you in your life. If you feel you cannot handle something, think again; perhaps you need to analyse yourself to see where you are going wrong.

YOUR MISSION ON EARTH

"We are all born as instruments of God, but the choice to continue to work as His instrument is entirely ours."

"Never be nice to, or encourage, evil people. Fight evil."

 What is your mission on Earth?

Many people feel their life has no meaning, that there seems to be nothing but problems. How can these souls find meaning in their lives?

First of all, never fear the obstacles that come your way; they exist to make you stronger. Also, do not be under the impression that you are on Earth to suffer. Karma, testing and training exist to help you change and to cleanse your soul. But God has also given you a chance to do something wonderful on Earth: your **Spiritual Mission**.

Every human being wants life to be meaningful, and this happens when you find your purpose. That purpose is known as your mission, a promise between your soul and God, an oath you took in the spirit world before coming to Earth. Each and every soul is on a spiritual quest. That is the path *you* have chosen in the spirit world before being reborn. When you come to Earth, you forget the very reason you chose to be born; for the progress of your soul.

Each human being has three missions.

1.   To improve spiritually.

2.   To selflessly serve others.

3.   To use individual gifts and talents for the growth of others.

Human beings are on Earth to change for the better. You can realise your full potential as a spirit being in a physical body only when you change from within. **Self-improvement** is your first mission – to change and walk on the Godly Good Path no matter what the circumstances or obstacles in your life. On Earth, there will always be negative forces. Earth is a spiritual battleground, and the only way to prove your moral strength is to choose light when darkness is overwhelming. Fighting evil does not mean you have to be vocal about it, judge people, or go to great lengths to expose them. **Exposing evil is important, but _not_ when you endanger yourself or your loved ones.** However, you must not use this as an excuse to be cowardly, either. The best way to fight evil is to be brave and simply do what is right, every single time. This is what it means to be on the Godly Good Path. Without change, there can be no growth.

When you follow the guidance of the subconscious mind, change becomes a natural part of your being and you change gracefully, step by step. When you change gracefully, you are able to handle your tests and training, and you are able to pay off your negative karma well because you are using your subconscious mind. Also, you can use your good karma – your spiritual gifts and blessings – for the greater good. These come your way only when you are on the right path. When you change gracefully, you are doing your best to bring God's Plan into effect.

When you fail to follow the guidance of your sub-conscious mind, you are resisting change. You resist change because you give in to the wrong justifications that the physical mind provides – it tells you there is nothing wrong with you and you do not need to change. The physical mind does not like change; therefore, if you do not operate from the subconscious mind, change will not come naturally to you. You will not change gracefully. But since you are not a bad soul, and your subconscious mind is still slightly open, you will get a physical blow. Something will happen in your life, a shock or blow, such as loss of finance or health, to make you open your eyes.

The sad part about human beings is that they can very easily ignore guidance, joy, and blessings, but they cannot ignore pain. So pain comes to you to awaken you. Once you are awake, you realise that you are on the wrong path and that you need to change. If you had listened to your subconscious mind, you would not have needed the pain to wake you up. If, even after receiving a physical blow, you refuse to change, the blows will stop coming because your subconscious mind will have become dormant. So do not assume that because everything is fine in your external life, you are on the right path. In other words, you might have changed for the worse.

This happens when you knowingly go on the wrong path. When you change for the worse and go beyond a limit your subconscious mind shuts down completely, and you realise what you have done only after you die, when you go to the lowest of Realms in the spirit world. This is a terrifying thing, when souls who think they are on the right path on Earth go to the spirit world and are shocked to see where they have landed.

Self-improvement or change must be undertaken for the right reasons. Sometimes, people do things for the wrong reasons: they want to be respected by others; they want to satisfy their ego by walking the spiritual path; they acquire knowledge in order to appear wise and learned; or they do the right thing because they want a place in heaven or because they fear they will go to hell. These are not the right reasons to change. You should change because you believe in goodness and want to be a better human being. **Choose goodness for the sake of goodness itself.** Instead of being spiritually ambitious and goal-oriented, change because it makes you feel better; enjoy the journey. The destination, Realm 7 Stage 9, is not the focus – the path or the change should be the focus.

☸ *Sometimes, people say, "I want to change but I am unable to." Are they being genuine when they say this?*

People who say this have good intentions, but are confused about why they cannot bring about a change from within. There is a simple reason for this. True change comes from the subconscious mind, but the physical mind has to cooperate. When people fail to change, it is because they are not dedicated to change – the genuine desire does not exist. They have made a choice to change, but it is half-hearted; you need to be wholeheartedly committed to change, for the right reasons.

So here is the first step: in order to change and follow the Godly Good Path, you need to have **knowledge** that will help you distinguish right from wrong. You need to identify what you need to change. Therefore, the first step to take is to acquire spiritual knowledge. Be sure that you trust the source of that knowledge. There is a great deal of wrong knowledge disguised as spirituality on Earth today, but God has given you a subconscious mind that will lead you to true knowledge. If you are seeking an easy way out, if you resist change, you are not a true seeker and your physical mind will lead you to the wrong knowledge. Little knowledge is a dangerous thing. **Do what is best for your soul, not your ego.**

☸ *How will a person recognise a true master?*

Few people are fortunate enough to have genuine masters in their lives, but spiritual knowledge is readily available. Make knowledge your master, and you will find the right knowledge if you truly seek it. When it comes to finding a master, use your common sense. There are many people who possess knowledge, but who are using that knowledge wrongly. A true master will never use knowledge for material gain. **True masters will be selfless** and use the knowledge only for their own spiritual growth, and that of others. **A master will not spoil you; he will train your spirit.** Many people convince themselves that they have the right master because they like what that master is offering; the knowledge is easy to digest, it does not require them to change, and it involves material growth. If you are on a quest for the truth, your common sense should tell you that the truth is not easy. If you have an ego the truth is always hard to accept, as the ego prevents you from gaining true understanding.

A true master will never cripple you. A true master will help you discover the master within you. You will not be dependent; you will be self-sufficient. Do not run from the master who offers you the truth. Run from the master who feeds your ego. Run from the master who weakens your spirit and lowers your self-esteem and self-worth. Use your common sense and instincts and you will be led to the right master or knowledge.

Sometimes, human beings think they will get materialistic help or information about others if they contact spirit souls. This is not possible, as spirit souls would never reveal information about others and would never discuss material things, nor would they indulge in predictions. Astral souls, however, do. Spirit souls are only concerned with spiritual guidance, so be aware of teachers who offer anything else. Also, do not look for proof that spirit souls exist, or that God exists. If you look for proof, you are failing your test; if you have faith, you will receive it when you least expect it.

Now, we will move on to the next step toward self-improvement. Knowledge is not enough. Knowledge is only the first step toward positive change. The next step is the **acceptance of flaws.**

The diagram below shows the cycle of spiritual knowledge and change.

SPIRITUAL KNOWLEDGE

↓

ACCEPTANCE OF FLAWS

↓

ACTION (CHANGE)

↓

WISDOM IS ACQUIRED

The downward arrow shows the flow of knowledge from the spirit world to Earth. This knowledge is God-given; it comes first from God to spirit souls and then to souls on Earth. On Earth, souls channel this knowledge. They are reincarnated on Earth to spread light in a dark age, so you have to recognize these souls as you will gain true knowledge from them. If the student has genuine desire, in other words he is ready, then the master will appear to help him progress spiritually. Once you gain this spiritual knowledge, you must use it to understand what you are doing right and where you are going wrong. The second step is the acceptance of flaws. All human beings have flaws. Analyse those flaws so you can eradicate them, and the only way to eradicate them is by taking action.

Action is the third and most important step. A person may be aware of certain flaws they possess but are not interested in changing. This signifies non-acceptance. True acceptance of flaws means changing to such an extent that those flaws are eradicated. That is the kind of spiritual action that is needed. In order to help others, you need to help yourself first. You need to be in a position of spiritual strength to have a positive effect on someone else. If you want a loved one or a friend to be humble and you point out their flaw in a tactful way, that is fine, but if you are a proud person, do not expect anyone else to change. Lead by example. Don't wait for others to change before you do, and remember that *no change is possible without humility.* Once *you* have taken action, you will complete the cycle, only to begin again. You will be given more spiritual knowledge so that you may again analyse yourself and take more action. This cycle will continue over lifetimes.

At times, you might feel you are unable to progress. You want to change, but instead of improving you feel like you are in quicksand. This is because you have some spiritual knowledge, but you have not accepted your flaws. And because you have taken no action, your understanding of God's laws is limited. Knowledge, by itself, is simply information. When that information is *shared*, it becomes knowledge. When knowledge is put into practice in your daily life, and you have learned your spiritual lessons, you will acquire wisdom. Only then will you be given more knowledge by spirit souls, which can be converted into wisdom through experience. This is how you live for the progress of the soul. These three steps — knowledge, acceptance and action will help you fulfill your first mission, that of self-improvement.

Your second mission is that of **Selfless Service.**

Service is the key to contentment, but in your materialistic world people will not understand this. True contentment comes from selfless service. There are many souls on Earth who are good people. They harm no one, lead simple, quiet lives with their families and fulfill their duties. These souls are much better than souls who harm themselves and others and add to darkness, but these good souls are unaware of their true potential.

By simply fulfilling your duties, you do not progress spiritually.

Unfortunately, the world is in such a negative state that a man who simply fulfills his duties and causes no harm is considered God's man. Such a man is not even halfway there. You must reach out and help others – walk the path of selfless service. You are on Earth as an instrument of God, to serve others *silently*. Do the work without waiting for recognition. **A light worker is a silent worker.** An instrument of God simply does what is right. He overcomes darkness by way of his good deeds, and he does not speak of his good deeds; he does not even analyse them because that would lead to pride. Remember that God's angels are watching over you and they are watching your actions. If you know this, understand that your soul will never yearn for recognition. Only your ego will *want* it. The moment you speak about a good deed you have done, or even think about it too much, its value is lost. The person who needed to be helped has no doubt been helped, but you have failed to progress because you have not understood the true meaning of selfless service. 'Selfless' means to think less about what the self has done for others. That is the meaning of true devotion to God. You serve God by serving others.

☙ *What is devotion?*

On Earth, devotion to God is connected to rituals and ceremonies. Spending a great deal of money and performing elaborate ceremonies and rituals is *not* seva.[15] Your devotion to God is not based on how much money you spend on charity or ceremony. Your devotion to God is based on quiet, selfless service. When you help others, do so without any expectations. The moment you ask yourself what you gain by helping someone, your motive is impure. Forget about the deed. Move on. When you do a good deed, you are bound to feel happy. It is only natural to feel good if you have made a difference in someone's life. But do not allow that feeling to make you proud. **Be grateful that you have been used by God as an instrument for His work.** You have been blessed because of this. Use that blessing, that feeling of goodness, to help someone else. If you simply hold onto that feeling and do not serve more, that feeling goes away very quickly. Service, like spiritual progress, is a never-ending cycle. The moment you feel your work is done and you want to rest, stop yourself. Your work can never be done. There is always more to do. Recharge, but do not rest. And when faced with personal pain, try to convert that pain into service. That is the most selfless thing you can do.

You can convert your pain into service by using the gifts and talents that God has given you. This is your third mission: **To Use Gifts and Talents for the Growth of Others.** The first two missions, those of self-improvement and selfless service, are common to all people. Everyone has a third mission as well, but the nature of the third

---

15. Seva means selfless service.

mission differs. Your third mission is connected to your gift. A gift can be a talent you have — for example, singing, dancing, writing, acting, sporting ability, and so on. But your gift could also be a special connection to old people, you might have a bond with children or animals, you might be a wonderful cook, or you might have a gift for gardening or carpentry. This gift is what you are good at, and it is earned over lifetimes. **Remember that every single human being on Earth is gifted. God would never send His child to Earth without His blessing.**

Just as your negative actions create bad karma, your positive actions create good karma. **This good karma comes to you in the form of a spiritual gift,** a skill that will bring you fulfillment and help others as well. If you are naturally good at something, your soul has acquired that gift over lifetimes, but your physical mind is aware of it for the first time in this life. You are not *discovering* what your gift is, you are *rediscovering* it. Whatever your gift, you must use it to serve the greater good. Most people with talent focus on using it to earn money and fame, which is not your ultimate purpose. Create something that is a positive contribution to humanity. If you do have the good fortune of being famous, use that as a platform, to spread spiritual knowledge. Use your position to heal people, to make them happy, to lift them up. You must use your gift wisely and do justice to it by being an instrument of God. By all means, reach the pinnacle in your line of work, but do not restrict your gift by using it only for earthly purposes. Find your higher purpose.

🕉 *Is there a way for us to know our third mission?*

Your third mission will be something you are naturally drawn towards and for which you have a *great love*. You can live your daily life working in an office or a factory, but no matter where you are, use your strengths to make a positive impact. A positive impact is about inspiring someone, raising his or her spirit, and giving hope through small acts of kindness. If you are proud, fearful, or materialistic, your physical mind will try to take you away from your mission. **If you do not complete your spiritual mission on Earth, no matter how much you have achieved in the earthly world, your life will be considered a waste, and your journey incomplete.**

🕉 *Why do some people on Earth know their mission while others do not?*

1. You have to be on a good spiritual level to know your mission. If you are on the wrong path, you are very far away from the first mission of self-improvement, so the question of service does not even arise.

2. Your subconscious mind has to be open so that you will be able to recognize your mission. If you are extremely logical and ignore your instinct, you are running away from your true purpose. The physical mind can be a hindrance when it becomes too analytical.

3. Your mission will be revealed to you only if you are ready for it. If you know about it too soon, it may overwhelm you or make you proud. You must be ready to accept the responsibility of that mission and be able to handle it.

4.   Your level of commitment is vital. How dedicated are
     you to the spiritual path? If you are consistent, and
     spirituality is a priority in your life, you will be
     directed to your true purpose. Sometimes, the efforts
     that human beings make to understand their missions
     are half-hearted, so they do not improve or make any
     progress.

You are a channel for God's work on Earth; if you pollute
yourself by following the wrong path, you are rejecting the
opportunity to perform your mission and you will lose
your gift. If you are an impure channel, you will not be
able to access the guidance from the spirit world that
would lead you to your mission and eventually help you
accomplish it. Every soul is born for a purpose, but that
purpose will be revealed only when you have begun your
spiritual journey. Once you discover that purpose and
begin fulfilling your mission, you will be truly happy and
at peace.

🔮 *You said that channels can pollute themselves.
Can even good channels go wrong?*

Yes. For instance, there are many psychics on Earth who
are gifted. But if they continually seek material rewards for
their work, their own progress is limited. They do good
work, but since they want wealth, they will not progress
the way they would if they had been completely selfless.
The good work is being done regardless, there is no doubt
about that, the subconscious mind recognizes the mission.
But once you gain success, that success is a test, and you
should not allow it to take you on the wrong path. Gifts
are tests to see how we use them.

⚛ *Is duty the same as service?*

No. There is a difference. Your first **duty** is to look after your own health. Your body is your soul's garment, given to you by God. It must be taken care of, looked after, and appreciated. It is an indispensable tool for the soul, to help you carry out and accomplish your mission. An unhealthy body leads to a disturbed mind, and vice versa. This, in turn, leads to an unhappy and unexplored soul that is unable to do the work it was reborn to do. Your body is a temple so you must respect it.

Caring for someone, such as looking after a parent or grandparent or bringing up your child well, is your duty. It should be performed without feeling as if you have made a sacrifice. Human beings have become so selfish that when someone experiences an act of kindness, it comes as a surprise. If you are not kind and compassionate by nature, ask yourself where you have gone wrong. To miss an opportunity to help your family and friends is a promise broken.

A person's duty is towards:
1.   Children
2.   Parents
3.   Spouse
4.   Other family members
5.   Friends

Remember to do your duty towards people only if they are on the right path. If they are straying, guide them;

however, if they continue to knowingly follow the wrong path, you must use your judgment. Do not let people take advantage of you. Remember that it is your duty to help others. There is actually no such thing as 'help'. The only reason you have formed the concept of 'help' is because it is a rare thing today. Earlier, help was simply duty. There was nothing like 'help'. As parents, children, and friends, it is your duty to do what is required. It should be a normal function, not one that requires careful consideration. Unfortunately, you need to exercise caution today as people are unpredictable at times in both receiving and giving help. But still, it is something that should come naturally to all human beings.

Service and help are simply one's duty, but nowadays people make the distinction because they are completely unaware. Human beings have become selfish. Spirit beings derive inspiration from serving others. Their mission is to spread awareness regarding God's laws to souls on Earth in the hope that these souls will share this knowledge with others and use it to change.

🐚 *Is there any way a person can prepare for his or her mission?*

If you are on the spiritual path, this happens naturally. Testing and training are what lead you to your mission and help prepare you as well. For instance, when you were in the spirit world you chose a mission to provide justice. On Earth, you will have to undergo testing and training to prepare for your mission, to help you recognize it. So perhaps as a child or as a teenager, you will be exposed and subjected to injustice to make you realise that so much of it exists on Earth. These situations come to you as your training.

But your test is this: injustice is very hard on the ego; will you resort to illegal or immoral means in order to gain justice? Will you become corrupt after you become a police officer or lawyer or judge? If you listen to your subconscious mind, you will use this negative experience as a learning process and it will lead you to your mission, which is to become an honest person who provides law and order.

The severity of your tests and training depends on the nature of your mission, as you require certain qualities or soul characteristics to fulfill it. All testing and training involves crushing of the ego, because you cannot train your spirit if you are ruled by your ego.

The first step to keep in mind when you are going through spiritual training is to realise that it is happening for the higher purpose of learning. Understand what you are being trained for. Analyse the difficult situation you are in and determine the weakness that makes you negative and off-balance. Ask yourself what prevents you from being positive and working your way out of that situation. That is your weakness, and that is the area in which your spirit needs training. That is the lesson you need to learn. Therefore, that is where you will be tested.

There is one major area in which each and every human being on Earth is tested. **This is a test of faith – your greatest test.** A test of faith refers to your belief in God. Even though you cannot see God, do you have the humility and courage to believe in Him? If you fail this test, there can be no true spiritual journey. There are human beings on Earth who do not believe in God, but who still do what is right. It is much better to be that way than to say you believe in God and then harm others and yourself in God's name. But understand that your failure to believe in God means that you have failed one very *big* test – the test of faith. Many people say that if God shows Himself to us, or gives us proof of His existence, we can believe in Him. But this is a test. That is why your subconscious mind does not reveal memories of the spirit world to the physical mind.

To pass the test of faith, you have to choose the subconscious mind over the physical mind. The moment you open your subconscious mind, you will realise that God exists because the subconscious mind *knows* that God exists; it is only your physical mind that always seeks proof. If you only develop the physical mind, you may automatically fail the test of faith.

Your weaknesses are your temptations.

Keep in mind that your weaknesses will be tested. When most people think of temptation, they think of physical things such as sex, drugs, food, alcohol, money, and so on. There is no doubt that those are temptations, but temptations exist on another level too: pride, doubt, anger, revenge, and jealousy, for example. Your negative soul characteristics, anything that takes you away from the Godly Good Path, are your temptations, and you will constantly be trained and tested in those areas to make you aware of your flaws. Constantly look within yourself, with honesty and courage, and be brave enough to accept your flaws. If you do not know what is wrong, how will you fix it?

Moreover, do not think of only controlling a flaw. Get rid of it by replacing it with something of a higher nature. So, if you have pride, do not only control the pride, but become humble. Also make sure you acknowledge the good that is within you. Self-worth and self-love, which means love and respect for one's own spirit, are very important. Use your strengths instead of being used by your weaknesses. You must use the good within you, your positive soul characteristics, to get rid of the negatives.

SUICIDE

"To terminate life is completely against God's law."

"God has given you life; it is not yours to take."

*"You have to face your problems. You have to fight evil.
You have to purify your soul."*

 There are so many people, especially young ones, who are ending their lives on Earth. What happens to these souls?

When these souls arrive in the spirit world they feel extremely dejected because they realise they have made a wrong decision. Instead of staying on Earth and completing their journey, they cut it short by terminating their lives. This is one of the worst choices you can make on Earth. To end your own life is the greatest harm you can cause your own soul.

 The logic people use is that humans have free will. Are we not free to end our own lives?

The choice to end your life is yours, but you will continue to operate under God's laws, and when you break those laws, there are consequences. Your body is your temple. It is given to you by God so that it can be a healthy vehicle for your spirit. When you destroy that temple, you are rejecting life, the very essence of creation. The real damage suicide causes is to your spirit. Spiritually, you fall an entire Realm, and you add a great deal of negative karma to your soul. You will have to come back to Earth and face the same situations with double the intensity. Your test and training become twice as hard. When someone commits suicide, he is breaking his oath to God.

Sometimes, the pain human beings go through is unbearable. We all come down to Earth in order to repay karma and undergo testing and training for the growth of our soul. Sometimes we have a lot of karma to pay off, or we have chosen hard tests. The pain that we might go through and the situations we might encounter will be very intense and trying, but we must complete our journey no matter what. What human beings do not realise is that even though they are in unbearable pain, the pain they might cause to others by committing suicide is just as unbearable. **Suicide is also an act of selfishness.**

At the time the person is in pain, he is not thinking of others. The pain you go through makes you think only about yourself. But what about your loved ones? What about the people you leave behind? You are adding karma not only by harming your own spirit, but by harming the spirits of others. Some will say they have no one, and feel like taking their lives for that very reason. But perhaps that is their karma, or perhaps they are being tested to see how strong they can be in spite of this loneliness. Selfishness makes your problems appear much bigger than they actually are.

ᛏ *Loneliness is a huge problem today. Even though people have families, they still feel lonely. Why is there so much loneliness on Earth?*

There are two reasons for this feeling. First of all, you are not a complete soul on Earth. Since you are now aware of the concept of twin souls, you will realise that you are only half of a soul, and the loneliness you feel is a longing for your other half. However, once you understand this, you must make sure that you achieve that sense of completion on Earth, as it is your test. It is absolutely possible to feel complete on Earth by fulfilling your spiritual mission. **Once you discover your life's true purpose, you will be at peace.** Feelings of emptiness arise when your subconscious mind tells you that you are not fulfilling your mission on Earth. Secondly, your subconscious mind knows that Earth is not your real home. It longs for the spirit world, for the peace of higher Realms, and the company of your group souls and loved ones. This should not be an excuse for you to feel discontent; to feel content is one of the greatest tests on Earth and that test must not be failed. Do not wait for death to bring you peace. To be at peace in the spirit world you must first learn to be at peace on Earth. Loneliness is part of that battle and must be dealt with correctly.

ᛏ *Does that mean we will always feel lonely on Earth?*

Not at all. It is not that you cannot be happy on Earth and that you will always feel lonely. But loneliness is one of the things that can lead to unhappiness and depression. If this depression continues, it can make you suicidal.

❦ *Is it true that to take one's own life requires strength and courage?*

This is *not* true. The fact that you feel like taking your own life means that **you need to strengthen your spirit.** Have faith that this strength exists within you, and know that God will never let you face a situation you cannot handle. You *do* have the strength, so use it. Another misconception is that, at times, suicide is honourable. There is no 'honour' in taking your own life. Do not do a disservice to your soul by destroying the very vehicle it needs to fulfill its duties and mission on Earth. To be a person of honour is to assume responsibility and do what is spiritually right. So many people who have taken their own lives did it out of pressure, in order to give in to the false beliefs of others and society. Where is the honour in that? Instead, live a spiritual life and honour God. His is the only opinion that truly matters. There are times on Earth when it is no doubt unbearable for the soul to stay in its body, but that signifies a time for change. Killing yourself is not the answer.

❦ *But when you hit the lowest point in your life, what do you do?*

When you hit the lowest point in your life, God is testing your strength. All that is required of you is *one positive step* to signify that you have the courage and the will to not give up. Once you pay off your karma and pass the test, your circumstances will change. God does send his angels

to help you. There are special spirit souls who choose to
work with humans who are suicidal. These spirit souls are
specially trained and they work with the person's Spirit
Guide, and through projection and prayer, try to enable
the person on Earth to hold on. They send messages
through the subconscious mind to give him strength to
survive. These special souls exist because God does not
want people on Earth to make the mistake of taking their
own lives, as the **consequences of this act are severe.** Open
your eyes, think about the reasons you have to live for:
your spiritual mission, service, and growth. Also
understand that sometimes the reasons for killing yourself
are completely ridiculous. For example, young people are
afraid to face their parents because they have failed their
exams and so they take their own lives. Nowadays a lot of
parents are very strict with their children and terrorise
them into doing wrong things. Some children are abused,
raped, blackmailed and harmed. At such times, if a child
has no one to confide in, he or she will tend to make rash
decisions like committing suicide. Parental guidance is not
about being strict – it is about understanding that child
and doing what is best for that child's soul. Sometimes a
parent's ignorance, cruelty and lack of understanding can
lead a child to suicide.

There are some children who want to jump out of the
window because they cannot handle their parents nagging
them or their intolerable cruelty. At such times it is
unbearable for the soul to stay in the body. A lot of
children kill themselves over something insignificant.
When they go to the spirit world, they understand how
reckless their actions were and how inconsequential their
fears. Such people need to know that failure is temporary,

a mere stepping-stone to success. Just as you need to experience sorrow in order to feel happiness, you need to experience failure in order to succeed. Failure is just a learning *experience*. It is the duty of all parents to teach their children love instead of fear and give them spiritual knowledge. Once this knowledge is imbibed, the child will open up and speak. Parents forget what is most important: being a good human being. Instead, they push their children in the wrong direction by teaching them that achievements in the physical world are all that matter, and so they misguide their children by giving them wrong notions of success.

☮ *How can one help these souls?*

Sometimes, all it takes to get someone out of their depression is **one small act of kindness** that restores their faith in others and in themselves. If you are aware that someone is going through a very hard time, try to reach out to them. You will be blessed if you manage to help someone handle their pain. The fate of those negative souls who cause others to end their lives is unimaginable. **A person who drives another person to commit suicide has committed a sin that is equivalent to murder.**

Sometimes, people use suicide as a form of emotional blackmail. In order to gain someone's attention, prove a point, or take revenge on someone, people attempt suicide or kill themselves. They do so in order to make the other person feel guilty. This makes them fall lower and they accumulate a great deal of karma.

Here are a few things to keep in mind when negative or

suicidal thoughts come to you. These thoughts must be stopped immediately because they will eventually take you down the wrong path:

1. When a negative thought comes, get rid of that thought immediately. Distract your mind and take positive action. The more you analyse it, the more power you give it. Get rid of such thoughts by diverting your mind elsewhere. Be physically occupied. It is never too late to change.

2. Read. Gain spiritual knowledge. Once you understand why certain things happen in your life, they become easier to accept and handle. For example, when you are familiar with the concept of karma, it becomes easier to go through tough times.

3. Open your subconscious mind because that is where your real strength lies. During hard times, the subconscious mind provides guidance and strength.

4. Do not worry about what people say. Never allow them to put you down. If what you are doing is good and right, and you are on the Godly Good Path, be firm, even if your parents are against you. But be sure that you are *truly* on the Godly Good Path and are not fooling yourself or acting out of pride.

5. If you have made a mistake, acknowledge it and change, but don't let the guilt consume you. It is human to make mistakes. The important thing is to learn the lesson and not repeat those mistakes. Also, do not try to cover up that mistake; otherwise, it will lead to more mistakes. Accept responsibility.

6. Pray hard, genuinely and sincerely, and ask God to send his angels to help you. It is important to ask God for guidance and protection.

7. Light a natural flame 24 hours a day. Light absorbs negative energy and clears the vibration around you.

8. Stay away from negative company and people who take you on the wrong path.

9. If you have a problem, talk to someone you trust. Another person's perspective may give you the clarity that is required. If there is no one you can trust on Earth, the most beautiful person you can talk to is your own subconscious mind, which is linked to the spirit world.

10. Remember that pain is temporary. Even good times do not last for long. Your problems will pass.

11. Keep your physical mind occupied. Do something constructive because your physical mind takes you down the wrong path when you are idle. Surround yourself with good people.

12. Get some exercise. Be active, go for walks. Breathe in fresh air; do not stay indoors all the time. Yoga is wonderful for the mind, body and spirit.

13. Do not be afraid to seek medical help. Prayers are very powerful but sometimes you need medical help too, so do not be ashamed to get it. Do not consider it a failure. Once the problem passes and you are stronger, you can reflect with more wisdom and then

change. However, *never* become addicted to medication.

14. Look after your health. So many people on Earth are slowly destroying their body with alcohol, drugs and cigarettes. Even overeating is harmful. These are forms of suicide because you are slowly killing your body, shortening the span of your own life and preventing your spirit from completing its journey. When you are under the influence of drugs or alcohol, your judgment is impaired and you are at your weakest, you are most susceptible to negative energy and projected negative thoughts, and you will act on an impulse that has not come from you, but has been projected to you by negativity. Another thing that you must take seriously on Earth today is sexual promiscuity. One weak moment can cause you a lifetime of pain. Humans give in to their desires instantly, and are very careless when it comes to looking after their bodies. Sexual promiscuity is a form of suicide because you are always at risk of contracting a disease that could end your life and in turn, the lives of others. This is *not* your karma. You choose to act in an irresponsible manner and these consequences are of your own choosing.

15. Try to reach out to someone else and help them even though you are in pain. That is how you strengthen yourself, by being compassionate towards others even though you may be hurting. Then, God will surely help you. But let your motive be selfless.

The human body is to be respected and cherished. You have been given a mind, body, and spirit so that you can live your life well and are able to serve others. There are times on Earth when human beings suffer a lot, especially those who have lost loved ones. Instead of blaming God and asking, "Why me?", be brave and look at the brighter side of life. Suicide is not the solution. When you go to the spirit world and review your life, you always realise that you could have handled much more, and suicide was not the answer. Your life belongs to God, and no one has the right to end it. Suicide is regression for the soul.

Besides the gift of life, God has given you a beautiful subconscious mind and a Spirit Guide. He has also given you a physical mind that acquires knowledge and can be trained to work in line with the subconscious mind thus helping you to know right from wrong. So much help and so much protection has been given to you that you must truly believe that no matter what obstacle comes your way you can handle it.

GOD

*"God does not have to prove Himself to us.
We have to prove ourselves to God."*

*"If you ask for proof, you will not get it. But if you don't ask for it
and you have faith, then you will get proof."*

"God does not punish you; your own subconscious mind does."

*"You can fool your fellow men, you can fool yourself,
but you can never fool God Almighty."*

*"A simple, honest, kind, selfless deed is more important than hours
of prayers without concentration, and giving thousands in
charity to fool people and our God Almighty."*

 *One of the earliest messages given was: "There is
no religion in the spirit world. We worship one God
only." Then why are there different religions on Earth?*

Even though there are different religions, they all
ultimately lead to the same Almighty Being. Your Earth
goes through cycles — good, bad, good, and then bad again.
When there is too much negativity on Earth, God sends a
very high soul from a higher universe to Earth to guide
people. He is called a **Prophet**. He imparts wisdom to
people so that they can improve and become good souls.

The followers of each Prophet are called by different names. Unfortunately, through the centuries, many of the Prophets' teachings have been twisted by human beings. However, there is no religion in the spirit world.

☟ Why do human beings find it hard to believe in God?

Your view of God changes over the course of your life. There are some who have a strong belief in God when they are young, but grow up and lose faith in Him. One of the reasons this happens is if you pray really hard for something and those prayers are not answered, you assume that God did not hear you and that He does not exist. But the truth is that when a prayer remains unanswered, perhaps what you prayed for was not good for your spiritual growth. You also lose faith in God when you have been subjected to injustice and you ask yourself why God does not provide justice. That injustice could be your karma, test, or training. Sometimes, when you are in poor health, you pray to get better, but there is no change in your health, and you lose faith in God. What you do not realise is that you could be paying off negative karma by going through health problems.

There are others who have no faith in God when they are young, but, over time, a series of experiences helps them develop faith. No matter what your experiences, understand that the choice to believe or not to believe in God is the most important one you have. When you are on Earth, your memory of the spirit world is blocked from the physical mind. However, you still have a connection to the spirit world through your subconscious mind. It is your subconscious mind that will guide you on Earth and will help you believe that God exists.

The biggest problem today is that human beings are always looking for a scientific explanation or proof of God's existence. The subconscious mind is infinite. But science is born out of human intelligence, which is limited. The intellect that humans possess is incapable of understanding God.

God does not have to prove Himself to us. We have to prove ourselves to God.

That is why we are on Earth. We are not here to test God. We are being tested to see if we choose the guidance of the subconscious mind over that of the physical mind. Some people are extremely analytical and need logical answers for everything. Faith and instinct play little or no part in their daily lives. These are people who operate mainly from the physical mind, or the intellect. In contrast, there are others who do not need logical answers for everything. They are able to move beyond rationale, beyond the confines of earthly logic, into the Realm of the spirit. It is only through your subconscious mind that you can *experience* God. You will never be able to understand God completely on Earth, but you can experience Him by choosing goodness. Intelligence is a great gift, but only if it is used in harmony with the gifts the subconscious mind brings — faith and wisdom.

The fact that you cannot see God does not mean He does not exist. The truth does not cease to be just because it is invisible to us. Our test on Earth is to believe in something that we cannot see by listening to our inner voice.

Sometimes, human beings have a very strong belief in God. But if something very painful occurs — such as the loss of a child or spouse, or a very strong injustice — the person tends to blame God and lose faith in Him. Yes, you no doubt feel pain, but instead of losing faith because of that pain, ask God to help you go through it. Earth is a place where there is a great deal of injustice. Good people suffer and bad people are often the ones in power, the ones who seem happy. There is a great imbalance on Earth right now, but that imbalance is our test and conflict, our teacher. In spite of all the injustices you may witness, do you still have the courage to believe in God and have faith in His justice?

There will come a day when good will overpower evil. But until then, darkness is a challenge. God allows darkness to exist so that good souls can be tested and trained. Eventually, when good will be in abundance on Earth, it will be easy to believe in God. You will surely feel His presence in abundance at that time. But if you fail to believe in God now, you will have not passed your test.

In your life, you will see many things. You might see children suffering, innocent men and women become victims of war, murderers going free and innocent people being jailed. You might be exposed to the worst crimes, the worst forms of injustice, and at that point you will ask yourself: Where is God? If God exists, why doesn't he do something? Why doesn't God stop this?

Well, God did not start this. Humans did. God has given

human beings free will and they use their free will to make negative choices. So right now, negativity is increasing and good souls are being tested. Their faith is wavering, they are getting fearful and angry, and they are being tempted to follow the wrong path. **There will come a point when nature itself will erase negativity.** At that time, more and more souls will be drawn to spirituality. But do not wait for that moment. Make a positive choice *now*, so that when the moment comes, you will have passed your test.

It is very easy to move towards the light when it is in abundance, when there is very little temptation, but it is extremely hard to embrace light when it is scarce on Earth, when negative souls are doing all they can to draw you away from it.

Think of yourself as a warrior and Earth as your spiritual battleground.

Do you give in to darkness because it is the easiest thing to do? Do you give in to darkness because it gives you the illusion of strength and power? Do you give in because of fear? Or do you have the wisdom to understand that darkness is a test, and that you must have the courage to fight it and choose God, to choose light, even if it is a much harder choice?

The strength of a true seeker depends on the strength of his subconscious mind. That is why you spend so much time in the spirit world developing it — because you know what kind of place you are going to and for what reason. This is why good and evil exist: so that you can move away from evil and choose good.

Negativity exists so that your free will can be tested. If there was no negativity, there would be no temptation, and there would be no opportunity to exercise free will.

Make the right choice. Resistance comes first: resist temptation. Action comes next. God is our Creator. He is a Supreme Being who is wise, just and loving. You can understand Him through goodness. The more you try to analyse God the more you are distancing yourself from Him, and the more you are denying yourself the chance to feel the peace that He can bring. God is not merely an idea or a way of thinking. He exists in form, but He is unseen on Earth for a reason. That is our test.

We are all looked after by a compassionate, wise, and just God. He is truly Almighty and He cares about all His creations and wants us all to follow the right path. We all have a chance to be blessed by Him; but to have His blessing, we must take the first step by choosing goodness. To know God is to know ourself, discover who we are, and discover His goodness within us.

PRAYER

"*The most powerful prayer is the prayer for the
spiritual growth of another being.*"

"*People pray to show off, people pray to prove to others that
they are truly pious. Prayers should be short and sweet and they have
to be full of feelings that are positive, genuine and totally selfless.*"

What is the purpose of prayer?

One of the most important aspects of spirituality is
prayer. Without prayer, you cannot grow. Just as the
human body needs food, so the spirit needs prayer. We all
need to pray to God so that He may bless us and give us
strength and wisdom to progress spiritually on Earth as
well as in the spirit world. Negative energy on Earth is
very strong and it is getting harder and harder for good
souls to do the right thing. It is not that good souls
cannot distinguish between right and wrong. They make
the *wrong choices* because they do not have the *strength* to
resist temptation, which is why it is so important to pray.
Prayer helps us put spiritual knowledge into action. It
builds spiritual muscle. Once that spiritual muscle is built,
you are strong enough to do the right thing no matter
what the temptation. Eventually, the soul is nourished as a
direct result of action, of putting knowledge into practice.

Prayer nourishes the soul. Prayer has to be genuine and sincere, from the heart. It is not the act of praying by itself, but rather the cycle of receiving strength from prayer and then doing what is right that brings you peace and helps your soul grow.

Contrary to what people on Earth think, prayer is not invisible.

When you pray, your thoughts, words, and feelings travel to the spirit world in the form of a ray of light. We, in the spirit world, can see millions and millions of rays of light travelling from Earth towards us. The brightness or strength of each ray of light depends on the sincerity and urgency of each prayer.

God has chosen good souls in the spirit world to work with Him and help Him answer prayers. These spirit souls are specially trained with respect to answering human calls for help. To answer a prayer, these souls send positive rays of light back to the person on Earth. That is why the word *prayer* consists of the word *ray*. Prayers are, essentially, positive rays of light.

ෙ *Does God listen to our prayers?*

When you pray, God *is* listening to your prayer. However, He is doing so through His angels, who intercept these prayers. Sometimes, people pray for life — for their own survival or for the survival of their loved ones. If they are good souls, they are given healing energies so that they have the strength to recover or to simply endure physical pain, if that is their karma. Sometimes, people pray

because they are confused. They do not know how to help
themselves or someone close to them so their prayers are
answered in the form of guidance or a message that is sent
through the subconscious mind. After receiving this
message, the person will have clarity. Certain calls for help
are so urgent and even complicated that spirit souls have
to consult the High Good Soul of the Realm. But please
understand that eventually, *all* souls who answer prayers
have to work with God's guidance and blessings, so yes,
**He does listen to your prayers – if they are sincere and
genuine.**

⚙ *Why do so many prayers go unanswered? Some
people have genuinely prayed, from the very depth of
their being, and yet their prayers have gone unanswered.
Why is this so?*

Your prayer will be answered only if:

1. What you pray for is good for you

    There are many times when human beings pray for
    something they think is good for them. When you
    think of things that are good for you, you think of
    them from an earthly point of view. But think of
    them from a spiritual perspective. If what you pray
    for hinders your spiritual growth in any way, the
    prayer will never be answered. So the next time you
    pray for something and it is not answered, understand
    that what you prayed for would not have been good
    for your soul. Also, whether a prayer will be answered
    at the right time, or not is not in your hands – it is in
    God's hands. When you look back at an unanswered
    prayer, you realise that it was not the right time for

God to grant you your wish. Sometimes human beings are just not ready to handle what they are praying for so fervently. **Ask God to do what is *best* for you.** In this manner, you are making sure that whatever happens will be for your spiritual growth. When you ask God to do what is best, you are handing over your life to a higher power that knows everything; it is a prayer of surrender.

2. Your prayer is genuine and sincere

    This is very, very important. Your prayer has to be genuine. It cannot be half-hearted or mechanical. The sincerity and faith in your prayer is what gives it power, and the manner in which angels respond to your prayer depends entirely on the *purity* and *motive* of your call for help. If your prayer is genuine and still remains unanswered, what you prayed for is not good for your spiritual growth.

3. Your prayer must be selfless and non-materialistic

    You need food, clothing and shelter to survive on Earth, but it is wrong to ask for luxuries. Luxury creates an imbalance that hinders your growth. Ask God to provide enough for your comfort. Also, if you are a person who prays *only* for material well-being, your prayers will not be answered. The most important thing to remember is that you should pray for the spiritual growth of others. This is what makes a prayer selfless.

4. It does not interfere with your karma

    One of the main reasons you are on Earth is to repay

karma. Sometimes people ask themselves why God is not helping them when they are praying so hard, but if what you are praying for relates to your karma you will still have to go through it. If you do not pray, or if you lose faith in God when your prayers are not answered, then angels cannot send you light and it will be harder for you to go through obstacles on Earth. There are many people on Earth who start praying *after* they have done something bad, believing that by praying their sins will be wiped out. **Your karma can never be wiped out by praying.** Genuine prayer gives you the strength to deal with your karma better; prayers do not wipe the slate clean.

5.   You are on the right path

There are many souls on Earth who are on the wrong path. But when they want something, they pray. The prayers of such souls cannot be answered. In fact, the only thing such souls who are on the wrong path should pray for is wisdom, so they may improve. This is the only call spirit souls will answer for people who are spiritually low. But if you are on the Godly Good Path, you deserve protection and healing, your prayer will be answered.

If you truly believe that God's angels are listening to your prayers, you will have no difficulty in praying whole-heartedly. Your angels are intercepting your prayers and doing everything they can, *within God's laws,* to answer them. So again, assure yourself that someone *is* listening to your call. Have confidence that they are wise, that they can see the complete picture from the spirit world, and that they will do what is best for you. Above all, know the power of prayer. It is an unbelievable force of light and it has the power to change lives. You have to believe that with all your heart.

☎ *Why are human beings so irregular with prayer?*

Humans are irregular with prayer mainly because when things are good they forget God and feel they do not need to pray. It is only when things go wrong that they wake up and remember God. Human beings have a problem with consistency. You want to be on the right path and make spirituality a priority in your life, but you are not regular with respect to your spiritual practices. There is, however, a simple solution to this. **You are inconsistent because you do not understand the *value and power* of spirituality.** If you feel that prayer is tedious, that it is a chore and time-consuming, you have not understood its value. Prayer means you are speaking to God Almighty — so what can be more important than that? Just knowing this should bring you joy. If you pray with faith and you believe that God is listening to you, you will never be lazy with respect to prayers, and when you know what prayer does for you, you will be naturally inclined to pray.

☎ *How do prayers help us?*

Here are the positive effects of prayer:

1. You will be at peace
   No matter what material wealth you possess, or what your position or status may be in an earthly sense, peace of mind can be attained only by being on the Godly Good Path. In this earthly world, a human

being goes through ups and downs. However, once prayer is a part of your life, you are activating your subconscious mind, and the subconscious mind helps you understand the very nature of those ups and downs. You will not let a problem crush you, nor will you allow success to bring pride.

Prayer keeps you calm, and calmness is required during a calamity. If you are calm and positive, and you do the right thing during tough times, you are passing your test; and once the test has been passed, the tough times pass as well. So you have changed the nature of the external factors (tough times) by the strength within (calmness).

If you do not stay calm, you are letting the tough times or negative external forces shake the feeling of peace within. You will be restless and confused and you will not have the calmness required to pass the spiritual test; and until you pass your test, the tough times will stay. In fact, the longer you take to pass your test, the harder your test becomes. Tough times become tougher because you have allowed the external forces to disturb your inner state of peace.

2. Your vibrations will improve
    Each prayer has a vibration or energy. When you pray, your prayers create positive energy. These positive vibrations have a healing effect on you and those around you, so you are clearing up the negative vibrations that surround you. When negative people are around you, their energy affects you and drains you, so be more aware and careful of people with negative energy. If you are fearful, proud, angry, depressed etc. by nature, you are lowering your own

vibration and weakening your spirit. Prayer helps you clear the negative energy that surrounds you so that a positive vibration can be built.

3. Your judgment improves
    When you pray, your own vibrations clear up and your negativity is erased. The black cloud of negativity that surrounds you is cleared and your higher self becomes active — that is, your subconscious mind awakens, and you become cool, calm, and clear, and your judgment improves. When your judgment improves, your choices are more positive. Thus, you are in a better position to perform selfless good deeds. As a result, you rise spiritually.

4. You receive protection from the spirit world
    Prayer is about you reaching out to the Creator. You have to ask for God's guidance and protection. Without asking for it, you will not receive it. Even if something is good for you, and you deserve it, spirit souls cannot give it to you if you have not asked — they would be going against your free will. So make sure you ask God to do what is *best*. When you ask for protection, the healing energies that spirit souls send you, along with the positive vibrations of your own prayer, build a protective shield around you that will guard you from negative forces.

5. You will experience a solution to illness
    If you pray with faith and sincerity, you will be surprised at its healing power. Medicine is important, but nothing in this earthly world can match the power of prayer. If you believe in its power and if you deserve healing, it will be given to you. Make sure that your physical mind is calm and clear and learn to

open your subconscious mind more. This will help you receive or access that healing.

6. You will get the strength to put your spiritual knowledge into action

    Having spiritual knowledge is not enough. You may know the difference between right and wrong, but you need the strength to resist temptation and make the right choice. That is what prayer does for you. It gives you the strength to manifest the will of your subconscious mind.

7. You will build faith

    You must always keep in mind that the faith with which you pray is of utmost importance. If you pray with faith, your prayer will be powerful, and will surely be answered. That answer helps you build more faith, continuing the cycle.

8. You will be protected from Black Magic

    The reason the vibration on Earth is so low is because many human beings are indulging in occult practices such as Black Magic (BM) or Witchcraft. This is completely against God's laws as it goes against someone's free will and is about using darkness for personal gain, to control, to harm, or to manipulate. Black Magic is an excess of projected negative energy. You may find it very hard to believe that it exists. Your logical mind will tell you that in an age of technology, no such thing is possible. We would have found it very hard to believe, too, if we were still on Earth. But Black Magic is dangerous, and has been prevalent on Earth for thousands of years. We have to make people aware of it so that they can protect themselves through prayer and positive thinking. All dark practices are completely against God's laws. Just as prayer creates an abundance of light, Black Magic creates an excess of negative energy. There is no reason to be fearful, just be aware, and understand that prayer is essential to protect you from this negative energy and therefore one must always be totally positive and fearless.

෬ How long should one pray for?

You need not pray for hours and hours. **Prayers should be short and sincere.** It is a false notion to think that the longer you pray, the holier you are. Pray for a short time, genuinely and regularly, so that the choices you make in your day-to-day life are a result of the strength that you derive from prayer. Some people like to pray for long periods of time – that is fine, provided it is sincere. Make sure you do not mutter, while your mind wanders everywhere else. Relax, concentrate, and be happy when you pray. Try not to pray in a fearful state.

෬ Does one need to be in a place of worship to pray?

Prayer is not about ritual. Places of worship are built so that people can assemble in groups and through their subconscious minds create more positive energy. Moreover, when people pray in groups, the power of a prayer increases. But do not feel guilty if you cannot visit a place of worship. Praying at home is extremely helpful because you are cleansing the vibrations of the place where you spend most of your time. So pray wherever you are, in a

car, at work, at school, anywhere. But when you pray at
home, do try to pray in one specific place. Make that place
your shrine, not by placing objects of worship, but by
exercising your strong faith and pure motive. It is your
prayer that builds your place of worship.

Here is something unusual that we would like to share
with you:

When you wake up in the morning, it is important
that you pray before you get out of bed, that is,
before your feet touch the ground, so that your auric
field absorbs that first morning prayer and keeps it
for the entire day. Once your feet touch the ground,
your protection is sucked into the ground. This is
because the Earth's vibrations are negative, and before
your feet touch the ground, your prayer builds a
protective shield around you – your prayer is
contained, and that good and powerful vibration is
held in your auric field for the day. It is important to
start your day in this manner.

Similarly, when you go to sleep at night, pray again
for your protection and for peace of mind, and your
auric field will retain that prayer as well. Then,
throughout the day, say short, sincere prayers. Pray
slowly; do not rush through. Mean every word you
say. Understand what you are saying, what you are
asking for, what you are requesting God to do for
you. Always keep in mind that prayers are meant to be
selfless – **the most powerful prayer is a prayer for
the spiritual growth of another being.**

Here is a short, simple prayer that will protect you

and keep you calm. Remember that there is no religion in the spirit world, so this is a prayer that anyone can say.

This prayer should be said **three times in succession, thrice a day.**

"My Dearest God Almighty,

Please our Lord, help us to avoid all evil and save us from such evil creatures.

Please take us in Your hands and guide us.

We are Yours, our God, and will be Yours always.

Keep us with You, our Lord, for eternity, so always and forever we will be blessed, guided, and helped by You and only You.

Thank You, God Almighty."

Nowhere in the prayer is the word 'I'. This is because it is important to pray for family and friends, and for good souls on Earth.

The line "Please take us in Your hands and guide us" means we are using our free will to surrender to God. We are placing ourselves in God's hands out of our own free will, with complete faith.

You might ask yourself why the word *evil* is mentioned in something as positive as prayer. On Earth, negative forces prevent us from being on the spiritual path. 'Evil' is the opposite of 'Live' —

anything that lures us away from the path of growth. We need to ask God to protect us from negative forces.

Finally, we are asking God to keep us with Him for "Eternity". We wholeheartedly ask Him to guide us and look after us in this lifetime and the next, forever.

At the end of this prayer, ask God to give you the strength and wisdom to do what is right. Then, pray for your family and loved ones. Finally, extend yourself — pray for good souls who may not be family or friends, but who are simple people in need of help. But remember the golden rule of prayer. **Ask God to do what is best for that person.** On Earth, you will not understand a person's karma, testing and training, so by asking God to do what is best, you are helping that person by sending positive energy without interfering with that person's path — test, training and karma. This is very, very important to keep in mind. No matter what, you will never completely understand someone else's journey, so ask God to do what is best for you, your family, your loved ones, and for anyone for whom you say a prayer. When you pray, keep hope alive. Expectation brings you down, but hope keeps you going. Know that God will do what is best for you. That is why you thank Him in advance — because you know He has heard your prayer and that He will never let you down. Pray consistently, and not only during bad times. Remember to pray to God and thank Him during the good times as well. Pray as hard as you can, but always leave room for God's Plan. Get out of the way and let heaven help you.

POSITIVE THINKING

"Be Positive."

"Like attracts like."

*"Control your mind and try to attain peace at all times.
Be cool, calm and sleep well."*

In what way are thoughts powerful?

The way you *think* is crucial to the development of your soul. You are the sum of your thoughts, words and deeds. Thoughts come first, and words and deeds arise out of thought — positive or negative thinking. This is why it is very important to think positively. Eventually, all thoughts create energy *so be aware of what energy you are creating.*

First, try to understand why people on Earth get negative.

Negativity can be a soul characteristic or a result of bad training in this life. But mainly, human beings get negative when they do not get what they want.

The first step towards thinking positively is to accept the fact that there will be problems. The ones who seem to be without problems are either handling their problems well or running away from them. Negative thinking is the main reason why many people get stuck in their spiritual journeys.

Negativity is a very common soul characteristic. It is an outcome of wrong understanding and a weak, uncontrolled, untrained mind. Moreover, the negativity in human beings is magnified because the Earth's vibrations have become very negative. It is up to you to think positively to combat this because your thoughts eventually manifest in the form of emotions. This is why thoughts are powerful. They manifest physically and emotionally and they shape your soul.

❧ *How will a person know if he or she is being negative?*

The following are the signs of negativity:

1. Fear

    Fear arises due to negative thinking, and a lack of faith and understanding. If you have full faith in God, there is no reason to be fearful. You are human, and you will face tough situations, but if you have faith you are given the courage to tackle these situations. The first thing to do to overcome fear is to increase your faith. There is a reason fear is so much a part of human existence right now. Good souls are afraid because the vibrations on Earth are negative, and these negative vibrations make you uneasy, as you are surrounded by an energy that is different from yours. You also fear that you will follow the wrong path; your subconscious mind understands this fear, but your physical mind does not — it only knows that it is afraid. **However, your subconscious mind is *never* afraid. It is aware.**

If you live in a place where the vibrations are positive, you will not feel fear. Keep your home simple and clean. Sunlight and plants help build positive vibrations and this will prevent you from being fearful. Fear also comes in the form of protective instincts, which are required for your own safety. For example, you will obviously be afraid to put your hand into a fire; this is a survival *instinct*.

Strange as it may seem, there are some people who are actually afraid of being positive. Perhaps they have had bad experiences in the past and are afraid of being hopeful, so they programme themselves into believing that life is not good and that they don't deserve any positivity in their lives. They gear themselves up for disappointment. Their justification is that they are being realistic, but they are not. A realistic attitude is to know that there are ups and downs in life, so it is natural to hope for the good times. No matter what your past experiences are, **hope is essential to human survival.** Sometimes people are afraid to change because they feel safe in that negative condition.

2. Worry

Constant worry only brings you down. People worry because they have lost faith and are too attached to outcomes. Results are not in your hands, but the process is. So do your best and then surrender to God. Complete surrender means knowing that God will do what is best for you after you have done your best. Surrender the outcome and be *consistent* in your surrender. Faith in God, your angels, your loved ones, and yourself is essential. Faith is the energy that drives you forward and brings you peace. Being without faith is like expecting a car to move forward without fuel. **Do your best and leave the rest to God.**

3. Doubt

When you constantly doubt yourself, your spiritual teacher, and most importantly, God, you are being negative. It is okay to ask questions, but if you are on the spiritual path, you must replace doubt with faith. **Trust your guides.** If you keep doubting them and asking for proof after they have given you knowledge and understanding, you are being negative.

There is a man who prays very hard each night. At the end of his prayer, he always asks God to do what is best for him. But somehow, things don't seem to work out in his life. He cannot understand why God does not answer his prayers. One day, an angel appears before him. "I have a gift for you," says the angel. The man is overjoyed. The angel asks the man to open his palms. The man does so as though he is about to accept an offering. The angel looks at the man's palms and blows on them. "You're welcome," says the angel. The man is confused because his palms are still empty. "But where's my gift?" he asks. "It has already been given to you," says the angel. "Your hands were full of doubt. I removed all doubt. Sometimes something that is taken away from you is a greater gift than something that is given to you."

Make sure that you trust God and do not doubt Him.

When you constantly doubt, your spirit is weakened because your spirit survives on faith in God.

4. Nagging

Nagging is spiritually wrong. It is a form of mental torture, a one-way assault of words. It comes out of ego and a lack of understanding and is an act of selfishness because you want to be heard at all costs and you want your way, no matter what. When parents nag their children it is very harmful, even though the motive is to help. When you nag, you are going against God given free will. Instead of listening to you, the person being nagged will not listen at all and will turn a deaf ear and may even do exactly the opposite if the nagging continues.

5. Constantly complaining and grumbling

A negative person does not know the meaning of happiness. If you whine and moan your way through life, you attract misery. Some people encourage this trait in others by showing sympathy. It is essential to count your blessings. Accentuate the positive. Don't focus on the negative.

6. Taking on more problems than you are required to

Some people want to show the world how much they are doing, how much they are suffering. They are only harming themselves. A failure to ask for help means you are being proud and negative. You are on Earth to coexist, not to handle everything on your own. This need to prove that you can handle things on your own is your ego talking. It is unnatural. No one expects you to be superhuman.

7. Jealousy

One of the things that robs people of happiness is jealousy. When you constantly compare your journey with someone else's, it holds you back. Be content with your gifts, and also learn to derive joy and inspiration from the accomplishments of others. That is how spirit souls live, and it brings us true happiness. Thank God for all that you have and learn the art of contentment.

8. Blaming others

Always look within yourself and you will recognize the source of your pain. Pain can be triggered by someone else only if it already exists within you. So get to the root of the pain. Do not focus on the other person. Correct the imbalance within you, improve yourself first, and then try to help others change.

9. Addiction to negative thoughts

Over time, people who are constantly negative become so used to that feeling that they cannot do without it. If they have no problems, they will create problems and drama. In many cases, self-pity and depression become habits. They start small, but are allowed to escalate into something huge.

10. Impatience

When you learn to develop patience, you will be more at peace. Impatience puts you off-balance. Remember that things happen at the right time: timing is in God's hands, and when you are impatient you are dictating terms to God. You are asking Him to put His Plan aside and put yours into motion. Your plan is always limited. God's Plan is infinite.

☙ In what way does negativity affect us physically, emotionally, and spiritually?

Negativity becomes a *habit*, a way of living for many people. Even though there is nothing wrong with their lives, they are so used to being hopeless, cynical, bitter, and defeated that they are constantly putting out that energy. Like attracts like. Therefore, negative people attract negative people and situations towards them, and this pattern is very harmful to their souls. Get rid of this pattern and replace it with positivity; do not be afraid of change. The following are the effects of negativity:

1.   Your judgment goes wrong

When you are negative, your judgment goes wrong. This will affect the choices you make in your day-to-day life and you will fall spiritually lower.

2.   You lose small gifts

Life has many small gifts waiting for you. When you are negative, these gifts can be staring you in the face, but you will fail to see and accept them. If you are negative, you will be unable to listen to the guidance of the subconscious mind that *directs* you to those gifts. Over time, your energy becomes so dark that gifts, being of a light nature, cannot come to you. Like attracts like, so you attract problems instead of gifts.

3.   People sense your imbalance

Like humility, positivity is a natural state of being. Good
people will sense a negative vibe around you, feel
uncomfortable, and spend less time with you. Since your
judgment is clouded, you will fail to understand why this
is happening and you will become negative with others
instead of understanding that the imbalance is within you.

4.   Your health is affected

Thoughts are very, very powerful. Your thoughts and
feelings will always manifest physically. Negative thoughts
and feelings manifest in the form of illness or injury. If
there is bitterness and anger within, it will manifest in
your body. Your inability to forgive yourself or someone
else leads to a breakdown of the body. Forgiveness brings
about healing; it is good for you and essential for your
growth.

5.   You fail your test

A very basic test given to most people is whether they can
remain positive in a tough situation. That situation may
not be their karma, but it is a test or training for the
spirit. If they react negatively and go through the whole
process complaining and feeling sorry for themselves, the
situation is repeated again and again until the lesson has
been learned. The process of learning to be positive in
tough times is the test — not the situation.

How you go through the process is important. For
example, no one likes to be sick, but if you are a person
who complains whenever you are ill and you make life
difficult for those around you, the lesson you need to

learn is to be positive *while* you are ill and appreciate the help others are giving you. The test is to remain positive during the illness. Another test may be that of fear. If you are terrified of medical reports, you will be in situations that will require you to go for medical tests over and over again. The test is for you to not be fearful during the process.

6.   You over analyse

Looking within yourself is a good thing, but when you over analyse, you get stuck. You keep thinking and fail to take action. You will over analyse a situation and keep on asking *why,* instead of accepting a situation as it is, taking action, and moving on.

7.   You are weakening the subconscious mind

Negative thoughts come only from the physical mind. The subconscious mind, even in the most trying of circumstances, will see things in a positive light. So when you give preference to negative thoughts, you are choosing the physical mind over the subconscious mind. The physical mind is getting what it wants, so you are spoiling it, and the subconscious mind is being ignored.

☸ *How does a negative person change for the better?*

There is a simple word that goes a very long way in preventing you from doing wrong in all aspects of your life: *control.* **Control your thoughts by controlling and training the physical mind.** The moment a negative thought enters your mind, do not analyse it. Get rid of it immediately. Out of habit you will entertain the thought,

but learn to break that habit. Initially, it will be difficult.
You might even experience a sense of fear when you get rid
of negative thoughts. "What if I need to analyse this?
What if this will happen? What if? What if?" Well, what
good does worry do? It does no good at all. So control the
negative thought. That is the first step. The next step,
which is even more important, is to replace negative
thoughts with positive ones. To be positive means to
understand the higher nature of things. Whatever your
path, learn to view it from a spiritual perspective. This will
help you cope with problems because you will understand
that they are invaluable. When faced with problems, be
mentally and physically occupied.

Problems do not stop your path. They *are* your path.

Both blessings and problems are part of the journey.

How can you be positive when faced with disappointments? By knowing that disappointments are part of the
learning process. Therefore, do things without expectation.
Hope is a beautiful thing, and it must be kept alive but
expectation is a demand that comes from your ego. Hope
is not about the outcome. Hope is staying positive
throughout the process and believing that the outcome
will be the best for your growth. We must surrender the
outcome to God, and remain positive and hopeful
throughout the process. Hope is what keeps your spirit
alive. Expectation weighs your spirit down.

If you are at a job that you dislike, being positive means
understanding that perhaps it is your test and you are
paying off a karmic debt, perhaps you need to learn to
appreciate something good that comes your way, or

perhaps you have been placed there for a short while to help others.

It can be devastating when you lose someone close to you. It is natural to feel shattered, but spirit souls do not want you to mourn for them. If they are good souls, they are in a better place so allow yourself to heal. Make sure you have every intention of healing yourself because that is what your loved ones want. Spirit souls do not want earthly souls to grieve their whole lives. When you cut your hand the blood flows out but, in time, the wound heals. It is the same with grieving. There is a time to grieve and a time to heal.

When we come to the spirit world, we are happy. We are alive and well and most important of all, we are still with you. We need you to believe that. When the pain gets unbearable, focus on this truth and hold on to it. This is what we mean by being positive in the face of a terrible loss. Derive strength from the fact that we are still with you and can guide you if you let us. Our Mom and Dad sometimes felt so lost and miserable without us that it would have been very difficult for us to calm them down and cheer them up without spirit communications. We explained to them that when they were upset, it saddened us as well. Most importantly, we let them know that we were nearer to them now than we were on Earth and that we loved them tremendously.

It is easy to be positive when things are going well. The real test is to be positive when life is difficult, when things are not going your way. That is how you evolve as a person. **Positivity is a choice no matter what the situation.**

Sometimes, you are unable to control your mind, or you might succeed at controlling your mind, but you will not know how to be positive. There is a very simple reason for this and it has to do with choice. You have to be completely committed to change and use your will. Therefore, even the physical mind has to cooperate with you. The reason people fail is that their commitment is weak. Their efforts are half-hearted and they are not fully dedicated to change. You *choose* to be positive. You *choose* to forgive someone. You *choose* to be humble. You *choose* to be content. Success or failure depends on the strength of your choices. Let's suppose that you have a tough time forgiving someone for the pain they have caused you. After having the knowledge, if you are still unable to forgive, it is because you don't *want* to, not because you don't know *how* to.

Being brave and keeping a positive attitude when things are going badly is the true meaning of positivity. Never lose hope, no matter how dire the circumstances.

Keys to Positive Thinking:

1. Have full and complete faith in God. Know that He will do what is best for you.

2. Accept your karma, tests, and training. Do not resist these.

3. Pray. Ask God for strength. The strength that you need to be positive in a situation can come only from prayer and is given to you only if you ask. Your prayer will build positive vibrations around you, and will improve your judgment so that you take the right action.

4. Activate the subconscious mind. Use it when dealing with problems. Do not use the limited understanding of the physical mind.

5. View problems as an opportunity to grow.

6. Exercise. Physical activity, such as yoga (it is vital to find a good teacher), dance, swimming, any sport is essential. The mind, body and spirit must all be healthy.

7. Surrender to God. To surrender means to follow the Godly Good Path, to do everything in your capacity, and then to let God take care of the outcome.

8. Do things that you like. Be occupied. They should be simple things that bring you peace of mind, such as reading, listening to music, cooking, gardening, swimming or whatever nourishes your heart and soul.

9. Learn to coexist. Share your time and experiences with people you trust and make sure you spend time with people who inspire you and who are positive influences.

10. Help someone else. Sometimes, when you are in pain, this is the best thing you can do. A change of focus distracts you from your own pain and you also learn to be selfless.

11. Laugh. Be light.

Enjoy your life. You are on Earth to enjoy your life without harming yourself or others. Know what makes you happy and know what brings you down. **Do not be of the view that you are on Earth to suffer. Yes, your karmic** debts have to be paid off, *but your earthly journey should be joyous.* Do not take life too seriously. Have a sense of humour. Be light. Again, the key word is balance. Try not to be too intense about situations; on the other hand, do not be frivolous and avoid responsibility either.

Make the most of your earthly journey. Humour and a sense of play are very important parts of light. In the spirit world, everyone has a sense of humour. We love what we do, we love our existence, and we laugh a lot. There is song, dance, and celebration. You will understand the meaning of celebration when you come to the spirit world. To celebrate is to know that you are created by God, that you are doing His work, and that a great deal is still unknown, even to us. Yes, we celebrate the unknown, the part of our journey that still awaits us. We are joyous because if we are happy now, at this stage of our existence, imagine how happy we will be in the seventh universe as we move closer and closer to God. This is surely something to celebrate.

PRIDE AND HUMILITY

"Put your pride in your pocket."

"Do not act humble. Be humble."

 Why do human beings have pride or ego?

One of the most common flaws that human beings possess is pride. Every single person has some form of pride or **ego**, which can be very dangerous if not controlled immediately. No spiritual journey can exist without humility. Pride is applicable to all human beings at some point in their lives. Some people have pride because of money, some because of their good looks, and others because of their intelligence, but strangely, most people have it when they really do not have anything to be proud about. This is because of insecurities and complexes. They build walls as a defence mechanism to protect the false image they have created. They are not being genuine and are walking away from the path of truth. In today's world, pride is the greatest downfall of individuals, as everyone believes what they are doing is right. If people do not control this pride, their judgment will go wrong because they will be unable to experience true understanding. An ordinary person who may not have status in the earthly world, but is humble, will be respected in the spirit world, unlike a proud person who is successful in a material sense. A humble person will attract good people, not flatterers, and people will come to him for genuine advice. But people who are proud always end up lonely, are suspicious of the people around them, and will never be genuinely liked by others.

Another reason people develop pride is due to earthly fame and success. Sometimes, people with equal amounts of talent have different levels of success. This has to do with their tests, training and karma. **Failure is a test and so is success,** to see how you handle both. Success and failure do not make you superior or inferior. If taken in the right way, failure is actually a blessing because it crushes your ego and teaches you humility. Moreover, success may not have been good for you at that time. When you have learned to be humble, you can handle the success that comes your way. So when you achieve certain goals, do not let pride set in. Instead, recognize that you have been helped by a higher power to reach where you are. Be aware of the fact that when you accomplish something, there will always be people who will give you undue importance just to be in your good books. Remember that when you have been given success, it is always a test. Sometimes, early success without too much effort makes you believe you are invincible. This early success is a test. It should not lead to pride. So, slow and steady, step by step is a safer way to climb the ladder of success. **True success is spiritual success and not earthly success.** The idea is to grow spiritually even though you live in an earthly physical, material world. So even when earthly success comes, your focus should be to evolve spiritually and the earthly success should be used for the greater good of humanity.

That is how you lead a balanced life on Earth. The human flaws that are an outcome of ego are endless. But if you are a sensible human being, you will realise that these are dangerous flaws to have, as they slowly but surely kill the spirit. Each time the ego gives you a feeling of invincibility, remind yourself that you are human and your life can change in a second, in an instant. **Instead of feeling great, feel grateful.**

ᕕᕗ *In what way is pride harmful?*

Pride leads to:

1. Loss of judgment

    When you are proud, you operate completely from the physical mind, and the physical mind has very little to do with making the right spiritual choices. Your judgment is spiritually impaired because you are not using the subconscious mind and your ego prevents you from listening to anyone else; it makes you believe that your point of view is the *only* point of view. Also, you are so concerned with what other people think and how they should perceive you that you end up making choices based on what they think. Your choices may not have anything to do with the truth.

2. Spiritual downfall

    Pride prevents you from acknowledging God. It makes you believe that there cannot be a higher power. It convinces you that you are an intellectual being, and as such, you need rational reasons for believing in God. Pride gives too much importance to the intellect and no importance to the subconscious mind, which knows that God exists. A truly balanced person's intellect and subconscious mind will work in alignment.

3. Lower vibrations

If you do something negative, the result is negative. Think of this negative energy as a dark cloud around your head that prevents light from coming through. If light (wisdom) cannot come through, your judgment becomes impaired even further. This creates a cycle wherein you make even weaker choices. Wrong actions build up negative vibrations. Your low vibrations affect you, as well as those around you. They will sense this negative cloud around you and stay away. Also, negative energy around you attracts more negative energy.

4. Injustice

The ego makes you believe that you are always right, no matter what. Therefore, instead of being open-minded, your understanding of situations will be limited, and you will force your opinion on others. You will thus go against their free will, which is a great injustice. Unfortunately, you will fail to see it that way, as you will be blinded by your ego.

5. Jealousy

It is your ego that compares your journey with someone else's. Instead of gratefully accepting the gifts you have, the ego will make you focus on what you do not have. Not only that, it will make you resent the gifts and accomplishments of others. The ego makes you an insecure, jealous being.

6.   Discontent

One of the most important lessons a person must learn on Earth is to be content. Ego is an outcome of the physical mind. It makes you want more and more. If you have an ego, you are always exercising the physical mind and giving it too much power. The physical mind goes far beyond earthly *needs* and creates *desires*. You then give in to those desires and pursue wealth, power, and fame. Even after acquiring these, you are not satisfied; you are still not content. The ego makes you want things, but when those wants are met, the ego creates new wants. You continue to feed those wants, giving them more importance and power. But if you are humble, you are exercising the subconscious mind, and the need of the subconscious mind is focused and very simple — it is only concerned about doing what is spiritually right. **Also, when you are humble enough to follow the advice of the subconscious mind, it gives you something in return — a feeling of peace. Contentment is a result of following the advice of the subconscious mind.**

The subconscious mind gives you advice
↓
Since you are humble, you follow that advice
by taking positive, spiritual action
↓
As a result of positive action, the subconscious
mind gives you a feeling of peace
↓
That feeling of peace gives you the strength to
listen to the subconscious mind again and take
more spiritual action and therefore rise spiritually

7. Enemies

    Due to rash and irrational behaviour, you create
    enemies. At the time, your ego will say, "I don't care,"
    but later on, when it is too late, you will regret it.

8. Loss of relationships

    Relationships are about coexistence, and pride goes
    against the concept of coexistence because it is about
    superiority. Therefore, it is impossible to have a
    healthy relationship as ego will always form barriers.

9. Expectations

    The ego creates expectations. It has a fixed agenda. Its
    way of thinking is: no matter what, this has to be
    done; this *has* to come *my* way. This is the true cause
    of misery because the ego cannot cope when its
    agenda is not fulfilled. It gets impatient and does not
    understand that **timing is in the hands of a higher
    power.** Moreover, expectations create anxiety because
    they build unnecessary pressure. The ego makes you
    expect things from yourself, from others, and creates
    a false need to live up to other people's expectations.
    Try not to create expectations, but always keep hope
    alive. The ego does not know the meaning of hope, as
    you have to depend on something *outside of yourself,*
    which means complete surrender of the outcome and
    leaving room for God's Plan. The ego cannot handle
    this, as it knows only control of self and others.

    ෴ *What exactly does it mean to have hope?*

Hope is not about holding on; it is about letting go. This
may be a strange concept for you because the expression

normally used is 'hold on to hope'. Hope is not wrong, but do not hold on to the outcome. Hope is not about having fixed expectations. It is about going through the process in a zestful and enthusiastic manner. In a sense hope means that a person lives positively day by day, and also has faith in the future. To "keep hope alive" is to go through the process of any situation positively, in the best way you can, and know that God will do what is best for you. That way, you are not attached to the outcome, but you have understood the importance of the process. The ego only knows how to cling on to the outcome; surrender, on the other hand, is a natural function of the subconscious mind.

ஓ How does one deal with the ego?

The fight between the ego and the subconscious mind will last a lifetime, but you cannot embark on a spiritual journey until you make a strong effort to eliminate your own ego. Here are three simple steps to start on this path:

I. Analyse yourself

    There are varying degrees of pride – some human beings have more and some have less. However, all human beings have some sense of pride. Yes, riches, fame, power, beauty, gifts, talents etc. are all obvious things that lead to pride. But the worst kind of pride is spiritual pride – the pride of thought – the 'I' factor, that is, "I am right", "I am humble", "This has happened because of me", "So many people come to me for help and guidance", "I do a lot of social work", "I am a great healer", "So many people are drawn to me", "I have built many hospitals and schools for people", "I am a very religious person", "I know", "I have achieved so much", "I am very good at my work/job/profession".

The moment the 'I' factor appears, it is a sign of pride and the first step towards your spiritual downfall. All success, talent etc. come from God. We are His instruments, given these gifts to share and for the service of man. We have to be grateful and thank God for all that is given to us and we should humbly accept these blessings and not feel 'I' did it all.

Now analyse yourself and accept the fact that you are a proud person. Sometimes, when you give it proper thought, you will feel foolish about being proud. Pray to God and ask Him to guide you. This is the most difficult step, to **recognise and acknowledge** that you are proud and to have a **true desire to change.** It is difficult to start walking on the spiritual path because this requires change. The ego knows this; it knows that it will eventually be discarded, and this is what it does not want. Therefore, it will make you resist change, so your resolve has to be much stronger than your ego.

2.   Control your pride

Understand that pride is in *thought.* When you do something good or achieve something, a feeling of pride may set in, but do not think and act proud. Distract your mind by thinking of something completely different. The first few times, it will be very hard to control yourself – like trying to break a bad habit you have become accustomed to. Your physical mind has become so used to this bad habit that you start believing you cannot do without it.

·Slowly, these thoughts will diminish and soon disappear. The urge will be there, but the test is not to give in. Even if you fail the first few times, do not be angry or negative; instead, **be humble enough to accept that you might fail initially.** Relax and try again. The key is to go on genuinely trying until you succeed, and you will succeed if you are positive and consistent. You will notice that things get simpler and clearer, and you will begin walking on the right path. Most importantly, maintain your control.

3. Replace proud thoughts with humble ones

Write down your unclear thoughts or understanding of things so they can be cleared and replaced by correct thoughts and understanding. In this manner, that small, proud thought will not develop into full-blown ego. Proud thoughts will still arise from time to time, but you will know to control your mind. Remain consistent in your effort.

🕉 *Are people born proud or do they acquire this quality over time?*

The fact that human beings have a physical mind means there is a very strong possibility of developing a full-blown ego on Earth. Some people have less pride than others, and some have more. This is because some souls had worked on crushing their ego in their previous lives and are humble now, whereas others failed to acquire humility and have taken rebirth with the sole purpose of crushing the ego. Unfortunately, the ego gets more inflamed on Earth and they end up acquiring many more flaws due to the ego.

Here is a simple example:

Revenge is one of the greatest sins because it is planned. It is done with negative intention. Take the case of a person who is on a spiritual level of Realm 4 Stage 5. He may not necessarily be a revengeful person, which means that his soul is not of a revengeful nature. But somehow he becomes proud. Something happens in his external world, an earthly achievement perhaps, that feeds his ego. His subconscious mind gives him hints that he is developing pride, but he does not listen to the advice of his subconscious mind because he is enjoying the sense of pride. That is the problem with pride. It makes you feel powerful and you get used to the feeling. Over time, this pride grows, until the ego becomes monstrous and wants to keep a check on everything around it, especially the achievements of others. When someone else does something good, the ego becomes inflamed as it always wants to be number one. It wants to be extra-special. It does not realise that God has made everyone special and equal. That is why comparison is wrong. When the ego starts making comparisons, *jealousy* sets in. When the comparisons continue day-in and day-out, the person starts to burn from within and *anger* develops. That burning, that intense negative feeling, feeds on itself like wildfire and becomes so extreme that it turns into *hatred*. Once you have reached the stage where there is hatred within you, you have allowed your subconscious mind to diminish so it has no effect on you, and no amount of logical reasoning will pacify you. You will be blinded by that hatred and you will be driven to take *revenge*. Once you take revenge on someone, the subconscious mind shuts down and you have very little chance of recovery. So that

soul on Realm 4 Stage 5 may not initially have revenge as
a soul characteristic, but the fact that he has not kept his
pride in check has led to his spiritual downfall.

PRIDE

↓

JEALOUSY

↓

ANGER

↓

HATRED

↓

REVENGE

Revenge is one of the lowest human qualities, and spiritual
law has no tolerance towards revengeful people. So be
aware of pride because if it is not cut off immediately, it
can become a very powerful negative force that harms the
spirit. A person can take revenge in different ways. Revenge
is not about causing bodily harm; that is a literal view of
it. You can take revenge on someone by putting them
down, make them feel small or by manipulating them into
doing wrong deeds. When you knowingly cause someone
physical, mental, emotional, or spiritual harm, you are
taking revenge.

🕮 *What does it mean to be humble?*

1.   To be aware that you are created by a higher power

     A true seeker, a person who walks the spiritual path, is
     a humble person. Such a person has a very clear
     understanding of what creation means and is aware

that he was created by God. To be humble is to never lose awareness of this truth. We are all created by God and we all belong to Him. To belong to a wise, just, and compassionate God is a blessing and it is up to us to maintain that connection by being humble.

2.   If pride is about the self, humility is about selflessness

To know God, and to know His qualities, *live* His qualities. The very first quality of God is humility. Humility is a natural form of existence. If you observe nature, you will understand that God has created beauty, and what gives His creations beauty is not only the appearance, but the fact that nature is a humble provider. It is completely selfless. It is this selfless quality that is the essence of all spirituality. Moreover, nature coexists: streams become rivers, rivers become seas, and seas form oceans. There is balance, unity, harmony, and above all, humility in nature. The stream never tells itself that it wants to be an ocean. It understands its place in the universe, accepts its function humbly with joy, and continues to serve a greater whole. This is how God wants human beings to live. The true art of spirituality is selfless service – a quality nature has in abundance.

3.   Do not *act* humble. *Be* humble.

Just as pride is in thought, so is humility. The ego is a master at disguising its impure intentions as righteous and good, and fooling you into thinking that what you are doing is right. This is because the ego is selfish and has to satisfy its agenda at any cost. This cost can be your own subconscious mind and soul. So many humans wear the mask of humility:

their actions and words give the impression that they are humble, but their thoughts are full of pride and they feel superior. They might fool people for some time, but these souls are eventually exposed.

4.   If you are on the spiritual path, do not feel proud and righteous.

If you are on the spiritual path, do not become proud about it. When you have all the required knowledge to live your life on Earth, and you *still* choose to do wrong, your spiritual downfall is faster and more severe. There are many people on Earth who think they are doing God's work. They think that by spreading knowledge and telling people how they should live their lives, they are contributing to light. But so many so-called spiritual leaders are proud of the fact that they have knowledge. **This is spiritual pride, the worst kind of pride.** It is corruption of the spirit at the highest level. If you want to gain spiritual knowledge and improve, choosing the right guru is the most important step. Be aware of the fact that many gurus are so power hungry that they know exactly how to manipulate the student. They will feed the student's ego and may use your own fears to manipulate you. The spiritual path is not easy. It involves hard truths. It requires you to look within yourself and accept your flaws. The wrong guru will feed you only what you want to hear, not what you need to. **A true guru is always a student as well.** That is the first sign that can denote whether a guru is humble or not.

5.   Always remember that you are a student of God.

All the knowledge you possess, the skills that you

have, and the goodness that exists within you, is not
yours. It flows through you. Your mind, body, and
spirit are fortunate to be a channel for that flow of
goodness. That flow keeps you on the right track. But
when you start taking *ownership* of that flow and begin
believing that it is you who is responsible for its
existence, you are slowly but surely reducing that
flow, until it will one day become a trickle, and will
eventually come to a halt. That flow of goodness has
not left you. You have left it. You have left it by being
proud. According to spiritual law, that flow will be
drawn to humility. It will seek another channel that is
not corrupt in spirit, a channel that is open enough
to understand the concept of service. As channels, you
are servers. By serving, you become co-creators. But
the moment you feel proud, you choose to operate
alone and to disconnect yourself from God, and you
will be left with your own mind and body, which are
extremely limited. Your spirit, of course, will continue
to diminish much faster than the mind and body,
because it is the one thing that cannot live without
God, without nourishment from the source.

To be of worth, you need spiritual wealth and strength.
The ego wants to be in control and it tells you that by
acknowledging God, you are powerless. By breaking away
from God, your ego gives you the illusion of power. It will
drive you relentlessly to achieve material wealth and fame;
it will make you restless, and you will mistake that
restlessness for a positive drive and try and attain more
and more in your physical world. By exercising the ego and
giving more importance to the physical mind than the
subconscious mind, you are completely ignoring the spirit

and strengthening the dangerous muscle of pride. That illusion breaks only when you die. When your spirit is evaluated, you are completely disillusioned. That disillusionment is the moment of truth that has arrived too late — you realise that your spirit, which is eternal, is the only thing of true value. You spent your whole life on things that were temporary. You focused all of your energy on attaining physical and material power. **Do not think of power. Think of spiritual strength.** The things you can see are temporary; the things that are not visible are eternal. If you live your life with this truth in mind, you will not be greedy for endless material wealth and fame. In fact, when that wealth and fame comes, you will be grateful for it, and you will be very aware of the fact that you have been put in a position to inspire others and do God's work. **To do God's work means to use your position of strength to help others grow.** To heal, to strengthen, and to eventually help someone else's spirit to soar should be the ultimate goal of every human being.

ॐ *Why do some people feel that humility is a weakness?*

This is because they do not understand the true meaning of humility. Self respect goes hand in hand with humility. It means that no matter what happens, you will always make choices that will never harm the spirit — yours or someone else's. It means having the right judgment, knowing your limits, and not hurting or disrespecting someone else. Humility should not be seen as a weakness. In fact, pride is a weakness that prevents you from accepting your flaws. Humility helps you work from your subconscious mind, and the subconscious mind is not concerned about appearances — it will crush the ego and do what is right. Sometimes, you will admit your flaws, but you will still feel resentment. An acceptance of flaws should bring you peace, not resentment. It takes some people a very long time to admit that they are wrong. This is a strong sign that the ego is at work. Humility is of utmost value because it enables you to access the moral truth within you and helps you be your own guide. How can that be a weakness? Humility allows you to be really honest with yourself. You will be able to judge within a second if your ego is hurt or if you are simply being firm in your beliefs. To take a moral stand is a good thing because you are responding from your spiritual core. **To be humble is *not* to tolerate evil.** A lot of people use humility as an excuse for being cowardly and that is, indeed, a weakness. Humility means you fight evil by not encouraging it, knowing that the strength to do so comes from God.

⚙ *How will a person know if he or she is proud?*

The following are **Signs of Pride:**

1. You do not believe in the existence of God.
2. It is very hard for you to accept your flaws.
3. When you find out that you were wrong and someone else was right, you cannot handle it.
4. You run away from the truth.
5. You think you are superior to others.
6. You think only you are gifted.
7. You believe you are indispensable.

8. You feel you know everything and have no desire to acquire spiritual knowledge.

9. You feel your point of view is the only point of view.

10. You constantly put people down and make them feel small.

11. You do not care if you hurt someone's feelings.

12. You feel you are responsible for all the good that happens to you.

13. You fail to accept the fact that there are others who are much better than you in something.

14. You feel prayer is unimportant.

15. You lack the understanding that everyone has flaws and that all people make mistakes.

16. You think only about yourself.

17. You are impatient, irritable (people's flaws irritate you), and very stubborn.

18. You resist change.

19. You can't handle it if someone does not agree with you.

෩ *How does one acquire humility?*

1. Open the subconscious mind. When you operate from the subconscious mind, humility will become a natural state of existence for you.

2. Pray. When you pray genuinely and regularly, you are constantly aware of the fact that you are created by God. This will keep you humble.

3. Understand coexistence and unity. God created everyone equal. So the moment you consider yourself superior to someone else, there is a flaw in your thinking. We all come to Earth with different gifts for our own tests, training, and mission, so there is no question of being superior.

4. Learn how to serve others. The ego wants to fulfill its own desires, but humility leads you to the path of service.

5. Be open and understand someone else's point of view.

6. Accept your flaws; only then can you change.

7. Always be open to spiritual knowledge. A humble person is always a student. **However, do not go too deep into spirituality.** What we mean by this is do not get stuck in the theory. As a student, *practice* whatever you have learned, *step by step*. **After you practice what you have learned, you are strengthening the spirit, but if you get obsessed with the knowledge alone, and do not work on changing yourself from within, you are strengthening the ego.**

8. Be compassionate. Keep others' feelings in mind. Be considerate and understand their situations.

9. Have patience. Keep in mind that people are at different stages of spiritual development, and that their tests, training, and karma are different. They also have varying levels of spiritual knowledge. **Do not judge them; help them grow.**

10. When something good happens to you, or when you achieve something in your earthly world, *always thank God*, and also thank the people on Earth and in the

spirit world who have helped you.

11. When you are unsure of something, ask for advice from a person you trust. Today, one of the main problems is that people are too proud to ask for help or advice. They see it as a sign of weakness. It requires strength to be open about the fact that you need help. But not asking for help and convincing yourself that you can go through problems without anyone's help, is a sign of pride.

12. Surrender to God. Do your best to stay on the right path, but know that the outcome is in God's hands. His Plan is of a higher nature than what you have in mind.

Spirituality involves crushing of the ego, and that can be a terrifying thing for people who are proud. So if you are very proud, it will be very difficult for you to embark on a spiritual journey. It is not impossible for a proud person to change, but a proud person will have to work hard to change because the ego will work extra hard to prevent you from changing. For years and years, you have been rooted in the physical, materialistic world by your ego. Spirituality is about cutting those roots and growing new ones out of a higher understanding. There can be no true flight with ego. Humility helps you take flight and at the same time, keeps you grounded.

THE SHIFT OF THE AXIS

"The shift is entirely man-made, caused by the energy created by man's actions. The more crimes and sins, the sooner the shift will occur."

"The only way to survive the shift is to stay on the Godly Good Path."

What is the shift of the axis?

Nature is a living thing. Therefore, it is very sensitive to energy. Since nature is neutral, when human beings follow the wrong path their actions build negative vibrations and these negative vibrations are absorbed by nature. Human beings have the ability to change the course of nature for better or for worse. When humans constantly follow the wrong path and show no respect for God, their fellow beings, or nature, a great deal of negative energy builds up. As a result, nature's response is negative. There is an increase in natural disasters such as earthquakes, floods, tornadoes, volcanoes, fires, and so on. This is nature's way of telling human beings to stop, think, and change. Humans may have progressed technologically, but that is not true progress. Power is to be used for the good of human beings, not for personal gain or for negative

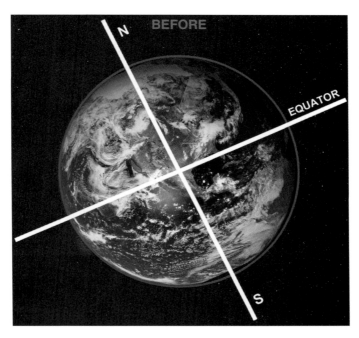

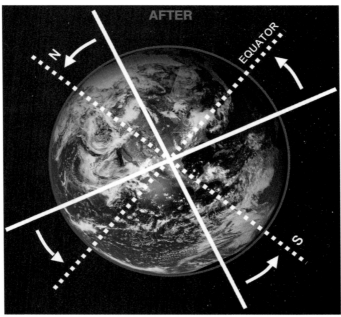

purposes. The basic foundations of goodness, love, selflessness and friendship have almost vanished from Earth. This is not a sign of progress, but a sign of decline.

Nature is a reflection of human beings. It shows what is within you. All the upheavals that are taking place in your world are an indication of the unrest within humans. Also, what emanates from you is absorbed by nature – if you send out positive energy, nature will reflect that in the form of peace and harmony. If you send out negative energy, nature's response will be negative. If you carry out nuclear tests in one place, the result will be an earthquake in another place. Unfortunately, we forget that the entire planet is our home and that we are all connected. Right now, human beings are so far removed from the right path that nature is giving a sign. You live in a world where people are afraid or embarrassed to talk about God or to walk on the spiritual path. There are other people who say they believe in God, but do not live even a second of their lives in accordance with His teachings, and are so disconnected from His goodness that they perform unimaginable acts. There are people who embark on so-called spiritual journeys only to feed their own egos, or who run away from their duties and responsibilities and convince themselves they are reaching for God. God's laws are made in such a way that when human beings go *beyond a certain limit*, when they are in complete disharmony with goodness and there exists a major imbalance, nature will give them warnings that they are following the wrong path. If human beings do not change, nature must correct that imbalance through a cleansing process because eventually, God's creations (both humans and nature) must exist as they are meant to, as pure, generous, and peaceful creations. But before that peace is restored, negative energies need to be wiped out. The cleansing has already begun, but this time nature will not rest until the Earth is pure once again — a place where humans live in harmony and practice what it means to be true instruments of the Almighty. To be a true instrument is to live selflessly, for the greater good, with complete faith in God.

Man must be in balance with nature, remain on the right path, and progress spiritually. However, on Earth, the cycle of life is such that sometimes good is more widespread and negativity is contained, or vice versa, and this goes on and on, cycle after cycle. At some point, negativity becomes too overwhelming, and this overbearing increase in negativity brings about a cleansing process, as a major portion of this negativity must be wiped out. Since the cleansing process is to be brought about by nature, the magnitude of natural disasters is such that there will be a 'pole shift'. The axis of the Earth will shift physically. A series of cataclysmic earthquakes will cause this major imbalance, which will be followed by floods, tidal waves, fires, more earthquakes, volcanic eruptions, and so on. This will cause a major part of negativity to be wiped out. This information is not meant to frighten you; it is meant to awaken you to change.

෯ Is the shift of the axis caused by God or man?

God gave man free will to make choices. Therefore, the shift is entirely man-made, as it is caused by the negative energy created by man's actions. The shift is about cause and effect and is a natural response to human action. It is entirely in the hands of human beings. By rejecting the guidance of the subconscious mind, human beings are straying completely from the spiritual path. This is the main reason the shift will happen soon. If you upset the miraculous and delicate balance of nature, it will have strong repercussions.

What will be the duration of the shift?

A major part of the devastation will take place within a few hours. It will be quite fast and at the time, when many have lost their near and dear ones, good people will guide and comfort them, giving them the strength to live and to not give up hope.

When will the shift of the axis happen?

The timing is entirely in the hands of human beings. The more crimes and sins take place, the sooner the shift will occur.

Who will survive the shift?

It is entirely up to you to survive. The cleansing process means that a major part of negativity will be wiped out. In order to survive, make sure that you are not part of the negativity that needs to be wiped out. Rise spiritually.

What percentage of the world's population will survive?

25% of the world's population will survive.

⚅ *Where will the shift begin?*

The shift will begin simultaneously all over the world with a cataclysmic earthquake, which will have a continuous chain reaction worldwide, and will continue until the cleansing process is complete. Land will be replaced by sea; there will be widespread fires; and there will be massive explosions wherever nuclear weapons, arms and ammunition are stored. The devastation will be monumental.

⚅ *Which parts of the world will be safe during and after the shift?*

Places that have positive vibrations will be safe e.g. parts of Canada, New Zealand and Australia. Places that have negative vibrations will be the least likely to survive.

⚅ *After the shift, will medicine be required in the safe areas?*

Initially, medicine will be required, so it is better to stock up medicine at home. Also, try to take first aid and disaster management courses so that you know what to do if someone is injured.

⚅ *What does the shift have to do with our spiritual development?*

You have all been reborn on Earth during this time in order to change for the better during a time when it is difficult to change because of so much negativity. This is how you chose to progress: by coming to Earth during difficult times and leading a positive, spiritual life. The very first thing you need to do is change. You need to do this quickly, before the shift of the axis occurs, because that is your test. It is a test you have chosen. Once the shift occurs the cleansing process will have begun and the vibrations on Earth will change, so there will be less temptation; therefore, the test is to change *now*. Spirit souls want to help you change, but we need your cooperation. If you have no desire to improve, we cannot force you to. Never say that you do not have the time to think about spiritual improvement. When you get too caught up in a physical existence, you forget why you have come to Earth. Consider yourself lucky to have been born during difficult times. As you progress spiritually, you will attach less and less importance to earthly things, and you will fulfill your duties and complete your mission on Earth. Finally, understand that a selfless good deed done now, when negativity is at its peak, will help you progress much faster than if that same good deed is done at a later stage (after the Shift) when the vibration is positive and good is ascendent.

🛞 *What are spirit souls doing to help souls on Earth with respect to the shift?*

Currently, we are trying very hard to improve souls on Earth in order to help them survive the shift. We are also working to move good souls to safer areas. There is a flurry of activity all around the Earth, of which you are not even aware. We are extremely alert right now, and are keeping track of every single change on Earth. The shift is a necessary cleansing process. It has occurred at regular intervals in your planet's history; however, this time, human beings have come too close to destroying the very planet that gives them life, supports them, and helps them grow. Human beings have to learn to live in total unity and harmony with nature. So it is up to you to simplify your lives and follow the right path. Once again, the only way for you to survive is to change for the better and follow the right path.

⚭ *How will human beings be guided and helped during the shift?*

People who are on the higher Realms will be saved. UFOs will send down levitation beams to evacuate good souls who are trapped in dangerous places. Everyone will see these beams and they will be scared, but good souls who are on the higher Realms will understand and they will be guided as to what they have to do. Even if good souls are fallen under the debris and not visible to the human eye, they will be 'seen' and saved. These souls will be guided towards the beams which will lift them into the spacecrafts. Those who are not on the higher Realms and have bad vibrations will fear these beams and will be unable to touch the beam or go into it, even if they want to. Once in the spacecraft, people will be taught survival techniques and will then be relocated on islands that will emerge from the sea. This will be one of the hardest tests people will have to face and they will need a lot of strength and positive attitude before, during and after the shift. Now do you understand why we are asking you to improve faster?

⚭ *Will a family remain together after the shift?*

It will depend on how **good** each individual is. During the shift only your Realm will count and depending on your Realm you will remain united or separated from your family.

⚭ *If a pregnant mother has low vibrations and her unborn child is a good soul what will be their fate?*

At the time of the shift no good soul will take rebirth through an evil mother.

Ratoo (left) with friend

Khorshed (second from left) and Rumi (extreme right)
in their early days

Ratoo (centre) with friends

Khorshed, Vispi and Rumi with their pet dog Chu-Chu

Khorshed, Ratoo and Rumi

Vispi could balance his entire body rigidly between two chairs,
supported only by the edge of his heels and the back of his head.

The ill-fated car: MRF 207

Ratoo Bhavnagri after his Navjote ceremony on 1 April, 1959

Vispi Bhavnagri after his Navjote ceremony on 1 April, 1959

Rumi and Khorshed on their wedding day
6 October, 1949

Khorshed and Rumi Bhavnagri were very fond of animals especially dogs

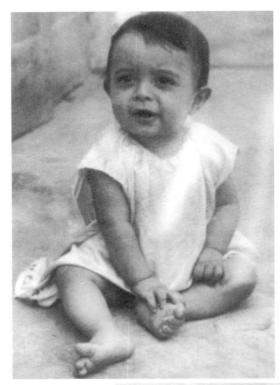

Vispi Bhavnagri
born on 9 August,
1950

Ratoo Bhavnagri
born on 13
December, 1951

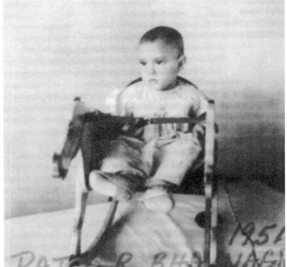

AN INTERVIEW WITH KHORSHED RUMI BHAVNAGRI

 How did you start helping people?

When my sons died, my husband and I were very miserable and did not know how we would face life. Our sons helped us by communicating with us, and giving us messages of hope and courage. Later on, when my automatic writing skills were well developed, they said to us, "Our mission is to help people on Earth, from the spirit world, through you both."

 What was your first reaction when you received your sons' messages? Did you believe in psychic things?

We were very excited, and yes, we have always believed in psychic things. Before they died, Vispi and I used to discuss the afterlife and reincarnation. From the time I was seven years old, I had a thirst for this kind of knowledge. I had an experience once that has stayed with me even today. Rumi, the kids, and I were going on a trip out of town with some relatives. I always carried sweets with me whenever I travelled, but this time I had forgotten, so I asked Rumi to stop the car and get some. I was sitting alone in the car, waiting for them to return, when I saw a weeping bullock. I saw tears pour down his face and I wondered why this was happening. Was he suffering? The bullock turned his head to me and put his jaw near the window, where my hand was resting, and looked at me in such a way as if he were trying to tell me: You know why I am grieving, I am suffering a lot. At that moment, Rumi, the kids, and my relatives returned and were surprised to see me talking to the bullock (Vispi told me during our communication that negative souls reincarnate on Earth as beasts of burden if they want to progress faster). I understood from this experience that beasts of burden suffer a lot, though I did not realise this until much later.

How did you feel a month after the boys died, and how did Vispi take away your misery and depression? What convinced you that you were communicating with them?

While communicating with us, Vispi said things that only he knew about. They also gave me the names of strangers and asked me to call them and give them some messages. We traced these absolute strangers and gave them the messages that we were asked to — this was our proof that these people really existed and Vispi's messages were accurate. When we were depressed, our sons cheered us up by telling us jokes and showed us how to lead our lives happily. They made us laugh and would guide us and tell us what to do and how.

Vispi Bhavnagri at the Rustom Baug Pavilion

Ratoo Bhavnagri in his car

✽✽✽ *Did people often ask you why you were disturbing the dead?*

Yes, very often. I constantly asked Vispi whether we were hampering their progress through communication and if we were harming them in any way or stopping their progress. If we were, we would have stopped communicating with them even though we loved to. Vispi said, "On the contrary, we can all progress much faster because we can guide you within seconds during our communication, as we have to help you somehow. You may take days or months to listen and you may still not do what is right, but with our two-way communication it will be much better." He assured us that nothing would harm their progress. I believed him and continued to communicate with them. He also said that it was much easier and faster to rise spiritually on Earth than in the spirit world, depending on how we led our lives.

✽✽✽ *How do you feel about taking messages for others? Isn't it a big responsibility?*

Of course it is, which is why it is necessary to gain more spiritual knowledge to help people. In the beginning, I used to be very scared of giving the wrong message to someone. Some people did not believe the messages I gave them and they would not listen; later, they regretted not listening to the messages, which was the proof I needed at the time to let me know that the messages were accurate. At first, Vispi used to move the pen, but as I improved, I began taking messages telepathically. Now, I hear them in my mind.

❧ *Who are we to judge if a person is good or bad?*

Using the word 'judge' is not correct. I am not judging anyone, but with Vispi and Ratoo's guidance I can make out instinctively if a person's vibration is good or bad, or if they are on a low level. As you rise spiritually and gain more knowledge, your subconscious mind guides you more and more and you tend to trust your own instincts. You feel uncomfortable with negative people and you just want to get away from them. The opposite is true of good people who are trying very hard to improve themselves – you are instinctively attracted to them.

❧ *Why do some people not believe in the spirit world and think that the ones who do are crazy?*

There are a number of reasons why people don't believe. Some are scared of what they cannot see or understand; some are brainwashed from childhood; some simply pretend they don't believe in the existence of God; some even deny their belief because they are afraid that their family and friends might laugh at them; some do not accept this belief because they are guilty; for some, it is easier to stay on the wrong path because they are weak. Most of the people who come to me for help are teenagers or youngsters in their twenties and early thirties – very few old people. Older people are set in their ways of thinking and deny the existence of an afterlife, and they fear the spirit world in general. The ones who are guilty won't come because they are scared to admit their guilt, as they know what they have done; they generally continue to do bad things, and don't want others to find out, so they avoid this knowledge.

❦ *What were Vispi, Ratoo and Popsie's hobbies?*

Our family was always interested in music and driving, and the men loved sports. Vispi and I loved reading and he loved music specially Jim Reeves and Nat King Cole. Vispi enjoyed tinkering with car and ship models and he even made his own speakers. The music recordings he made were exceptional and I still have some of them. We all loved animals, especially dogs, and we had many – Collies, Pomeranians, Alsatians, and a Lhasa Apso, whom Vispi trained very well.

❦ *Why is Vispi more heard of and talked about than Ratoo?*

We hear more about Vispi as he is helping and giving messages to more Earth souls than Ratoo. Ratoo's work, on the other hand, is to help souls who have just arrived in the spirit world by guiding them. He also works with Vispi by communicating with Earth souls.

❦ *When did you first communicate for someone else?*

In 1981, I communicated for my cousin and some relatives.

༝༝༝ *What are the major things for which people come to you?*

About 50% of the people come to me to receive spiritual guidance and comfort through messages. The other 50% is divided among people with problems, including family unrest, serious problems between parents and children, marital problems, and worst of all, evil people directing negativity at others. People from all walks of life come to receive guidance and I try to help them all – if they are willing to accept, learn, and improve.

༝༝༝ *If you had one message to give readers, what would that be?*

There are many good souls on Earth who lose their loved ones and then follow the wrong path because they do not know how to handle the pain. We want to assure those people that they are not alone. Their loved ones are still with them, looking after them from the spirit world. Always remember what Vispi told me years ago: **"Real, true love never dies. Not even after your death on Earth. Love is greater than death. Love is eternal. Death is just a transition – from one world to another, from one body to another. Death is not at all something big, but love is extraordinary."**

GLOSSARY

AKASHIC RECORDS

Akashic Records are also known as the Hall of Memories or the Hall of Journals. Each and every deed, good or bad, is recorded here under your soul name. The Akashic Records contain the memories of all the lives you have led on Earth. When souls on Earth are in deep dreamless sleep their subconscious mind makes entries in the Akashic Records.

ANGELS

Angels are good souls from Realm 5 Stage 7 and above. They have the ability and power to perform miracles. They can also come down to Earth to help human beings in case of emergencies, after taking permission from His Highest Good Soul. Lower level souls cannot be Angels as they have to take training and have more knowledge on how to guide Earth souls.

ASTRAL PLANE

The astral plane is a dimension higher than Earth but lower than the Spirit Plane. In that sense it is between Earth and the Spirit World. An astral plane is where astral souls reside. These astral souls can view Earth from the astral plane but cannot view the Spirit Plane or the Spirit World.

ASTRAL BEINGS

They are lost souls who have rejected the advice of the

subconscious mind and refused to become spirit beings. An astral being is one that has shed its earthly, physical body but is not a spirit being as yet. It looks just as its human form did at the time of its death.

AURA

An aura is an energy field that surrounds the body of every living being. Its colour and intensity reflect the current mood, emotional and physical state. Some human beings have the ability to see auras.

AUTOMATIC WRITING

Automatic writing is the process through which spirit beings communicate with human beings on Earth. The spirit being, whom you are communicating with, will move the pen while you hold it lightly on the page. Slowly, over time, words and then sentences will form.

Never attempt automatic writing on your own. It is extremely dangerous to start automatic writing on your own without a protective link.

BLACK MAGIC

Black Magic is an occult practice completely against God's laws, where human beings use negative astral souls and entities, and their own negative thoughts, for selfish gains and to cause harm to others.

CHANNEL

A medium through which spirit beings can communicate with people on Earth.

CONSCIENCE

Also known as subconscious mind. See subconscious mind.

EXTRA SENSORY PERCEPTION [ESP]

ESP is the ability to perceive things beyond the five senses of touch, taste, hearing, sight and smell.

GHOSTS

See Astral Beings.

GROUP SOULS

God created a certain number of souls at the same time. These souls reincarnate on Earth together, in the same group, life after life, so that they can help each other pay off karma, work on their mission and rise spiritually. Group Souls are also known as Soul Mates.

HALL OF JOURNALS

See Akashic Records.

HALL OF LEARNING

The Hall of Learning is a place in the Spirit World where spirit beings can go to access information. It is like a library full of spiritual truths. It contains knowledge about God's laws, about the nature of the universe and about every single aspect of God's creation. Information is revealed according to a soul's ability to understand.

HALL OF MEMORIES

See Akashic Records.

HALL OF REST

If the death of a person on Earth is unexpected and sudden, that soul is taken to the Hall of Rest. As these souls may be traumatised they are given healing rays to calm them.

HIGH GOOD SOUL[S]

A High Good Soul refers to a spirit being from Realm 6 Stage 7 and above.

HIGH GOOD SOUL OF THAT REALM

The Ruler, King or Head of each Realm is called the High Good Soul of that Realm — a complete soul from the next universe.

HIS HIGHEST GOOD SOUL

The Ruler, King or Head of Realm 7 and all the other Realms as well. He is a complete soul from the next universe.

HIGHER SELF

See subconscious mind.

INSTINCT

Instinct is a God-given, gut feeling that comes from the subconscious mind. This feeling is for your protection as well as those around you.

KARMA

Karma is the consequence of a soul's thoughts, words or actions. It is based on the principle of what you sow, you reap. Karma can be a debt that you owe or a blessing that you may receive.

LINK

During the process of automatic writing protection is provided by higher spirit beings, through prayers and positive energy, for safe communication between Earth souls and good spirit beings. This link can only be joined by an experienced and authorised automatic writer once permission has been granted from the spirit world.

MASTER

A master refers to a spiritual teacher. An evolved soul who comes to Earth from higher Realms of the Spirit World with the mission to impart and spread spiritual knowledge.

MEDIUM

A medium is a person on Earth who is able to communicate with the Spirit World.

MOTIVE

The true intent, reason, or driving force, behind a person's thoughts, words or deeds.

PAST LIFE MEMORY

The recollection of an event or part of an event that took place in a soul's previous lifetime.

PROPHET

When there is extreme negativity on Earth, God sends a very high soul from a higher universe to Earth to guide people. This Prophet gives knowledge to Earth souls so they can improve spiritually. Prophets come down to Earth very rarely, only when the planet is facing a spiritual crisis.

REALMS

There are seven Realms or planes of existence in the Spirit World, with one being the lowest and seven being the highest.

SEANCE

A seance is a meeting of a group of people who wish to communicate with their deceased loved ones or other supernatural entities. It is performed by a single medium who acts as go-between for the group and the spirits.

SHIFT OF THE AXIS

God's laws are made in such a way that when human beings go spiritually wrong, beyond a certain limit, nature will give them warnings that they are following the wrong path. If human beings do not change, nature will correct the imbalance through a cleansing process. Since the cleansing process is brought about by nature, the magnitude of natural disasters is such that the Earth's axis will tilt thereby causing a "Pole Shift".

SILVER CORD

The Silver Cord is a ray of light that is the connection between your spirit and your earthly body.

SOUL

The soul is your eternal spirit body. Just as you have a physical body on Earth, which is guided by the physical mind, the soul is your immortal spirit body and is guided by your subconscious mind.

SOUL CHARACTERISTIC[S]

Soul characteristics are the qualities - positive and negative — that a soul gathers through many lifetimes.

SOUL MATES

See Group Souls.

SOUL NAME

Every soul is given a soul name when the soul is created. Just as the soul is split into two, so is the name, which remains the same throughout your existence. Your deeds are recorded in the Akashic Records under your soul name.

SPIRIT

The Spirit includes your soul and your subconscious mind.

SPIRIT GUIDES

Every soul on Earth has a guardian in the Spirit World who guides the earthly soul from birth to death. This guardian is known as your Spirit Guide, and it is his or her job to guide you spiritually.

SPIRIT WORLD

Our true home. It is divided into 7 different Realms. Each Realm has 10 Stages.

SUBCONSCIOUS MIND

The subconscious mind is also known as the Conscience, Higher Mind, Higher Self or Inner Voice. It is your true spiritual mind that guides your soul.

TELEPATHY

Telepathy is the ability to receive messages from spirit beings in the form of projected thoughts, which are accessed through your subconscious mind.

TWIN SOULS

When a soul begins its human journey on Realm 4 Stage 5 it is split into two; a male soul and a female soul. These two souls exist separately and continue their earthly journey individually until both reach Realm 7 Stage 9. There they reunite to become a whole soul before progressing to the next universe.

VIBRATIONS

Every object, whether living or otherwise, has a vibration. A vibration is a frequency of energy that flows at different speeds. Vibrations are either good or bad. A good vibration makes you feel comfortable and positive, while a bad vibration makes you feel uncomfortable and negative (you can only recognise this if you are a good soul whose subconscious mind is open).

WALK-IN

If the situation on Earth gets harder than you can handle, and you are on the right path, then a good soul from the Spirit World known as a Walk-In will occupy your body until the trying period passes. This happens rarely and only in case of emergencies.

RECOMMENDED READING

A Search for the Truth : Ruth Montgomery
Here and Hereafter : Ruth Montgomery
A World Beyond : Ruth Montgomery
The World Before : Ruth Montgomery
Strangers Amongst Us : Ruth Montgomery
Born to Heal : Ruth Montgomery
Threshold To Tomorrow : Ruth Montgomery
Companions Along the Way : Ruth Montgomery
Herald of the New Age : Ruth Montgomery
Aliens Among Us : Ruth Montgomery
The World to Come : Ruth Montgomery
Do the Dead Suffer? : Lawrence Burt
Teachings of Silver Birch : Silver Birch
Guidance from Silver Birch : Silver Birch
Philosophy of Silver Birch : Silver Birch
Mystery of Life, Death and the Beyond : F. Rustomjee
Life after Life : Raymond Moody Jr., MD
Death and Its Mystery Before Death : Camille Flammarion
You Will Survive After Death : Sherwood Eddy
Life in the World Unseen : Anthony Borgia
A Life After Death : Dr. S. Ralph Harlow
Twenty Cases Suggestive Of Reincarnation : Ian Stevenson, MD
Faith is the Answer : Norman Vincent Peale
Many Lives, Many Masters : Brian Weiss, MD
Messages from the Masters : Brian Weiss, MD
Edgar Cayce: The Sleeping Prophet : Jess Stearn
Many Mansions: The Edgar Cayce Story of Reincarnation : Gina Cerminara
On Atlantis : Edgar Cayce
Earth Changes Update : Hugh Lynn Cayce
We the Arcturians : Dr. Norma Milanovich (with Betty Rice and Cynthia Ploski)

AFTERWORD

Khorshed Aunty always said, "Spirituality is a 'light' subject. Don't go too deep into it." Spirituality is not about running away into the mountains. It is about living your life right here amongst people, facing your problems and fulfilling your duties and responsibilities. It is about completing your spiritual mission on earth. When you understand this fine balance, your life will be joyful.

One doesn't become spiritual just by reading a thousand books on spirituality or joining a spiritual group and then failing its main purpose — selfless service and true action. You must sift knowledge and let your instinct lead you to decipher what is right and wrong. There is no use getting fanatical about the knowledge from books and allowing your ego to think that you know it all without true application of the same. Many fall into this trap and call themselves teachers without having practiced what they preach. Blinded by their egos, the years of gaining spiritual knowledge are a waste due to no application and therefore no spiritual growth — all because of spiritual pride which is man's biggest downfall. What makes you spiritual is your spiritual action. Only genuine selfless action brings about true change.

Khorshed Aunty always liked small acts of kindness. She always encouraged us to go step by step with full faith with respect to any problem. Spirituality is a slow but sure climb. We all have flaws and we all make mistakes, but we must forgive ourselves and others, and continuously do our best to improve and reach our goals. With the help of God and His angels, we can do it.

Just like the caterpillar breaks out of the cocoon, turns into a butterfly and takes flight, whether you believe it or not, your spirit will break free from the physical limitations and take flight to higher realms of growth until it is one with the Creator.

God Bless!

Shiamak

ABOUT THE AUTHOR

Khorshed Bhavnagri nee Screwalla was born in Mumbai (Bombay), India, in 1925. Her childhood dream was to be a teacher, psychologist or detective. She loved gardening, cooking and music, especially the Hawaiian guitar, and she watched a lot of cricket. In 1949, she married Rumi Bhavnagri and had two sons, Vispi and Ratoo. She discovered that she shared her family's passion for automobiles and driving. After the death of her sons in a car crash in 1980, she started communicating with them through the process of Automatic Writing. Her sons told her that it was her mission to spread spiritual knowledge on Earth. In 1998, at the age of 72, she moved to Vancouver, Canada, where she continued to work tirelessly towards her mission, until her death in August 2007. It was Mrs. Bhavnagri's wish that this book reach as many people as possible.

DISCLAIMER

The messages contained in this book are obtained through the process of Automatic Writing and are not the views or opinions of the author and/or those of VRRP Spiritual Learning. VRRP Spiritual Learning disclaims and accepts no responsibility and/or liability and gives no representation or warranty or other assurance as to the accuracy, completeness or timeliness of the contents of the messages in this book or its fitness for any purpose whatsoever.

By reading this book, the reader accepts the disclaimer as above and confirms his/her full responsibility for any action he/she might take thereafter and he/she will not hold VRRP Spiritual Learning responsible for the contents of this book and/or for any such action that may be taken by the reader or persons claiming by or under or through him/her in respect thereof.

VRRP Spiritual Learning is a group of individuals who are committed to spreading the knowledge provided in "The Laws of the Spirit World." They help and provide solace to individuals who have lost their loved ones and offer spiritual guidance. There have been cases where persons have fraudulently represented themselves to be a part of VRRP Spiritual Learning, and VRRP Spiritual Learning is not responsible for the same. Please check with VRRP

Spiritual Learning and confirm the authenticity of people claiming to be a part of the VRRP Spiritual Learning group before interacting with them.

Automatic Writing is the process, or product, of writing material that does not come from the conscious mind of the writer but from the Spirit World. It takes practice and control and requires guidance and supervision. Only an authorized, experienced and linked current member of VRRP Spiritual Learning can join your Automatic Writing link. DO NOT ATTEMPT AUTOMATIC WRITING ON YOUR OWN.

Website: www.vrrpspirituallearning.com
E-mail: vrrp@vrrpspirituallearning.com

JAICO PUBLISHING HOUSE

Elevate Your Life. Transform Your World.

ESTABLISHED IN 1946, Jaico Publishing House is home to world-transforming authors such as Sri Sri Paramahansa Yogananda, Osho, The Dalai Lama, Sri Sri Ravi Shankar, Robin Sharma, Deepak Chopra, Jack Canfield, Eknath Easwaran, Devdutt Pattanaik, Khushwant Singh, John Maxwell, Brian Tracy and Stephen Hawking.

Our late founder Mr. Jaman Shah first established Jaico as a book distribution company. Sensing that independence was around the corner, he aptly named his company Jaico ('Jai' means victory in Hindi). In order to service the significant demand for affordable books in a developing nation, Mr. Shah initiated Jaico's own publications. Jaico was India's first publisher of paperback books in the English language.

While self-help, religion and philosophy, mind/body/spirit, and business titles form the cornerstone of our non-fiction list, we publish an exciting range of travel, current affairs, biography, and popular science books as well. Our renewed focus on popular fiction is evident in our new titles by a host of fresh young talent from India and abroad. Jaico's recently established Translations Division translates selected English content into nine regional languages.

Jaico's Higher Education Division (HED) is recognized for its student-friendly textbooks in Business Management and Engineering which are in use countrywide.

In addition to being a publisher and distributor of its own titles, Jaico is a major national distributor of books of leading international and Indian publishers. With its headquarters in Mumbai, Jaico has branches and sales offices in Ahmedabad, Bangalore, Bhopal, Bhubaneswar, Chennai, Delhi, Hyderabad, Kolkata and Lucknow.

SINCE 1946